The English Prisoner

Tig Hague works in the City of London. He lives with his partner Lucy and their young daughter in London.

The English Prisoner

TIG HAGUE

PENGUIN BOOKS

KS

Group
WC2R ORL, England
w York, New York 10014, USA
Penguin Group (Canada), 90 Eglinton Avenue East, Suite 700, Toronto, Ontario, Canada M4P 2Y3
(a division of Pearson Penguin Canada Inc.)
Penguin Ireland, 25 St Stephen's Green, Dublin 2, Ireland (a division of Penguin Books Ltd)
Penguin Group (Australia), 250 Camberwell Road, Camberwell, Victoria 3124, Australia
(a division of Pearson Australia Group Pty Ltd)
Penguin Books India Pvt Ltd, 11 Community Centre, Panchsheel Park, New Delhi – 110 017, India
Penguin Group (NZ), 67 Apollo Drive, Rosedale, North Shore 0632, New Zealand
(a division of Pearson New Zealand Ltd)
Penguin Books (South Africa) (Pty) Ltd, 24 Sturdee Avenue,
Rosebank, Johannesburg 2196, South Africa

Penguin Books Ltd, Registered Offices: 80 Strand, London WC2R ORL, England

www.penguin.com

First published as *Zone 22* by Michael Joseph 2008
Published in Penguin Books 2009

2

Copyright © Tig Hague, 2008
All rights reserved

The moral right of the author has been asserted

Set in Monotype Garamond
Typeset by Rowland Phototypesetting Ltd, Bury St Edmunds, Suffolk
Printed in England by Clays Ltd, St Ives plc

ISBN: 978–0–141–03393–8

www.greenpenguin.co.uk

Penguin Books is committed to a sustainable future
for our business, our readers and our planet.
The book in your hands is made from paper
certified by the Forest Stewardship Council.

In memory of Sandra

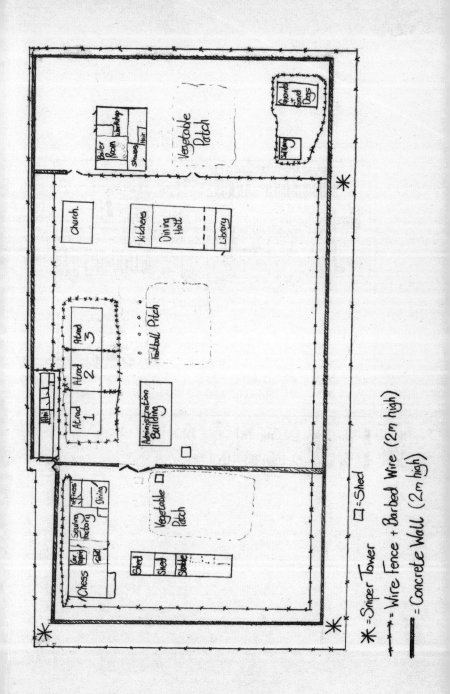

Vegetable Patch

Boiler Room | Workshop
Shoes | Hair

Gourds + Good Dogs

Solitary

Church

Kitchens | Dining Hall | Library

Football Pitch

A.rad 1 | A.rad 2 | A.rad 3

Administration Building

Vegetable Patch

offices
Sewing | Dining
Factory
Car Repair | Gym
Chess

Shed | Shed | Stable

* = Sniper Tower

☐ = Shed

✳ = Wire Fence + Barbed Wire (2m high)

▬ = Concrete Wall (2m high)

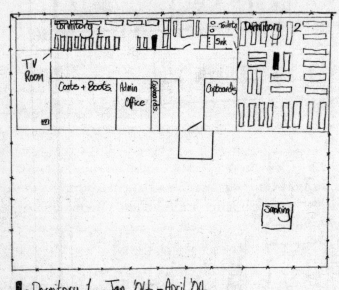

My Beds:
■ = Dormitory 1   Jan '04 – April '04
■ = Dormitory 2   May '04 – April '05

Moscow

The bump and skid of the wheels woke me up with a jolt as we touched down at Moscow's Sheremetyevo 2 airport. I squinted through the window at the watery grey clouds enveloping the skies over the Russian capital. It was just after six Moscow time, three hours ahead of the UK, and my aching body was telling me it was actually three in the morning and this was no time to be starting a day. My bum was numb and my head thick with sleep, or the lack of it, after a fitful night squirming in my uncomfortable Aeroflot seat. My mouth was dry and sticky but my water bottle was empty and I was just going to have to wait until we passed through Customs. I was still paying for the stag party and wedding at the weekend, and this was one business trip to Moscow I could've really done without. Garban Icap, though, didn't become 'the world's largest derivatives broker' by letting one of its junior brokers cancel three days of meetings with leading clients just because he had a dog of a hangover.

Half asleep I tidied up my notes, snapped my briefcase shut and sank into my seat as the plane began to taxi slowly back towards its docking bay. I stared out of the window, thinking of Lucy yesterday morning back in bed at Mum's house when I nuzzled into her warm neck as she dozed under her mop of wavy brown hair.

'Sweetheart, how am I going to spend four days without you?' That was the last thing she'd said and I smiled as I recalled it.

It usually takes about an hour, or sometimes two, to reach the front of the passport and visa queue at Sheremetyevo 2, and there's always pushing and shoving as people start to lose their patience. I was one of the first into the Arrivals building and I reached the man in the booth in a personal best time of 30 minutes – only to be told I hadn't filled in my form properly. I was dispatched with a grunt and a wave of the hand to join the back of the queue and I was annoyed that I couldn't quickly scribble out a new form there and then, which would have taken under a minute. I rolled my eyes, sighed loudly and sloped off like a naughty schoolboy.

I glanced anxiously at the clock on my mobile. Time was getting a little tight. I needed to get through the terrible Moscow traffic to my hotel for a shower, a shave and a change of clothes before I headed off to the first meeting of the day. I hadn't touched my razor for three days, and what with my puffy, black-ringed eyes I didn't want to be shaking hands with some of our most important clients looking like a Chechen separatist on the run, albeit one dressed in a smart light-blue shirt and a pair of tailor-made dark trousers.

The queue I rejoined after filling in a new form had become something of a scrum and I elbowed and shoved as politely as the next man to reach the booths, but by the time I finally made it into the baggage reclaim area I was one of the last passengers left in the cavernous grey hall.

There were just a few bags left on the carousel, but my large black suitcase wasn't among them. It was sitting on the floor with two or three other cases. Weird. What was all that about? Running late, I walked quickly towards the screened-off Customs area with my two Duty Free bags, dragging the case behind me.

A dozen or so officials wandered around in a variety of uniforms, while roughly the same number of passengers shuffled towards the exit. No one was smiling. Just beyond the screens, a set of electronic glass doors opened into the Arrivals area and I headed straight for them, craning my neck to see if I could spot my driver for the trip. It always gave me a small thrill to come through into the concourse and see a man holding a board with my name emblazoned across it: TIG HAGUE!

I was dimly aware that there was a group of other passengers over to my left, but I just kept walking, thinking nothing of it. I was about five yards from the door when a man started shouting in Russian. I turned around. He was shouting at me. I didn't understand what he was saying, but he was waving his hands around and pointing to the back of the queue. 'Am I ever going to get out of this shithole?' I muttered to myself. Everyone was being asked to put their bags through an X-ray machine. I had never seen luggage being scanned on the way *out* of an airport. Then I remembered the previous week's news story about the twenty people who'd been killed by two female Chechen suicide bombers at an open-air rock concert in the city. Fair enough. Besides, the queue was moving fairly fast and I'd be away in a couple of minutes.

The middle-aged official who took my bag was the

same one who pulled me up just as I was about to head through the automatic doors. He looked like he'd been there all night. He was very small, no more than about five foot two, and he had dark greasy hair, big blood-shot eyes, skinny arms and the expression of a man who just wanted to get home and put his feet up.

As my suitcase emerged on to the rollers from the other end of the scanner, he pointed to my two Duty Free bags, one containing a box of Marlboro Lights and another of Marlboro Reds, a pen and some perfume, and the other, two bottles of whisky; presents for my clients. I handed them over to him, knowing that that was the last bureaucratic obstacle I had to hurdle. Within seconds, I'd be through those doors. He peered inside the bags and said something in Russian. I shook my head and looked quizzical. 'I'm sorry, pal, but I don't understand Russian,' I said in English, smiling.

He replied sternly: 'Two whisky, two cigarettes, NO!'

That amount had never been a problem on previous trips and I told him that, even though I knew he wouldn't understand. He looked around the room and over his shoulder, leant towards me and rubbed his fingers and thumb together. I didn't twig that he was inviting me to bribe him. I thought he was asking whether I was carrying large sums of cash in my luggage. The Russians are very strict about how much money you can take in and out of the country; when you fill in the visa form on arrival you have to declare how much cash you have and what credit cards you are carrying. I had about 500 US dollars – two months' wages for this guy but hardly enough to put me in smuggler class.

I was too tired, too rushed for protracted negotiations, and I said in a 'fuck-you-just-get-on-with-it' kind of way: 'No! ... I ... no ... have ... money. Me-No-Money!'

He didn't like that. He stabbed a finger at my suitcase and then at the metal inspection table at the end of the scanning machine. 'Oh, for God's sake,' I mumbled and lifted the large black case on to the table. He spun the case around and snapped it open while fixing me with an icy stare. Half a dozen officials stood nearby chatting among themselves. Dozens of people milled around beyond the glass doors and I hoped one of them was my driver.

He started taking out my clothes, piece by piece, hanging them up on the screen behind him. He was in no hurry now, and showing me that. I was the last passenger left in the hall. All my clothes were on hangers so I could put them straight into the wardrobe at the hotel. He hung up a couple of shirts and T-shirts. Then he picked up my jeans.

I froze.

I

Images tumbled through my mind like a video on fast-forward: stag party ... pub garden ... scrap of hash in Rizla paper ... light blue jeans ... change pocket ... SHIT!!! ... Adrenaline burst into my body: my heart raced, my head swam, I tried to suck air into my lungs as the blood in my head dropped into my feet ... The world went into slow motion, like I had just plunged into deep, icy water from a great height. I watched spellbound as he lifted out the jeans and began to run his hands through the pockets. I felt the acid building up in my stomach and spreading out through my chest like fire.

He put his index and middle finger into the change pocket. He turned his head halfway round in the vague direction of his colleagues nearer the exit. He let out a low groan and then barked something in Russian in a raised voice. I had no idea what, but I took it to mean: 'We've got one here, guys!'

I was muttering to myself: 'Shut Up! Just shut the hell up! Shut your face, you greasy little jerk!'

Uniforms were walking towards me. Two huge men in army fatigues with sub-machine guns were on either side of me. They had berets, twelve-holed combat boots and Para belts. It was just a blur of images, like an old-fashioned cine-film. Another guy strode towards me: Mr Meathead, a great bear of a man in a dark blue jacket emblazoned with important-looking badges. With his military cap on, he was touching six foot eight, about three feet wide at the shoulders and he had a head the size of a medicine ball. I suddenly felt very small.

I was terrified for the first time in my life: it wasn't just fear or panic, it was sheer terror. I tried to think clearly but my mind was awash. So much was crowding in and jockeying for attention in my head that I couldn't separate one thought from another. Thoughts rattled and collided in my head like an asteroid storm. What's Lucy going to think? What are Mum and Dad going to say? How am I going to tell my boss at work? What am I going to tell my clients? They're going to send me home in disgrace … I'm going to be deported and never allowed back into Russia … My boss is going to go mental … I'm going to get sacked here … We won't get the mortgage … We're going to lose the house we have set our hearts on … We've exchanged but not completed … Lucy's going to go mad … I'm in serious trouble here … If I lose my job in the City, I'm as good as un-employable … I'll have to get a job as a brickie working for Dad … Hang on. Cool it. Calm down, Tig. Deep breaths. I know what I'll do, I'll just tell them I fell ill on the plane and they had to send me home, I'll take a couple of days off sick at work, I'll make up some illness and say that they wouldn't let me into the country in case I sneezed and infected someone else.

The commotion was getting louder. Everyone was talking at once. They were asking me questions in Russian. 'I don't speak Russian,' I kept saying. Meathead took the hash and pushed it towards my face. It was so small in his giant fat fingers it looked like a brown pinhead. 'What this?' he asked in English. 'WHAT THIS?'

'It's hashish,' I said. What else could I say? He asked me if it was mine and I replied: 'Yes, it is. I didn't mean to bring it to Moscow. It was a mistake. I was at a stag party and ...' At which point, the conversation erupted round me again. They sounded jubilant, like a bunch of fisherman on a riverbank who'd finally reeled one in. I was the one that didn't get away.

Flanked by the two camo guys with the sub-machine guns, and with Meathead pushing me in the back, I was frogmarched round the corner into a small area that had been screened off on all sides. There were sofas along two of the walls, a desk littered with papers, and an office chair behind it. Some strip lights were stacked in one corner and some old filing cabinets lined one wall. As a one-man office it would feel cramped, but with all four of us squeezed in, it felt claustrophobic. My heart was trying to burst, it was pounding so hard.

I was told to sit on a sofa. I turned to Meathead, who was now sitting behind the desk, and said: 'I need to speak to the British Embassy or a lawyer.' He laughed and said something in Russian to the guards, who joined in the laughter. Another man arrived, clearly the most senior of them all, with his olive-coloured officer's uniform and a big heavily peaked army cap. You look absurd in that massive hat, I thought. I looked up at him as he stood right over me, hoping I might find a more sympathetic response, but I could only hold eye contact with him for a second or two. His face told me it was not, as a rule, one to which desperate people were inclined to look for sympathy or clemency. He motioned for me to stand up and take my clothes off.

I felt a bit unsteady as I got to my feet and slowly removed my clothes, starting with my loafers. Embarrassment and fear spread over me like a chill. The floor beneath my bare feet was cold. When I got down to my boxer shorts, he signalled that I had gone far enough, and I felt a mild sensation of relief that no one was going to give me a 'digital rectum' exam right then. I covered my genitals like a footballer in a defensive wall waiting for a free kick to be taken.

Without looking up from the papers on the desk before him, Meathead said: 'Tell me why you are hashish.' He began writing as I leant forward and tried my best to explain about the stag party. I wanted him to look at me, but his head stayed down. He didn't understand, or want to understand, anything I said. 'Well, I was at a stag party for a very old friend from university, we'd just finished clay-pigeon shooting and we're sitting in a pub garden in Hertfordshire which is a county near London . . .' And so I went on. Meathead was barely paying attention and only glanced in my direction from time to time in between adding the odd scribble in his file. I was speaking quickly and nervously, in step with my racing heartbeat, blurting out my explanation in staccato bursts of semi-Cockney, dropping my T's and my H's because I was talking so fast. I realized I was just talking to the air as Meathead glazed over and drifted off to Narnia behind his desk. He asked me a few questions about the purpose of my trip to Russia, and then made it perfectly clear he wasn't listening to a single fucking thing I was saying by looking around the room and yawning. Then he sat back in his chair to signal he had heard quite enough, thank you, and dismissed me back to the sofa with a backhand wave. I slumped into the sofa and felt the cold of the plastic on my naked back.

No one uttered a word for several minutes. Another man appeared holding a small glass test tube. Meathead pointed to my suitcase, which had been brought in earlier, and showed him the small scrap of hashish that they'd placed on top of my jeans. The man took out a knife and, placing the hash on the desk, sliced off a thin sliver, which he found quite difficult because the hash was so small he couldn't get a decent grip on it. He placed the sliver, the size of a baby's fingernail, into the test tube, then poured in a small amount of liquid from a bottle, shook it up and placed it on the desk. For several minutes everyone in the room stared at the little glass vial in complete silence, waiting for something to happen: Meathead, Twat-in-the-Hat, the two guards, the laboratory geezer and me, all transfixed by this tiny little glass tube. I'm not a religious man, but I found myself in prayer. 'Please God, Please God, you've got to help me out here ...' repeating it over and over again as the minutes ticked away and no one said a word. Then the liquid began to change colour, and the Russians all started nodding at each other. Meathead smiled in satisfaction and motioned to me to put my clothes back on.

The two guards led me from the room and walked me round the corner into what looked like some kind of medical room. Like everything else in the airport, all the furnishings, decor and paraphernalia were distinctly

11

1950s: drab, functional, tired. The only connection with the modern world was a large set of electronic scales and an unsophisticated computer. There were two plump, oldish women in there, one sitting at the desk tapping away at the computer keyboard, and the other making some kind of hot beverage. I needed a drink myself. My mouth and throat were like sandpaper, and my stomach was starting to ache with hunger.

They were the first women I'd seen since I'd been stopped in the Customs hall two hours earlier – or was it three? Or one? I was overwhelmed with shame at the sight of them for some reason. They both looked at me with disgust, like I was the lowest of the low, a horrible little scumbag. Meathead came in and handed one of the women the piece of hashish. She went to a cupboard and took out a thick black bag made of heavy polythene. Into the bottom of the bag she dropped the tiny blim of hash – enough for one joint, maybe two if you're a student – wrapped it into a ball, took out a roll of tape, and proceeded to bind it around the bag until there was almost more tape visible than bag. When she'd finally finished she picked up a seal with a tag on it and attached it to the top of the bag, carried the package over to the electronic scales and dropped it on to the weighing platform. I couldn't see the numbers it was registering, but after a few seconds she let out a little wolf whistle, as if to say: 'Wow, this lad's carrying a serious load of drugs.' Everything went into slow motion again as the realization hit me: I was being fitted up.

An exchange took place between Meathead and the other woman, who wrote something on to a form.

Meathead put the form in front of me and handed me a pen. I hadn't had a sensible, rational thought from the moment the bureaucratic nightmare began. I was in a state of shock, I suppose. At the very least, I was confused and tired and getting more and more freaked out by the minute. The two armed guards were standing at my side, and Meathead was fixing me with a glare as he held out the pen in front of me. 'I don't know what it says. I don't speak Russian,' I whispered feebly.

But what if I don't sign? I was thinking. No one knows where I am! They can just take me away if they want to. They could beat the hell out of me, even kill me, claiming I'd attacked them, or they could frame me with a consignment of heroin, or charge me with anything they damn well like, or they could simply make me 'disappear'. It was perfectly clear by then that I wasn't dealing with what you might call a clear and transparent judicial system in there.

'What is this?' I asked, mustering a little courage.

'Sign,' he replied.

'But I don't understand what it says,' I pleaded.

'SIGN!' he snapped.

'I need a lawyer or the British Embassy. I'm not signing anything else if I don't know what the forms say!'

Meathead ignored me and carried on holding out the pen over the form that he'd laid out in front of me on the desk. I looked at the pen for about five seconds. Fear got the better of me. You're a pathetic coward. Your brother Rob would be ashamed of you. Rob would've been throwing punches by now, or more likely sitting in the corner taunting them and refusing to do a thing until a lawyer or Embassy official arrived. I snatched the pen, and quickly scribbled at the bottom of the page: 'I've flown to Moscow, there was hashish in my suitcase, the hashish is mine but I did not intend to bring it to Moscow.' I signed my message, and then I signed along the dotted line. I had no idea what the form said. For all I knew, it read: 'I'm here to kill President Putin.'

Why the fuck did I do that? And of all the things I might have written, why the bollocks did I write that? I suppose I was still thinking like an Englishman. I couldn't fathom why there was such a palaver over a piece of wacky-baccy the size of a drawing-pin, enough to make one man feel a little mellow for an hour or two, the equivalent perhaps of three pints of bitter. In England these days, the coppers wouldn't even bother to issue a warning. They would just send me on my way with a flea in my ear.

I handed back the pen and one of the guards stepped forward, holding a pair of handcuffs, and motioned to me to put my arms out in front of me. Wearing handcuffs was a first for me. Three of them, a guard on either side with Meathead at my rear, led me through a series of doors, offices and corridors and I suddenly found myself out in the concourse of the airport. Passengers were hurrying to and fro as airport workers went about their daily business. I was walked through the throng; people glanced and gawped at me. I was so embarrassed I tried to pull my shirt cuffs down to hide the handcuffs, which were biting into the skin on my wrists. It was as if I was having an out-of-body experience, like I was watching a film. It was as if it was happening to somebody else.

We headed up a set of escalators and through a

corridor of shops. Through the mezzanine window I was able to see planes taxiing in and out of their bays and along the runway, and one had just lifted off, rising steeply as it disappeared into the low grey clouds. I could feel my guts churning and I thought I was going to crap myself. I clenched my buttocks and my walk turned into a waddle. We went up a further flight of stairs, leaving behind the echoing din and bustle of the airport. Doors closed behind us as I was led down a dark corridor into a dingy administration area, with little offices off to each side.

Meathead had his great ham of a hand on my shoulder and he was starting to exert more pressure as he pushed me down the corridor, the proud sheriff arriving back in town with his captured outlaw. I was pushed into a very small office where a man in a suit sat behind a desk by a small window. The man didn't look up as Meathead pushed me down on to a wooden bench along the side wall and left the room. It was very gloomy and the room was thick with the man's cheap cigarette smoke. He must be a chain-smoker to create this much fog, I thought. The office was a picture of disorganization. A couple of tired old pictures hung on the walls at slight angles. The surfaces were strewn with papers and files and personal knick-knacks, including porcelain figures of animals and small trophies made from poor-quality metal, the kind you find in a gift shop in a seaside resort. It looked like my dad's office down at the building site.

The man behind the desk was obviously the airport's top security man. There was a long silence as he sat there looking down at the papers that Meathead handed him, drawing deeply on his cigarette and exhaling in great clouds without raising his head. I tried to weigh up the possible scenarios, veering from wild optimism to deep pessimism. The best-case scenario, I figured, was a fine for 1,000 dollars or so and a warning that I could expect to be dealt with severely if I stepped out of line again during my trip. The thought flashed through my mind: maybe this guy would take a backhander. The worst-case scenario, I feared, was a few nights in the airport police cell, followed by conviction in some kind of magistrates' court, a heavy fine and deportation home in disgrace. If that happened, then I kissed goodbye to my job, we lost the house we were halfway through buying, and Lucy did her nut.

The man behind the desk said something to me in Russian. Why did they keep talking to me in Russian? The only words I knew were *da* for 'yes', *nyet* for 'no' and *spasiba* for 'thank you', which I'd picked up from going out to restaurants. I shrugged and said for the hundredth time that I was unable to speak Russian. He made a five-second phone call and then we sat there in silence again, just the two of us. A junior official put his head around the door and peered at me like I was some kind of exhibit in a fucking freak show. He made a strange smiling face at me, and I couldn't work out whether he was mocking me or showing some sympathy. A few minutes later there was a knock on the open door and a very large woman in her mid-fifties walked into the room. Her clothes suggested she was a sales assistant and the name badge on her left breast was written in English. I couldn't quite make out what it said, but it was definitely English.

They talked for a moment before she turned to me and said, 'I am be translator.'

'Fantastic! At last, thank you,' I said, my face erupting into its first smile of the day. A sense of relief washed through me.

'You smuggle drugs,' she said curtly and then turned to the man, nodded and walked out of the room.

'No! No! No! No! I'm not a drugs smuggler!' I shouted after her as she disappeared down the dim corridor. A surge of alarm and anger rose up in me and I turned to the man and said to him as forcefully as I'd said anything over the previous few hours: 'I need the British Embassy. Now!'

'Later, later,' he said, patting the air with both hands as if to say, 'Calm down, calm down.'

The junior clerk character who'd stuck his head in a few minutes earlier came into the room and I blurted out: 'I need a lawyer!' I was beginning to panic. There was a pause as the clerk went to the desk and wrote down a telephone number on a piece of paper and handed it to me.

'English lawyer?' I asked, my heart filling with hope. After a pause, the pair of them burst out laughing. The bastards were taking the fucking piss out of me.

'No. No lawyer,' said the boss, chuckling.

He barked a sharp order and the two armed guards who'd been chaperoning me all morning re-emerged from the corridor outside the office. They took an elbow each as they hoisted me off the bench and led me further down the long corridor and into another room with two makeshift cells next to each other against the wall opposite the door. The room was obviously a storeroom of some sort where they dumped all the crap that had no obvious home. It was full of cardboard boxes and what looked like a pile of gym mats stacked up to one side. There were no windows. They opened the door to the left-hand cell and sat me down on a wooden bench with metal legs. Another guard came in and threw my suitcase into the cell while another removed my handcuffs and then locked the cell door before they filed out in silence.

I tried not to look at the bars as I sat, unable to accept that I was a detainee. I put my head in my hands and stared vacantly at the suitcase for several minutes before it hit me: my mobile phone was in there! Excitement and fear gripped me as one. This was a chance, but also a risk. I quickly turned it on and put it under my leg to smother the noise of the greeting tune.

I sat there for about five minutes, wrestling with what to do. Who did I call? Lucy? Mum and Dad? My boss, John? Rob? The prospect of breaking the news to any of them filled me with dread. At the back of my mind, I was clinging on to the hope that the nightmare was going to be over very shortly and everything would just go back to normal. My eyes began to well up and my breathing became shorter and faster. Strangely, calling home was making me more frightened than anything else that had happened this morning. I found myself dialling John at the office.

'Hey, Tig, I've been trying to get hold of you. You all set up for the day?'

'I've been fucking arrested, John. I'm in a cell at the airport. The Customs guys found a pinhead of hashish in my jeans. It's not looking good. They're treating me like I had a stash of heroin strapped to me. You've got to do something. You've got to help. It's a nightmare. They won't let me have a lawyer or the Embassy. They're beyond bribing now. There's too many of the bastards now. I'm too deep into the system. They're going to fucking hang me out to dry here. I'm freaked out, John. Please do something. Ring Lucy will you? Please. Shit, shit, shit, shit, shit, shit . . .'

'OK, OK, Tig, stay cool. We'll get the ball rolling this end. Be calm. We're going to make sure you're going to be all right. I'll talk to the guys upstairs and see if we can get a lawyer sorted for you . . .'

The door began to open and I switched the phone off and quickly shoved it under my clothes in the suitcase. An armed guard I'd not seen before walked over and put his face up to the bars, like he was in Moscow State Zoo and I was some kind of weird animal. I could feel the warm tears running down my cheeks and my stubble as they dripped on to the floor. I looked at him, hoping for a small gesture of kindness. He leant forward to the bars, smiled, and then lifted up his right hand and started to make a syringe-injecting motion into his other arm. I jumped off the bench. 'No, I don't,' I said to him. 'I don't do drugs! I don't do drugs! I'm not a junkie, I'm not a smuggler! Please, help me!'

He stared at me impassively and then walked slowly from the room, reappearing a few minutes later with two more guards. They put my handcuffs back on and led me back out into the labyrinth of corridors and offices, through the shops, down the escalator and back on to the main public concourse. I just looked straight ahead and paid no attention to the people I knew were gawping at me. Where the fuck are they taking me now? Suddenly, I was standing outside and a blast of aviation fuel hit my nostrils and the back of my throat. A big black official-looking car, a Volga, had its engine running.

The guard opened the rear door and pushed my head down as he bundled me on to the back seat. The door was slammed shut. The two men in the front seats turned round. One had short hair and chiselled features and the other a round face with a huge fuzzy perm and a big moustache. They said nothing as the car pulled out into the airport traffic. We were heading into Moscow. I knew that road. I looked out of the window. Muscovites were going about their business. Kids were playing on street corners, mothers with heavy shopping bags filled the pavements and grandmothers sat on benches, their heads wrapped in scarves, watching the world go by.

'Where am I going? Please tell me where I'm going?' I pleaded as I leant forward between the two of them.

The one with the perm, who was driving, half-turned his head and whispered: 'Smuggle drug Russia? You go prison seven year.'

I slumped back into the seat and my chest began to heave. I could barely breathe. I began to sob uncontrollably.

2

I was lying on the metal bench when the eye-slot on the door slid open with a metallic click and I could see an eyeball fixing me. I must have finally fallen asleep. I was in a cell in a very quiet building in some kind of military or police complex about an hour from the airport. After my arrest they'd taken me to a medical centre somewhere outside central Moscow. The plain-clothes cops couldn't find it at first and so they had to pull over and ask a little old lady in a headscarf, a proper old babushka, to hop in the back next to me and give them directions. It was a strange episode, me sitting there in cuffs and tears and this nice wrinkled lady talking to the police guys and then turning to me from time to time with a sympathetic look.

At the medical place I was given a full physical examination, which involved standing around in the buff while various people in white coats played around with my body. They put a syringe in my arm and took some blood, they pulled the skin down below my eyes and had a good look inside, I stuck my tongue out and said 'Aaagh', someone put two fingers up my arse and had a little rummage, they took my pulse and blood pressure, and I weed into a bottle for them. The whole process took a couple of hours, including the hanging around in between tests – and the weirdest thing was that no one said a fucking word to me throughout. They just prodded and probed me like farmers at a cattle market, weighing up whether to make a bid. Then the Bodie and Doyle guys drove me back to the airport and I was marched through the public concourse and back up into my makeshift cell like I was Carlos the fucking Jackal or some bigshot Chechen separatist. I wondered if the people staring at me would have laughed if they knew I was, in fact, a junior broker on the emerging markets desk at Garban Icap, caught with a pinprick of poor quality hash in my pocket after a stag party.

They left me in there for an hour or two and the longer I sat there the more convinced I became that they'd brought me back to the airport because they were going to deport me. I got that funny feeling in my stomach – like when you go over a humpback bridge in a car – as the hope spread out through my body. Why else would they have taken me back there but to put me on a flight? I heard myself singing under my breath, to the tune of 'Three Lions on a Shirt': I'm going home, I'm going home, Hague is going home ... But as soon as the guards came back in and cuffed me again I could tell by their faces and manner that London was not my next stop. They led me out to a minibus with a police driver who took me to a compound surrounded by trees and barbed wire. It was a huge place but it was so quiet it felt like I was the only person there, bar a couple of guards.

Night was falling by the time we arrived and, for the third time since my arrival in Russia, I was told to strip naked. I almost laughed. Maybe it was an old Russian custom to take off your clothes every time you arrived somewhere new. Once they were absolutely sure that I hadn't managed to get any knives and guns on the way from the airport and hidden them about my person, they handed back my clothes. Except my shoes, for some reason. Maybe they thought I was going to batter myself to death with my penny loafers.

It was the first time I'd been in a proper cell and it looked pretty much how I'd always imagined one to look: dirty without being disgusting, graffiti on the peeling walls, small, barred window high up on one wall, wide bench for sitting and sleeping, low-wattage bulb hanging from the roof near the door. I spent most of the night staring at two flies circling the bulb, over and over, like they were on a long-distance aerial racetrack. My panic had turned to blank exhaustion after the drama earlier in the day and I lay on my back with my hands behind my head watching the fly race in a daze, thinking about Lucy, and Mum and Dad. I hated myself for all the grief I must've been causing them. I kept thinking, How many more days will they have to sit there fretting about me?

It felt very cold in the cell, but I couldn't work out whether that was the temperature, or just me being tired and hungry. I was seriously hungry and thirsty. Nothing had passed my lips since I'd had a bowl of pasta, a glass of red wine and a cappuccino at Heathrow on the Wednesday night. That was about thirty-six hours. I curled up in a ball on the bench facing the door and I could feel the salt from my tears of the night caking the skin around my eyes when, after a while, the eye-slot opened and a hand passed through a steaming metal mug and a piece of black soda bread. Ah, the Continental breakfast. The sweet black tea was delicious. I tried to eat the bread but it was very stale and I had a smoke instead. There was a tinny radio playing further down the corridor and the silly Russian pop songs didn't agree with my mood, but then 'At Night' by Shakedown – Rob's song, a funky electro-pop number – came on and I found myself tapping my foot and mouthing the lyrics through my cigarette smoke.

It was the song Rob had been playing all the time when I went to visit him in Spain last summer. We used to listen to it driving around in the evening heat, windows down, shades on, tapping the doors of the car, as we headed out to his favourite bars on the coast.

The upbeat, familiar tune lifted my mood and a flood of positive thoughts washed over me: Garban will have rolled out the heavy guns of their legal department by now, the Embassy will be straightening it all out with the relevant authorities, Mum and Dad will have put in some calls, maybe one of my Russian client friends has taken care of it all ... The cell door opened and the guard threw me my loafers. Great, it's all over now. Let's get home.

Two uniformed policemen handcuffed me and escorted me to a black minibus. I was driven back into and around Moscow for at least an hour in total silence but for the noise of the rush-hour traffic outside. Not a word had passed between the three of us when we finally turned off the main road and on to a very long straight tree-lined road somewhere in the city suburbs. At the end of the road I could see a large international-style hotel and my heart quickened at the thought that they'd been ordered to leave me there to be collected by one of my clients, or the Embassy. But about 200 yards before the hotel the car pulled over and the cops got out and walked up a path into a small low red-brick building. They were getting my release papers and/or the caution from the authorities, I guessed. It was weirdly quiet outside. Just one car passed by in twenty minutes. The thought kept crossing my mind: do a runner, do a runner . . .

One of the cops came back and opened the door of the van and I followed him into the building and into the first room on the right, a small office with a desk and computer in the centre of the room and a few chairs and shelves lining the walls. The cuffs were removed again and I sat waiting for fifteen minutes or so, fidgeting and squirming a little, stretching my neck, cracking my knuckles and opening my eyes as wide as they'd go to shake off the fatigue, dreaming of a bacon sandwich and a strong cappuccino. The door opened and in breezed a couple of cool-looking dudes, both in their mid-twenties: one with collar-length blond hair and wearing jeans, T-shirt and trainers, the other with short-cropped brown hair, collared shirt, jeans and leather jacket. They dress like I do at the weekends, I thought. They could be my mates. They smiled, invited me to sit down as they took their seats behind the desk, and the blond one, with the hint of an American accent, said: 'Hey, how you doin'? We are here to help you out with your little problem, to find out what's really going on and sort it out. I used to work at the US Embassy and I have spent a lot of time over in the States. My colleague also speaks good English, so you will be able to explain everything to us and we will understand.'

This is looking *very* promising, I thought: both lads

speak good English, they've both smiled at me, one's got his feet on the desk, the other is leaning up against the wall looking very chilled ... I felt the tension ebbing away, my shoulders relaxing a little. A middle-aged man with greying hair and moustache, dressed a little more formally, came in and sat down on a chair along the wall by the door. He nodded to me and exchanged a few words in Russian with the other two.

The conversation began casually and they asked me dozens of general questions about my life in England. The blond was doing most of the talking and he seemed genuinely curious and interested in my life back home, about England, my family, my mates, my job, London, the pubs, my football team Arsenal ... We chatted away like two like-minded guys who had fallen into easy conversation on a long train journey. Every now and then the short-haired guy tapped something into the keyboard. The questions came fast and I answered them all honestly and politely. I figured these guys must have some connection with the Embassy, or the Consulate.

After ten minutes I asked: 'So who exactly are you guys?'

'We've been asked to come down and help sort out your problem. Straighten out the facts,' said the blond guy.

'Great, and who sent you?'

'The authorities involved in your case,' he said, pinning me with a friendly grin.

'Do you work with the diplomatic service?'

'Yeah, kind of.'

'Do the Embassy know about me?'

'They sure do. We'll take you to them later.'

The conversation continued with plenty of half-jokes, chuckles and casual banter amid the questions. We got on to the subject of my arrest at the airport and I told them the truth: I'd been to a stag party, drunk a lot of beer, smoked a bit of puff, put a piece of hash wrapped up in Rizla to smoke later into my change pocket. I'd then fallen asleep as soon as I went back to the room where I was sleeping and had completely forgotten about it when I came to pack my jeans for this business trip to Moscow. 'It was just one of those stupid, absent-minded things and I'm really, really sorry for all the bother it seems to have caused,' I finished.

We chatted about recreational drugs back in England and I explained that, as they probably already knew, millions of people smoked hash these days, that there was a more relaxed attitude to cannabis, and that the police no longer really bothered about people carrying hash for their own personal use and there was a policy of virtual tolerance towards it. They were more concerned with those trafficking the heavy drugs like heroin and ecstasy, I explained.

'I used to smoke a few joints when I was at university, but nowadays it's only when I'm at a party and some-body's handing one round,' I added, filling a pause in the conversation.

Drug use, it turned out, was the last subject of our conversation, which made me feel a bit uncomfortable as I was reminded that that was why we were all there in the first place. The moustachioed man walked across the room and whispered some comments to the guy on the computer, pointing to the screen from time to time. The younger guy then, ad-libbing, read out a tightly condensed summary of our conversation, ninety minutes of chat squeezed into two or three minutes. There was nothing blatantly incorrect in the plain facts that he read out: I lived in London, I worked at Garban Icap, I went to a stag party, I smoked hash with my friends sometimes, I came to Moscow on business ... but somehow it didn't sound quite the same as it had when we were chatting. All the nuance and subtlety of it had gone. It was just a list of bare facts.

'Have I got anything wrong, Mr Hague?' asked the crop-haired character on the computer.

'Er ... not quite ... yeah ... roughly. I mean, I wouldn't have put it exactly like that myself but ...'

'Very good, then we'll print it off.'

The blond one left the room and came back a couple of minutes later with two pieces of typescript in Russian. 'This is a copy of the summary we just read out to you,' he smiled. 'We need you to sign this before we can go any further. Please ...'

Standing by the desk he beckoned me forward with the pen.

'No problem ... fine,' I said, all relaxed. There was a silence as I leant towards the document on the desk and I tried to fill it with a joke. 'I'm probably signing my own death certificate here!' We all chuckled, apart from the grey-haired man with the moustache and the policeman on the door who didn't understand. I signed the document, and the moustachioed man put it into his briefcase.

3

We returned to the minibus and the terrible Moscow traffic but I had no idea where they were planning to take me. Airport? Police station? Courtroom? British Embassy? Back to my cell? We drove for over an hour and the mounting uncertainty started to fray my nerves once again. It was almost forty-eight hours since I'd eaten any food and I was feeling light-headed and nauseous as I looked out of the window at the drab, grey streets of Moscow. I leant forward towards the two silent cops in the front, holding myself steady by pressing my cuffed hands against the bench seat in front.

'Excusy ... *spasiba* ... Excuse me ... Where we go? ... Please ... We go Embassy? ... Angliski Embassy? ...'

But they carried on looking straight ahead, saying nothing. They had no English, I had no Russian and I guess they weren't going to try to explain what was happening with hand gestures. The silence said: you'll find out soon enough.

We entered a large tree-lined square, full of smart town houses made from attractive grey stone, not regulation concrete like the rest of Moscow. It looked like a posh London square, the kind you find in Chelsea or Knights-bridge. As the minibus pulled over I saw half a dozen people standing in a small group about twenty yards away, all of them looking towards us. There were five men, dressed in suits and ties, and a young girl with long brown hair, smartly turned out in a dark twinset. They were all wearing sunglasses except for a tall guy with silver hair who had little round Gandhi glasses. It was like a cast of extras from *Reservoir Dogs*.

The cop opened the door for me and as I stepped out on to the pavement, the posse started walking towards me. The tall guy was smiling at me sympathetically as he strode out of the group to greet me. I went to shake hands, forgetting I was cuffed, and looked away, embarrassed.

'Hi, I'm Peter Smith from the British Embassy,' he said with a mild northern accent. The sound of an English voice was reassuring. 'Your family contacted us and told us what had happened. We heard you had a spot of bother at the airport. We'll be coming to the court hearing with you,' he added, pointing to the building behind.

Courtroom! I closed my eyes and exhaled loudly, thinking, well, that's my career in the City gone.

'How are you bearing up?' asked Smith, sensing my dejection.

'Not brilliant, to be honest.'

Smith introduced the other four, who were all lawyers. Four lawyers! The older, skinny-looking guy with a tash and glasses was my Russian lawyer. He had the reassuringly English name of Alfred Piskin. I didn't catch the names of the younger two guys, but I got that they were Russians working for one of the world's biggest law firms. The English girl, Julia, was a trainee at the firm and was going to translate for me in court. As he introduced each of them I felt my spirits rising, thinking: I'm walking right out of here. The *Reservoir Dogs* boys are taking charge. Mum, Dad, Luce and John at work had clearly been reacting quickly to blow this daft episode out of the water before the system had a chance to take it any further.

'Wow, that's quite a team we've got,' I smiled. 'I can't quite believe that such a tiny piece of pot has caused such a palaver. Mad, isn't it?'

As one, we all moved up on to the steps of the courtroom, and Smith started asking me how the police had been treating me, whether I'd been beaten or abused and so on. I was in a daze of excitement and nerves and I wasn't concentrating. All I could think about was getting out of the courtroom, into a hotel, and speaking to Luce and Mum and Dad and then getting the first fucking flight out of there. I just wanted to be home. I found myself leading the way up the steps, eager to get the hearing over and done with.

The words rushed from my mouth in a torrent as I told them about my arrest. I was aware that I wasn't making much sense, but they were making all the right-sounding noises: 'Is that right ... really? ... what a shock ... well, don't worry ... be calm ...' As we headed down the wood-panelled corridor in the courtroom I saw the two young casual lads from the office, who had been so laid-back and friendly earlier, chatting in hushed tones. I tried to make eye contact with them as we brushed past but they didn't look my way. In the smart, sober surroundings of the courthouse a wave of embarrassment spread over me as I realized how filthy and haggard I must look. Four days of thick, dark stubble covered my face and my eyes were puffy and bloodshot from crying and sleeplessness. I was going to court on a drugs charge looking like a bloody junkie!

'We'll see you after the hearing,' said Smith as he and the lawyers – my legal team! – disappeared through a set of wooden doors. My hands were still cuffed in front of me as the policeman took me by the upper arm and led me round the corner and through a side door. I shivered as I stood in the dock. It felt unreal. I started to sway a little as the panic spread over me and I pressed my legs against the wooden railing of the dock to steady myself. The room was roughly fifty feet square and the walls were panelled with wood. The dock was at the side of the room and, almost opposite me, in the corner slightly to my left, was the judge's bench, which looked down on the rows of tables and benches in front. My legal team took their seats at the long desk nearest to me. At the table beyond them, the two friendly young dudes took theirs with two older, smarter guys, one of them the silent guy with the tash from the meeting earlier. I realized with a jolt that the 'friendly' guys were not that friendly after all. They had to be cops, or prosecutors, or investigators, working on behalf of the state. Shit, shit, shit! What the hell did I tell them?

Julia the translator smiled at me as she sat down right in front of me on the other side of the dock. The court fell silent as a handful of officials entered the room. The usher invited everyone to stand for the judge and I was taken aback to see a woman in her mid-forties emerge from a door on the opposite wall. I'd never seen a real judge, let alone a Russian one, but for some reason I'd been expecting an elderly man with white hair and half-moon glasses, not a slim, stylish woman with short brown hair that she'd fashioned into neat crescents curling down and then back up her cheeks, like a pair of microphones. She looked like a character from *Blake's Seven* or *Star Trek*, but her being a woman made me feel confident for some reason.

Then it began, with a flurry of exchanges in Russian. Julia, trying to keep pace, whispered rushed snippets of translation to me through the wooden railings. I leant forward to hear what she was saying but I caught only every other word or so, or whole phrases of legalese that meant sod all to me. It all sounded very technical and procedural. Charges were solemnly read out with the names and numbers and clauses of acts and codes. The lawyers exchanged words with the judge in hushed, earnest tones. The translator mentioned the word 'smuggling' and I was seized with alarm. Smuggling! I'm not a smuggler! A fucking drugs mule! I'm a derivatives broker in the City. I wanted to butt in and say: 'Hey! Let's just slow right down and see it for what it is, can we? This is getting way, way out of hand! Smuggling – you're kidding me ...'

But I might as well not have been in the room, because no one was even looking at me, let alone including me in the exchanges. There must have been a dozen people at the hearing, and a sensation of dread ran straight through me as the realization struck me that with so many of them involved, they weren't just going to let me walk out of here with a slapped wrist. They were going to make me come back for a fuller hearing of some sort. You didn't assemble that many professionals from all over the city, make them sit in a room for half an hour or however long, and then send them all home without *doing* something to justify them all being there in the first place. They were all having to give the impression that the matter in hand was, in fact, a matter of the very greatest seriousness. I'd been to enough business meetings to know that when you assemble a room full of people, it can only come to an end once there is satisfaction that something has been *done*, or has been arranged to be done. That's what we all get paid for: playing at being serious, diligent professionals.

'Hague was smuggling 28.9 grams of hashish ...' the translator continued. 28.9 grams! Adrenaline exploded through my body like an electric shock and I found myself getting to my feet. That's an ounce! An ounce! There wasn't so much as a twentieth of an ounce. An ounce is 100 quids' worth of gear. You can't even get an ounce into the change pocket of a pair of trousers ...

'But that's not true!' I shouted. 'It's not true! There was nothing like an ounce. That's a bloody lie!' I went to throw my hands out to the side as if to say: 'Come on! This is ridiculous!' but again I forgot my cuffs were on and I lost my balance a little as my arms pulled me forward. Everyone in the room was staring at me now. The judge scowled at me and motioned for me to sit down and at the same time someone in the room let out a loud 'Shhhh!'

'Say something, will you?' I whispered at the three lawyers, whose heads were all turned in my direction.

One of the law firm guys tilted his head and patted the air over the table, telling me to calm down and implying that everything was going to be fine if I just sat the fuck down and listened.

I was breathing heavily and fast and I felt I was going to start crying like a baby again as a prosecution lawyer started reading out the summary of my conversation with the two young guys earlier that morning. The translator whispered that it was my 'statement to the police' – and the statement certainly wasn't coming across too well in translation. It was all about drugs. Drugs. Drugs. Drugs. Me and drugs. About me smoking drugs at home with friends. About me having smoked drugs since I was at university. About me not thinking drugs were wrong. About me smuggling drugs into Moscow ... As the young girl translated through the railings at a rate of knots, it was clear that what the judge and the court were hearing was a heavily edited and abridged version of what I'd said to the blond guy, a grim mixture of half-truths, shorn of all context and wider detail and with all mitigating facts removed. From where I was sitting, it sounded like this: Tig Hague admits he smokes hashish; he 'smuggled' a large amount of it into Russia; he doesn't think smoking cannabis is a big deal; he has smoked it for over ten years; Tig Hague is one big mother-fucking dope smoker ...

I tried again to get the attention of my lawyers, to get them to say or do something, to challenge what was being said, but they sat there with long faces, just listening. I began to panic. I was standing up and talking directly to the judge. I heard myself say: 'Excuse me, excuse me, your honour – please listen to me, it was just a silly mistake. I'm not a habitual drug user. I have the odd toke on a joint occasionally but that's it. So does half of Britain. In the UK this wouldn't even be treated as a misdemeanour, let alone a crime. It's not that serious. Please. I wouldn't be arrested for such a tiny amount. The policeman would just take it off me and that would be the end of the matter. I didn't have an ounce, it was enough for one joint, barely even that. It wouldn't even get my dog stoned . . .'

It was running away from me now. I'd lost it. I was rambling, barely aware of what I was saying. It was just an incoherent appeal for clemency, for common sense and decency to prevail. The judge cut off the translator relaying my garbled plea, with the question: 'So you can buy "hashish" in shops in England, can you?'

'Well, no,' I stammered. 'But such a small amount . . .'

She turned to Pete Smith and asked him the same question.

'Er, no. No, you can't,' he replied, looking a little uncomfortable.

'Fucking cheers, Pete,' I muttered.

One of my lawyers – the older one called Piskin – got to his feet. Finally! And he looked the part too, with his grey hair, round wire-rimmed glasses and serious face. My yo-yoing hopes rose again. He'd addressed the judge for half a minute or so when the translator whispered through the railings: 'He's putting in a bail application for you . . .'

'*Bail?*' I blurted out, and the whole court heard. 'They're not seriously thinking of detaining me, are they?

You've got to be kidding me,' I said more quietly through the railings to the translator.

'He says you have some friends and clients who have said they are happy to put you up ahead of the main trial,' she continued.

'Main trial?' I cried out, loudly again. 'This is ridiculous!'

Piskin sat back down, and there was silence while the judge looked down at her notes and scribbled something. The court usher motioned to me to stand up. The judge spoke clearly in two bursts, allowing the translator to relay the message. Sentence One: 'No bail is granted.' Pause. Sentence Two: 'You will be detained for two months while the state investigates your case, the standard for foreigners.'

I felt dizzy and my chest began to tighten. I started falling. I saw the translator's alarm as I lurched towards her. A hand grabbed my upper arm and yanked me back. It was the policeman. He steered me through the door and back into the corridor. Tears streamed down my cheeks and the back of my throat was sore. I was aware of Pete Smith and the legal team standing around me, trying to reassure me: 'You'll be OK, we're going to help you … we'll keep your family informed … chin up, it won't be as bad as you think … we'll come and visit and make sure you're not maltreated in there … just keep your head down, avoid confrontation, do what they say …'

All I could manage, shaking my head and looking at the ground, was: 'But this is absurd, this is absurd …' We began walking down a dark stairwell, all six of us, our careful footsteps echoing off the stone walls. It was so dark I could barely see. A buzzer sounded and suddenly we were standing in bright sunlight and I shielded my eyes with my cuffed hands. One of the young lawyers put a packet of Parliament cigarettes in my pocket and said with a smile: 'Don't worry, you're going to be all right. Some people would pay good money for an experience like this. Don't drink and don't play cards and you should be OK.'

He walked off towards the cars parked outside the courthouse and it was clear that all of them were in a hurry to move off. Pete Smith gave me a sympathetic look and said: 'We'll come and see you at the beginning of next week. Chin up, old chap.'

I stood on the pavement with the sunlight pouring through the trees as the two cars disappeared round the corner.

My body was quivering so much I couldn't lift the cigarette to my mouth with my cuffed hands. The young policeman who'd driven me from court lifted my arms for me and guided the cigarette between my trembling lips, but I was crying so hard I couldn't inhale. I spat it on to the floor and fell to my knees. He helped me up and sat me down in the back of the car. Why was this one being nice to me? I wondered. He looked genuinely upset.

I was outside the giant gates of Piet Central prison. I could hear banging and shouting, reverberating from its towering walls. Two men in uniform emerged from a small door built into the gates and started walking towards the car. They were coming to get me. I tried to climb back in, pulling my knees up to my chest, but the bigger of the two grabbed my arm and pulled me out. I couldn't walk properly, or didn't want to (I couldn't tell which), so they had to drag me across the road and inside the massive walls. We passed through three or four barred gates, which closed behind us with a loud metallic crash that echoed down the endless corridor. The human sounds were getting louder and louder. At first I could hear only murmuring and a dull din somewhere in the distance but as we headed deeper into the gaol the noises became more distinct and coherent. There was shouting and groaning. It was clear that there were a lot of people in there somewhere.

We stopped outside a door and the guard gestured to me to take my clothes off. They took off my cuffs but I couldn't undo my shirt buttons because my arms and hands were trembling so badly. One of the guards had to undo them for me. When I was naked the other guard opened the door and pushed me into the dark and the door slammed behind me. I couldn't see anything in the pitch black and I stood there for a minute or so, too frightened to move. My eyes started to adjust and I made out a kind of arch in the wall beyond which a tap was dripping. The room stank of shit and the ammonia of old piss and beneath my feet it was cold and slimy. I stood underneath the freezing cold trickle that was my shower and I was so thirsty I craned my neck backwards and opened my mouth. The moisture in my parched gums was glorious.

Unable to stand the cold any longer, I shuffled across the greasy floor back into the first room. I had no towel and no clothes. There was a thin wooden bench along the far wall and I lay down on it on my side, shivering. I was happier now. I was safe in there. I didn't mind that hours seemed to be passing. I felt delirious and occasionally a warm, dreamy feeling swept over me. It was all going to be OK now. This was the beginning of the end.

I heard the key in the door, which opened to reveal the dark silhouette of a guard against the light. '*Anglichanin!*' I was terrified again. I just wanted to stay where I was. I walked slowly across the room and re-emerged into the dim, unnatural light of the corridor, covering my balls. The other guard opened a door almost opposite and pushed me into another tiny cell.

A light bulb hung from the ceiling, casting a dim light over the filth on the floor and the walls. There was a pile of shit in one corner and what looked like an old half-eaten orange in the middle of the room. The walls were covered with graffiti and smeared with stains. I stood retching and swallowing back the bile from my cramping stomach. I was naked, quivering with cold and fear. I stood in the middle of the room, unsure what to do. After a few minutes I heard shouts and screams outside and the door was flung open. I jumped backwards as the guards threw in two young skinheads. Their Doc Marten boots were laced up to the knees. Their heads and faces were covered in blood, some of it fresh, some of it congealed and matted on to their skin and hair and T-shirts. One of them had blood pouring from his mouth; the other could barely see because his eyes were so swollen from the beating he must have taken.

They were highly distressed and high as kites, jabbering

to themselves as they paced up and down the room, like animals in a cage. They didn't even acknowledge me as I leant against the wall. They didn't seem to know I was there. They walked past me, brushing me as they went, touching the wall, then turning and walking back the other way. Over and over again. Talking, talking, talking. I was petrified. I didn't move a muscle for half an hour as I clung to the damp wall. Was this what I would be like before they'd finished with me?

I felt the sudden onset of a dark madness. I couldn't take this! I couldn't fucking take this! I'd been staring at two wires sticking out of the ceiling where a light must once have hung. The two skinheads were about to turn at either end of the cell and I jumped into the middle of the room and grabbed the wires, which came loose and scattered plaster into my eyes. With one hand I held the two wires and then I lifted up the wrist of the other towards the frayed metal wiring sticking out of the plastic tubing. I was shaking harder than ever, but I couldn't cry any more. I'd shed all the tears I could and my eyes were parched and itchy. And then I heard Lucy's sweet voice and saw her smiling face somewhere in my head. 'Tig, what the hell are you doing, my love?' Then everything was black.

4

I have no idea how long I lay there. It could have been five minutes or two hours. When I came round, woken by the slamming of doors and the shouting of the guards, the skinheads were gone and, through the small grimy window high up on the wall, I could see that night had started to descend over Moscow. I was lying on the filthy floor, naked and shivering, my arms and chest covered in a light dusting of plaster from the ceiling. Had I really tried to top myself?

I was getting to my feet when a guard opened the door, lobbed my clothes at me and then disappeared, leaving the door wide open. I was balancing on one foot trying to put on a sock when he came back, holding a thin brown mattress rolled into a tube. Even in the gloom I could see it was a disgusting object, covered in patches and holes and stains. The stuffing, bursting from every seam and gash, looked like the contents of a Hoover bag. Fuck knows how many prisoners had slept on it and sweated and dribbled into it over the years. As the guard threw it at me, I recoiled and parried it to the ground. He laughed, turned away and came back a minute later to hand me a metal bowl, a spoon and a heavily stained cup, with a smile that said: 'Welcome to your new home. These will be your material comforts over the coming months.'

Carrying my bundle I followed him out into the long

corridor and through a series of large metal gates, slowly moving deeper into the bowels of a huge labyrinth of corridors and cells, each of the gates shutting behind us with a heavy clunk that reverberated along the stone walls. We passed cell after cell, on either side of the corridor, and from behind the doors I could hear a dim murmur of voices, like the rumble of distant traffic. But there was another noise too, a faint but rhythmic tapping, deliberate and structured, like Morse code. Three clear taps, pause, two clear taps, pause, three clear taps, pause … This wasn't the random creaking and groaning of an old building, but a crude form of communication. The cells were talking to each other.

We had passed through a fourth gate into the last section of the corridor when the guard stopped in front of the last cell door but one on the right-hand side. He opened the eye-slot and pressed his face against the peeling green door, then he lifted up his giant hedgehog of keys and – with a noise that couldn't have sounded more like a key turning in a lock if it had tried – turned his hand and pushed the door open. I suddenly became aware of my heart thumping against my ribcage. He motioned me to go in. As I reached the doorway I felt his hand shove me between the shoulder-blades. I stumbled forward, clutching my mattress and eating utensils, and as I corrected myself the door slammed behind me and the loud lock turned again.

Through the gloom I could see roughly two dozen faces staring at me, most of them registering barely a flicker of interest in the latest addition to their cramped world. The room was small, and the number of bodies in there made it feel even smaller. It wasn't a difficult calculation to work out that there were roughly twice as many men here as there were wooden shelves to sleep on. Each 'bunk' was occupied by a prostrate body, but most people were crowded together on the floor, crouching down on their haunches with their bums just above the ground and their arms resting on their knees. Half the crouchers were smoking and the room was thick with cheap tobacco, but through the fug there was a powerful stench of shit and ammonia and body odour, stale and fresh. The air was hot and damp and I was breathing it heavily. I stood at the door squeezing my mattress to my chest, paralysed by indecision and fear. The room had two barred windows high up on the wall opposite me, one of them with a pane of glass, the other open to the elements – the ventilation system, presumably.

The rows of double bunk shelves were on the walls to the left and right and straight ahead. Squeezed between the bunks in the far left-hand corner there was a toilet area behind a low brick wall, surrounded by a large puddle that leaked into the centre of the room in a meandering stream through the crouching bodies. I knew it was a toilet of some sort because I could see the head and shoulders of a man crouched behind the wall, and I could hear him farting and grunting.

No one stirred as I walked the few steps towards some space in the middle of the cell and got down on my haunches, holding on to my stinking bedding so that it didn't touch the filthy damp floor and at the same time trying to avoid bumping into anyone. As I lowered myself down, the muscles in my lower leg and knees stretched so tight they felt like they were going to snap. I bounced as gently as possible on the balls of my feet, trying not to fall forward into the gaunt man with long matted hair crouched no more than two feet in front of me. By the look and smell of him, he was some kind of vagrant and/or junkie. As far as I could see everyone was wearing trainers or slippers, tracksuit bottoms and T-shirts of various different colours and designs, even the older-looking characters. Two guys had bruised, cut faces and one of them, a fat guy who must have been at least fifty, had eyes so badly swollen that there was no way he was able to see out of them.

After about two minutes I had to stand up because the pain in my legs was becoming unbearable, but I felt very self-conscious standing there in the murky stillness. By the sound of it, the guy taking a shit behind the wall, about six feet from where I was trying to squat, had a bad case of diarrhoea. When he stood up and pulled up his trousers he filled a bowl of water from the tap on the wall and threw it over the floor where he'd been crouching. He repeated this a couple of times and then began to curse as the liquid oozed out from behind the wall. There was clearly a problem with the drainage and I watched him scraping at the floor with his feet in an apparent attempt to push his waste down the hole in the ground.

I still felt unsettled by the looks I was starting to draw as I tried to get comfortable, shifting from foot to foot, then squatting, standing up again, over and over ... up, down, up, down ... for about half an hour. I guessed once you'd been in there a while your squatting muscles loosened up a bit, and it became easier. I was starting to fret about how I was going to find a place to lie down and sleep when a very young fresh-faced guy with cropped blond hair climbed off one of the bottom bunks and, with a kind smile, motioned to me to take his place. Stepping this way and that between the squatting figures on the floor I reached the bunk and the young guy said something in Russian, pointing to the bed. I sat down – and so did he, right next to me. I smiled at him nervously and he smiled back. He asked me something in Russian, but I could only shrug and make a silly, apologetic face in reply.

The thought that he might be offering himself to me in some way passed uncomfortably through my mind. Wasn't that kind of thing rife in prisons? Don't bend over for the soap and all that. I pulled out the packet of Parliament cigarettes one of the lawyers had given me and offered them to him in an attempt to show I appreciated his thoughtfulness. Within seconds there were half a dozen guys forming a circle around me, some patting me, others putting their hands together as if in prayer, all of them with an air of desperation. Within two minutes, the whole pack had gone. As he pulled out a cigarette, a guy with an eye-patch and two slash scars running right across his face said, 'Merci beaucoup, monsieur. Gentil.'

'Pas de problème. C'est mon plaisir,' I replied instantly, jumping on the opportunity to communicate with someone. It had been so long since I'd spoken that I had to clear my throat halfway through.

We began to exchange small talk in near-whispers so as not to stir up the moody silence hanging over the room.

I'd studied French at Leeds University, and I was able to speak it freely, but his grasp of the language, I quickly learned, was pretty limited. He asked to see my court papers and immediately a couple of others gathered around him, reading over his shoulder, to find out what I was in for. Their reaction to what they were reading was surprise, bordering on astonishment. One of them started laughing with incredulity, pointing his finger at me and exclaiming, 'Anglia! Anglia!' The other guy held out his hand and rubbed his fingers against his thumb, just like the Customs guy at the airport. The general message seemed to be: 'What the fuck's an English businessman doing in this hellhole? And why the fuck didn't you just bribe your way out of it, you fool?' I could only shrug and blow out my cheeks.

The young blond guy took the papers and handed them back to me, then pointed at the bed and put his hands to one side of his head, indicating that I should take the chance to sleep. He continued with a series of hand signals and I eventually twigged: I was to sleep there now, then it would be his turn. We were to be bunk partners. I laid out my sordid thin mattress and, not wanting to put my face anywhere near it, stretched out on my back, being careful not to kick the head of the guy in the bunk along from me.

I must have fallen asleep within seconds, and I had the feeling it was the dead of night when I woke up with a start, almost hitting my head on the bunk above, however many hours later. Most of the room was asleep, including the majority of the guys on the floor, who had given up their squatting positions and were now either curled up in a ball on their side or – like my bunk partner – were sitting on their backsides leaning up against the bunks behind. I lay there for a few minutes, listening to the tapping on the water pipes, a series of calls and answers, being passed between neighbouring cells. What the hell were they saying to each other? It was another language, or code, that I didn't understand.

Someone had wrapped a small piece of wire around the slats of the bunk above me and, without thinking, I unravelled it and immediately used it to start writing on the back of my court papers. In the half-light of the room I couldn't quite make out the impressions I was making on the paper but I was scribbling furiously, trying to recall and record every last detail of what had happened to me since arriving in Moscow. I was trying to make sense of the experience.

Every now and then I cursed under my breath at my stupidity. If only I had realized that all that greasy little Customs guy had wanted me to do was slip him a couple of hundred dollars, that would have been the end of the matter – and instead of lying in a cramped, squalid, shit-soaked, pissy cell with twenty-five low-lifes, I'd be in one of Russia's finest hotels, sleeping off a night out with the boys, dreaming about my beautiful girlfriend. Why didn't I stand my ground at the airport and insist on a lawyer or an Embassy official? Why did I admit it was my dope and why the hell did I admit that I smoked it back in England? Why didn't I call one of my Russian clients to come down to the airport, rather than just blub down the phone to my boss like a big fucking baby?

It was the first time since arriving that I had been able

to gather my thoughts, and the realization crept over me like a shadow that at every single turn I had made the wrong call. How had I been so bloody naïve? What the hell was I thinking? Had I just been plain scared and put my hands up in the air before a shot had even been fired? A coward who couldn't stand up for himself when it came to the crunch? Or was it that I simply couldn't believe that such a fuss could be made over a miserably small piece of hash and that being a reasonable person, I'd expected everyone else to be reasonable and that common sense, common decency and natural justice would prevail?

I scrawled manically, and all the while the images of Lucy and my mum and dad kept coming back at me, harder and harder, as my eyes began to well up again at the thought of what they were doing right that moment. They'd still be awake back in England, worrying their hearts out, especially Mum, who I knew would be sobbing into her hankie in front of the telly, or into her pillow. Dad would be putting on a brave face trying to reassure her, cracking a few jokes, giving it the bravado. Deep down, though, he'd be as worried shitless as Mum. And Lucy, dear Luce – what nightmare had I plunged my gorgeous babe into? Would she stay with me through this? How the hell could I have done this to them all? The reality was bad enough for me, but in a way I'd rather have been in my shoes than theirs, imagining the most horrible things happening to me. Fucking idiot, Tig Hague! Idiot! Idiot!

I'd covered the equivalent of three and half pages of A4 when the young blond guy walked towards me and indicated that it was his turn to use the bunk. I thanked him with a nod and a smile, rolled up my mattress and made my way to the space on the floor he'd vacated by the bunks on the adjoining wall close to the toilet area. The tramp guy was on my right between me and the toilet and there was little more than two feet between us as I crouched down and lit up one of the few Marlboro Reds I had left. There were still only a few guys awake and, but for the sound of snoring, the room was silent. There were three men squatting on the floor, all smoking cigarettes, and all staring at me without either embarrassment or great curiosity, just blankly taking me in: the English guy in the natty shirt, jeans and loafers. How precious my clothes must have looked among all the grubby tracksuits and T-shirts.

My legs, especially my knees, soon began to ache and I realized there was simply no way I was going to be able to crouch like that for long periods. Moreover, my body was crying out for more sleep and I knew I needed to be as strong and calm as possible over the coming days and weeks. Standing up, I unrolled the mattress and then folded it in half lengthways because there wasn't enough room to fully extend myself. I lay down on my side, my upper body on the mattress and my legs on the floor, pulled up towards my chest like a big embryo.

The crash of the hatch on the door opening woke me up however many hours later and I could tell by the watery natural light in the room that it was early morning. My eyelids were pasty with sleep, my head was thick and my upper right arm was half-sore, half-numb from lying on it. When I'd woken up in the night the stench of shit and piss seemed to have got better – probably, I figured, because my nose had got accustomed to it – but now it was worse than ever, like it was right under my nose. When I pulled myself up to sit on my mattress I realized why: the toilet area had leaked badly in the night, soaking my right trouser leg with waste. I leapt to my feet, holding my hand over my mouth and nose as I retched. It was lucky my stomach had nothing to offer in response.

In those same few moments, I noticed out of the corner of my eye that over to my left a guard had put a large bowl with a ladle in it through the hatch on to the fold-down tray, and I could see his hand now holding out a smaller bowl, waiting, it seemed, for someone to go and collect it. No one stirred a muscle in those few seconds, and I felt a sudden panic that as the new boy in the cell it was my job to go and collect the breakfast. I trod carefully through the bodies, but went as quickly as possible to get to the door on the other side, the wet of the toilet waste clinging to my leg. The little bowl had sugar in it and I took it from the guard, placed it on the long thin table against the wall next to the door, then put the larger bowl, containing a grey, runny, porridgy mixture, next to it. A couple of the guys were now forming a queue at the table and someone shouted '*Bilander!*' ('Food!'), causing those still in their beds to sit up and get to their feet. As I moved away I watched closely as they each put one ladle of the slop into their bowls and sprinkled it with about half a teaspoon of sugar.

I hadn't eaten for three days and my stomach was starting to ache with hunger. I had to eat something, not least to try to regain some strength. When it was my turn at the big bowl, I was careful to take only a modest amount of porridge and sugar so as not to upset anyone and then I moved over to the bunk where my 'bunk buddy' was already sitting. He smiled and indicated I sit down next to him. I put one mouthful of the porridge in my mouth and instantly, but quietly, spat it back on to the spoon and into the bowl, swallowing back down another empty retch. It wasn't my decision; it was my body's. It just didn't want the watery, lumpy filth, no matter how hungry I was. I put the bowl on the floor between my legs and then put my head in my hands and rubbed my face up and down in exasperation. How the fuck was I going to survive, living off that shit, in this shithole?

I looked up and the fat guy, squinting through his swollen eyes, was standing in front of me holding out his empty bowl. I went to take it, thinking he was telling me to wash it up, but he pulled it away and pointed at my bowl on the floor. He wanted my porridge. Dilemma: did I try and explain with hand and mouth gestures that I had spat in it, or did I just hand it to him and hope no one else had seen what I'd done and tell him? He pointed at it again – as I couldn't see his eyes it was difficult to know if he was being aggressive or urgent – so I handed it to him and he quickly scooped out the contents into his bowl, nodded and smiled his gratitude, and handed back my bowl.

My bunk buddy stood up and held out his upturned hand, telling me to wait right there. Like I was going any-where. He went to the cupboard above the table and took out some kind of metal and wire contraption, a primitive heating element with a plastic handle strapped on with tape. Taking a large metal cup off the cupboard shelf, he filled it up from the tap in the toilet area and plugged the element into a socket on the floor by the cupboard. It took ages for the water to heat, and I was quietly willing it to hurry up, partly because I was nervous about what he might present me with, and that I'd be obliged to consume it for fear of rebuffing his generosity, and partly because, in a room with nothing else happening in it, the heating of the water in the mug had become something of a spectacle for half the men in there. After half an hour it was ready and the young boy, beaming from ear to ear, held out the steaming mug with one hand and four oatmeal-style biscuits with the other. One of the squatters a few feet away turned to me and with a toothy grin, cackled: 'English boy like tea and biscuits.'

I ate the biscuits with an almost obscene relish, and gulped the sweet black tea down as fast as its heat allowed me. As soon as I'd finished, I took out my Marlboros so that no one else could see them this time and passed one to the young guy, nodding at him a few times in gratitude for his kindness. He extended his hand to me and said: 'Gennady.'

I shook his hand, replying with a smile: 'Me Tig, thank you, *spasiba*.'

We had soup for lunch, or rather everyone else did. It looked suspiciously similar to the porridge, only with added bits of see-through cabbage and one or two dubious items of vegetation, and I couldn't bring myself to consume it. Gennady swapped four more biscuits for a Marlboro Red, and that was enough to do away with the hunger cramps. Lunch had triggered a small flurry of activity, but half an hour after everyone had eaten, washed their bowls under the tap and used the toilet, the room was still and quiet again, except for those sitting up and crouching having a fag. It struck me that the reason it was so quiet was that none of us knew each other. We were just a room full of strangers, brought together by our crimes and misdemeanours, keeping our heads down and killing time.

At some point in the afternoon, all heads turned at the loud, slightly shocking sound of the key in the lock. A guard in khaki shirt and trousers took one step into the room, pointed at five people, including me, and barked something in Russian, motioning to us to follow him out of the room. I made sure I was the last out of the cell so I could watch and follow what the others did. We walked a little way down the corridor until the guard said something and we all stopped. We formed a line with our backs against the wall, legs apart, looking at the floor and, one by one, at intervals of five minutes, we were led into a little room opposite that looked like some kind of medical office.

When I was summoned, a man in a white coat tugged his shirt and clicked his fingers with a dramatic flourish, meaning, I guessed, 'Strip off, scumbag, I need to look up your bum.' It was a small room and I felt particularly uncomfortable as I undressed because the two guards and the medical officer were standing very close and there was little room for manoeuvre. For such a vast prison, why were all the rooms so bloody cramped, I wondered, balancing on one leg like a flamingo as I tried to take off a sock.

With my clothes piled on to the bed opposite I stood in the middle of the room, hands at my sides, cock beating a retreat into my pubes, while the medic began his examination. For the second day running I felt the horrible intrusion of rubbered fingers in my arse – I knew it was coming but I still felt myself tensing all over and my buttocks clamped on his hand like a vice. There's nothing pleasant about a general body search or 'exam' but there's something particularly humiliating about a stranger putting his hand up your backside, and right then I had to swallow down a powerful urge to shout and thrash out. He then lifted up my cock and my scrotum, checking for God knows what, each time picking them up with thumb and forefinger, like he was holding a china teacup, as he peered underneath.

'You are Manchesters United or Liverpool?' he asked as he let go of my cock and peeled off his rubber glove.

'I like Arsenal. I'm a Gooner,' I replied.

'Ah, Terry Onri. Good goals. Fast.'

'Yes, Thierry's very fast,' I said.

'Goodbye.'

I put my clothes on, trying not to touch the stripe of dried shit down the right leg of my trousers, and returned to the corridor. When all five of us had been seen, we were taken further down the corridor back towards the shower area I'd come from yesterday. Again, we lined up against the wall and one by one were directed into a room opposite. This one was for fingerprints and ID photographs. The guard took me by the wrist, made me spread out my fingers and then pressed them first into a large ink sponge and then on to the appropriate finger spaces of an official document. We repeated the process with my other hand and I was then told to stand against the bare wall while he took my picture. The camera he took out from under the table was very large and very old with a big flash on top, the kind you see news photographers using in American films of the 1940s and 1950s. He took one of me face on and one of my left profile, each time the flash and the sound of the shutter making me jump a little.

I was a proper criminal now. With each burst of the flash I took another step deeper into the system and that much further away from home. The fingerprinting and the photos were a ritual initiation into my new world. I was being given a new identity. It was official: I was a prisoner in Russia. That was the main point about me now. Mum and Dad could no longer say, with pride: 'Tig's a broker in the City with a top American firm.' They'd have to say: 'Tig's in gaol in Moscow on drugs charges.' That was my character now, and it was time to start learning my lines.

5

Two dozen heads looked up as one as the key turned in the lock and a broad shaft of light from the corridor cut across the cell, lighting up the thick, acrid smoke as the door swung wide open. A grey silhouette stepped into the room and snapped: 'Hague! Tig!' I slowly walked over to him but he pointed back to my bedding, saying: '*Matras!*'

Where the hell was I going now? The cell was a squalid dump, but my instinctive reaction was that I didn't want to leave, just as I hadn't wanted to leave the filthy shower room the day before. I was safe in there at least. No one had threatened or disturbed me – they'd barely even registered my existence, except the young boy, Gennady, who had given me the tea and biscuits. He smiled and jerked his head upwards in farewell. I did the same. No one else in the room so much as looked or flinched. They just carried on smoking, crouching, sitting or lying.

I quickly rolled up my metal eating utensils inside my mattress and walked into the corridor, where the sight of roughly ten other prisoners in a line against the wall – each holding his mattress to his chest and looking solemnly down at the floor – made me stop in my tracks. They were a sorry sight, barely a flicker of life or energy between them, and I noticed that the guy nearest to me was dribbling down his chin and not bothering to wipe it off. It just drooled on to his T-shirt and mattress. I joined the back of the column, and with one guard at the front and one at the back we walked the short distance to the end of the corridor, through a metal gate and a door out into a stairwell. Up we went, floor by floor, slowly trudging up the steps, our numbers gradually reducing as we deposited prisoners at the entrance to each long corridor where two guards were waiting to take them away. In the stairwell I noticed the odd cigarette left in the right angle or side of a step or on the window ledge between floors. It seemed that they had been left deliberately for others to collect.

By the time we reached the third floor I was breathing heavily, partly because I was weak and short of breath but more because I was growing increasingly anxious about where I was heading. I was learning quickly that the fear of the unknown, the uncertainty of what was going to happen next, was causing me greater stress than any actual experience I had – to the extent that I'd rather have stayed in that shitty, rank, crowded cell than be moved. Better the devil you know. I was having some kind of panic attack, virtually hyperventilating, when we stopped at the door on the third floor and one of the guards said, 'Hague, Tig.' The way the guards pronounced it, it sounded like 'hectic'. I followed the guards into the corridor and walked past two doors, one on either side, then we stopped and one of them rifled through the bunch on his belt for the right key.

He opened the door and said: '*Franceuse*,' stepping aside for me to enter. The room opened up to the right. The only person I could see was a tall, wiry black man with a little pot belly, a shaved head and a moustache that dropped down to the sides of his mouth. From twenty feet away he looked like a dead ringer for Errol Brown, the lead singer of the 1970s soul band Hot Chocolate.

'Ah, so we have a French dude coming to stay,' the man said in excellent English with an American twang, walking towards me and holding out his hand.

'English, actually,' I said nervously.

'Hey, an English boy! Welcome!' he laughed. A big, friendly smile spread over his face as we shook hands.

'Hi, I'm Zubi, welcome to Piet Central.'

'Tig. How d'you do?'

I'd only been in the room ten seconds but my immediate impressions were very positive. The cell was the same size as the other one, but most of the bunks looked unoccupied. It didn't stink of shit, the floor looked clean and dry, no one was smoking cheap Russian fags – in fact there was no smoke at all. There was bags of room and plenty of bunks to choose from, and some effort had been made to make the place comfortable. The wall on the door side, weirdly, had been decorated with old newspapers and magazines, layer upon layer of images and script from over the years all jumbled up on top of each other. A few of the images were of naked female bodies, a tit here, some buttocks there, and several shots of Jordan sticking out her enormous rack. People had also scrawled graffiti over it in places. It was the kind of work that wouldn't look out of place in a student art exhibition. To the left, in the far corner, was the toilet area, which had been screened off all the way round with sheets, and along the left-hand wall there was a big metal cupboard above a worktop. In the centre of the room there was a metal table fixed to the floor with a bench on either side, each capable of sitting three people at a squeeze. Behind the door there was a small black and white television with a flickering screen, which right then was showing some kind of Russian game show with the volume down low.

From behind the bunk sheets two faces appeared, one white, one brown. A very young Indian-looking guy, probably barely out of his teens, emerged from one bunk and introduced himself softly. 'Hey man, how you doin'? Nice to meet you. I'm Ranjit,' he said with a shy giggle. His English sounded very good too.

'Come and meet Pasha. He's Czech – we think. He doesn't give too much away,' Zubi said, taking a few paces and pulling back a sheet over a bunk in the corner.

Pasha was a wiry, pale young hippy-looking character with shaved blond hair. He was sitting in the lotus position, wearing a T-shirt and a sarong, and he barely twitched a muscle as Zubi introduced me. He stared at me vacantly, moronically almost, with giant ice-blue eyes. The words 'space cadet' popped into my head as I shook his outstretched hand.

I felt much calmer than I had done just moments earlier but I was still breathing hard and I must have looked a little bewildered because Zubi took my mattress, set it down, then put his arm on my shoulder and said in a very soothing voice: 'Calm down, it's cool, my friend. We'll look after you, you're with us now. You're in the foreigners' cell.'

Zubi told Ranjit to go and boil some water, and with a big toothy grin that sent his moustache shooting across his face, he said: 'Man, you look like shit! I'm going to tell you everything you need to know about this place and how to get the fuck out of it. But before we have a chat, we need to get you washed, shaved, dressed and fed.'

He went to one of the bunks and started searching through a giant checked laundry bag with handles. 'These, my friend, are called *sumkas* and that's where you'll end up keeping all your worldly possessions.' He came back and handed me some soap, a new toothbrush, a tube of toothpaste, a bottle of Timotei shampoo, and a clean towel.

'We're going to have to wash those shitty trousers and that shirt of yours,' he continued, heading back to his *sumka*. 'You'll need those for your court appearances. Here, take this,' he said, throwing me a clean pair of dark tracksuit bottoms and a brown and yellow T-shirt. Ranjit walked over and presented me with a grey fleece top and a pair of brown and red tartan slippers. When the large bowl of water, with two elements in it, had boiled, Zubi said: 'Right, go get cleaned up,' and he pulled back the screen around the toilet. Plastered over the wall were more images of semi-naked girls, and there was Jordan again, grinning and squeezing her mighty boobs out towards me.

I'd barely spoken a word in the fifteen minutes since my arrival, muttering only, 'Great ... brilliant ... God, thanks ... cheers, mate ... wow ... lovely ...' At the back of my mind I kept wondering if there was some elaborate con trick being played. Was I being stitched up in some way? The experiences of the previous few days had made me nervous and suspicious of everyone. But these guys seemed genuine, and they were foreign, which was reassuring, and they spoke English.

'Go on, my man, we're not going to jump you ...' said Zubi, holding the screen open for me. I walked in and he passed through the bowl of steaming hot water. I stripped off quickly and started washing furiously, squeezing the shampoo into my hair and lathering the soap into my skin. The feeling of hot water was magical as I splashed and rubbed it all over my sticky body and grimy hair. When I'd finished I poured the remainder of the water over my head and stood and savoured the feeling of cleanliness for a minute or so.

'You ready for a shave now?' said Zubi, passing through a smaller bowl of hot water, a razor and some Gillette shaving gel. The razor was new but it was still painful removing five days of stubble. I emerged from behind the sheet screen, washed and scrubbed from head to toe, comfortable but a little awkward in my new clothes. Zubi exclaimed: 'Food now! You must be hungry!'

'I'm bloody ravenous!' I replied.

'Hey, the guy says "bloody", Ranjit. He may look Italian but he really is English. Make the gentleman some supper.'

Zubi took my dirty clothes from me, put them in the large washing bowl with some powder and water, and left them to soak on the floor. I watched Ranjit open up the large, deep cupboard screwed into the wall ...

'Fucking hell!' I blurted, my eyes popping out as he pulled back the two doors to reveal three shelves groaning with food. I could see dozens of packets of noodles,

I could see salamis, and garlic cloves, and onions, some biscuits, a few oranges and lemons and apples . . .

'Treat this as your own,' said Zubi. 'Take whatever you want. *Mi casa es su casa.* We all share in here. When you get a delivery, it all goes in there. All for one and one for all.'

Twenty minutes later Ranjit presented me with a bowl of steaming noodles, containing chunks of salami, onion and bits of garlic. 'The house speciality,' he smiled, as he put it down on the metal table. I launched myself at it, bolting it like a dog, and finishing it in no more than two or three minutes. It was the most delicious meal I'd ever eaten.

'Would Sir enjoy a cigarette after his dinner?' asked Zubi, holding open a shopping bag half full of individual cigarettes. There must have been at least 400 in there.

I took one and sparked it up, leaning back and blowing the smoke high into the air, and I could feel the muscles starting to release their iron grip on my neck and shoulders. Zubi sat down on the bench facing me and said, 'So, tell me your story, English boy, and I tell you how to get out of here. Trust me, I'm an expert.'

Zubi and I sat up into the small hours of the morning, and I hung on to his every word as he explained about Russian gaols: how they operated, how to survive them and how to get out of them. We sat on his bunk behind the overhanging sheet, talking in hushed tones so that the night guard patrolling outside couldn't hear us. The dull murmur of the prison had given way to a crisp silence, broken only by the rhythmical tapping of the pipes. I knew roughly how long we talked because I heard the guard pull back the eye-slot for his hourly check at least five times. By the time I slumped back to my bunk, my head was swimming with knowledge, advice, warnings, handy tips ... Boy, the man could talk, and he certainly seemed to know what he was talking about. Zubi was a proper drugs dealer, who had come to Moscow from Nigeria to make his illicit fortune. He had married a Moscow girl about five years ago, and he was now as good as fluent in Russian. With tears in his eyes and emotion in his voice he twice showed me a picture of his pretty little daughter and told me that one day, when he was a rich man, he was going to take her back to Lagos and drive her around in an open-top sports car. He had been caught with five or six grams of heroin two months earlier and was looking at up to twelve years if convicted. His advice to me was to start learning the language as fast as possible. 'The better you communicate,' he said, 'the better the chance you have of getting by and of getting out. Misunderstandings are dangerous. If you can't speak or understand, you are powerless. You may as well be a deaf mute.'

He explained that there are two types of prison in Russia: Krastnaya Zona ('Red Zone') and Churnaya Zona ('Black Zone'). Piet was a Red Zone, meaning that the prison was effectively controlled by a hardcore of prisoners led by the '*volk*', which is Russian for 'wolf'. His authority was absolute. If you had a problem with another prisoner you got word to the *volk*; if the *volk* asked you to do something, you just did it. Piss off the *volk*, or one of his people, and your life was on the line.

The prison guards had no real control over day-to-day

life in Piet. They were just minor officials who unlocked doors, delivered the food and took prisoners down to the interview rooms or the wash area for the weekly shower. That didn't mean you could ignore them or show disrespect to them, because they had the capacity to make life very uncomfortable, it was just that the real power didn't lie with them, but with the *volk* and his henchmen. 'Every few weeks, though,' Zubi continued, 'the authorities like to assert themselves and send in their riot cop hooligans, known as the *shmon*, who turn the place over in a frenzied search for drugs, needles, weapons, mobile phones and any other illegal possessions . . .'

The Black Zones, meanwhile, were prisons controlled by the KGB, or FSB as they are known today, and in there the guards had total control over day-to-day life. It wasn't a case of one type of prison being more preferable to live in than another, Zubi stressed; each presented its own survival challenges and it was more a question of understanding how the systems worked and learning how to play the game. Get it wrong with the *volk*, and you ended up with a knife hanging out of your back. Get it wrong with the guards and you ended up in 'Razburg', the penal block in the basement where all rights were taken away and where you either lived in solitary confinement or you shared a windowless booth with another prisoner. 'Razburg's basically a dungeon. There's no daily walk up on the roof, you go weeks without a shower and your visits are restricted. In Razburg, you're left to rot.'

Each cell had a '*smatriashi*', which meant 'watcher' or 'monitor', who was in charge of life in that room and reported to the *volk*. 'I'm our *smatriashi*, but as we're a foreign cell, we're not as strictly controlled by the *volk* as the Russian cells,' he added. The *smatriashi* settled disputes within his cell, and with so many desperate men living in such crowded conditions with so little to do, flare-ups were almost daily occurrences. The *smatriashi* also oversaw the contributions each prisoner made to the '*obshi*' (general or shared) running of the cell, whether that was in the form of goods from the outside such as cigarettes or food, or in tasks performed such as cleaning, or collecting the food at the hatch from the *bilander* man.

'Most of the Russian cells also have a *peederaz* – and that's one fucking prison job you don't want!' said Zubi, bursting into nervous laughter. '*Peederaz* means queer. In here he's an inmate chosen by the long-term prisoners to abuse, rape and humiliate as and when they feel the urge. The *peederaz* sleeps on the floor, he doesn't sit at the table with the others or shower with them. He cleans everything in the cell and he's forced to have sex with anyone who wants it. If somebody wants a blowjob, the *peederaz* gives it to them. If they want a bugger, the *peederaz* bends over for them. If the *peederaz* refuses or complains, then he's beaten up or stabbed, and the hardcore guys simply choose another one. The *peederaz* is normally a new arrival in the cell and he's normally young and good-looking . . .'

When Zubi moved on to examine my court papers, he seemed genuinely taken aback that I had managed to end up so far into the system for such a comparatively minor offence, just as the guys in the first cell had been. Perhaps he was trying to cheer me up after all his tales of riots and buggery and solitary confinement, but he was convinced that, if I played the system right and took his advice, I'd be back at home in time for Christmas.

'Christmas!' I yelled. 'You're fucking having me on – that's almost six months away! They said it'd take two months to investigate my case . . .'

'Man, don't be a pussy!' Zubi howled, then immediately covered his mouth in case he had attracted the attention of the night guard. 'This is the Russian judicial system you're dealing with here,' he continued in a whisper. 'It ain't the Swiss rail network where all the trains run on time. They'll get round to you eventually, but you gotta be prepared for the waiting or the delays are gonna drive you outta your mind . . .'

Encouragingly, my case was almost exactly the same as Ranjit's. Like me, Ranjit had been caught with a small amount of hash at the same airport when he arrived from India to visit his brothers living in Moscow. The only difference was that from the moment he was arrested he had denied all knowledge of how the little lump had found its way into his suitcase. The other crucial factor was that Ranjit's family were well off and they had paid their lawyer 20,000 US dollars to bribe the prosecutor and the judge to secure his freedom. 'If you got money, you should walk every time,' Zubi said. 'Ranjit's trial is later this week, and I guarantee he won't be coming back here when it's over. And, English boy, like Ranjit, you're a millionaire compared to everyone else in here. It's all about the money, and if you've got it, or you can get it, you gotta use it. It's the only guaranteed way out of here. You gotta get yourself a lawyer who's prepared to play the bribery game, or they're gonna fuck you. You'll end up in a camp in the middle of fucking nowhere for fuck knows how many years where they'll just leave you to decompose or go crazy. You can't afford to gamble with the system, or expect the court to be fair and reasonable, 'cos they don't give a shit about you. To Russians, human rights is just something that happens to other people. Man, this country has sent more of its own people to camps than the rest of the world put together. To them, you're just an English pussy drug smuggler. But right now, for the next few weeks, your first priority is to learn how to survive in here, and Zubi's gonna show you how it is. Watch what I do, listen to what I say and trust me, and you're gonna be just fine. Zubi's gonna look after you. Zubi's the man.'

6

It was barely light when I found myself leaping to my feet at the crash of the hatch in the door. God knows what time it was when we'd gone to bed but we couldn't have had more than three or four hours' sleep. Zubi rolled out of bed from behind his drape in one motion and, walking towards the cupboard, looked at me and pointed to his eyes, as if to say, 'Look and learn.' He picked up the large metal bowl and took a cigarette from the shopping bag. When he placed the bowl on the fold-down hatch, a hand appeared from the other side, ladled out four servings of porridge gruel and then passed through a little bowl of sugar. Zubi put the fag into the hand and there followed a short exchange in Russian that ended with both men laughing. Zubi pulled the hatch up and, carrying the bowl over to the table, said: 'You can't let these mother-fucking pussies get the upper hand on you. If they say something to you, come back at them with a wisecrack. Make them laugh. Dominate them with banter, because if you play the wet pussy with them, they'll walk all over you. Talk the talk with them and they'll show you a bit of respect.

'Rule number two: keep the *bilander* man sweet with cigarettes and coffee, and occasionally he'll bring you an onion, or a potato, or some bones for making stock, or even the odd piece of meat. You want to look after your nutrition in here, or you're gonna get sick like a dog. There ain't nothing but shit in them bowls. Keep all the guards sweet when you can afford to, because there's not one of them that doesn't take a bribe. These guys are poor and they want stuff just like everyone else. One day you'll need them to do you a favour . . .'

'Rule number three: always take the food they offer you, even if you ain't gonna eat it 'cos your embassy has brought you your shopping that month. If you turn down your food, it sends out the wrong message. They don't like it, and they'll start giving you a hard time for not playing the game. If he puts shit in your bowl, you thank him, then chuck it down the toilet hole when he ain't looking and go make yourself some noodles.'

I watched Zubi like a hawk the whole day, and asked him endless questions about life in the prison, desperately trying to gather as much information as possible. Ranjit chipped in occasionally but otherwise lay on his bunk, reading his court papers and preparing answers for his cross-examination. Pasha, meanwhile, said nothing. He just sat and stared vacantly, or lay and stared vacantly, or walked around and stared vacantly. 'Fried his head in India,' said Zubi. 'He's away with the fairies now. Didn't even bother to hide the dope he was smuggling. He was changing flights in Moscow when they caught him.' Zubi tapped his temple and raised his eyebrows, just in case I didn't get it that Pasha wasn't all there upstairs.

It was difficult to know the exact time at any point in the day because there was no clock in the cell and nobody had a watch, but the day's schedule went like this: breakfast at six, followed by 'cell check' between eight and nine, soup at around midday, an hour-long walk on the roof at some point in the afternoon, cell check at about five or six, into bed by eleven.

During the cell checks the guards looked for 'contraband', which meant anything prisoners weren't allowed: drugs, mobiles, alcohol, tools, wires, ropes, syringes ... and the only reason they gave a shit and made an effort, Zubi explained, was because if they ever found something, behind a brick or stuffed in a mattress, for instance, they would sell it back to the cell, or the prisoner, a few days later. In preparation for their first visit of the day, we made our beds, tidied up the cell, and folded away all the sheets that hung over our bunks and the toilet area as privacy screens. They knew we had the sheets because they could see them every time they looked through the eye-slot, Zubi explained, but it was prison ritual that we hid them for the cell check.

I could tell when it was almost our time to be checked, because I could hear a low commotion that grew louder as they moved along the corridor from one cell to the next, towards ours, virtually at the end. I was starting to feel nervous as the key turned in the lock. 'Just do what I do,' said Zubi, shooting me a reassuring look. 'If in doubt, just nod and say "*Spasiba, nachalnik.*" It means "Thanks, boss."' Three guards strolled in, each holding a truncheon in his right hand, and all four of us got off our bunks and stood to attention. All three guards walked past me slowly, looking me up and down as I stood staring at the wall opposite. Zubi began bantering with them, trying to draw their attention from me, I guessed, and then we filed out into the corridor where we stood facing the wall with our hands behind our backs for about ten minutes while the guards hunted for their contraband. I could hear scraping and grinding and swearing and banging and the odd burst of conversation. I shot Zubi a worried look, wondering whether this was normal, and he winked back at me. When the guards re-emerged and motioned us back in, Zubi made some cocky comment, triggering a mock argument between the four of them.

'I told the mother-fuckers they'd never find my Kalashnikov or my heroin,' said Zubi smiling. 'Looks like the fuckers have helped themselves again,' he added, looking over at the cupboard where packets of noodles and sachets of coffee lay strewn over the shelves. The room looked as if a small typhoon had passed through. All our beds had been stripped and my *matras* had been slashed open, all its revolting stuffing scattered over the bunk and the floor below.

'Welcome to cell 310,' said Zubi, handing me a needle and a ball of coarse thread from the cupboard. 'They just want the new boy to know from the start that they're gonna be watching him carefully. Man, you think this is bad, you wait till the *shmon* show up.'

In the late afternoon, a guard entered the room and we all jumped off our bunks and stood to attention.

'*Gulet?*' he asked Zubi.

'You guys fancy a walk on the roof today?' Zubi asked, turning to the three of us. 'English boy, the daily walk rule is that we all go or we all stay.'

From the look on their faces, the others weren't exactly wetting themselves with excitement at the prospect, but

I'd been looking forward to exercise hour all day, up there on the roof, stretching my legs with the sky above my head and maybe even a good view across Moscow.

'Yeah, lovely, I fancy a bit of fresh air,' I said.

I had it stuck in my imagination that the yard was going to be like the ones you see in the films: a couple of guys doing some weights, a few others playing basketball or football, others walking, chatting and smoking, all of them happy to be out of the confinement of their cells. The reality was something else. The outdoor exercise area, two floors above our cell, was barely outside at all. It was a dingy, corrugated iron shack, almost entirely enclosed from the elements. There was a one-foot gap between the roof and the top of the walls, which were far too high to see over, and there were also a few narrow cracks between the joins of the iron sheets through which I could just about make out the city in the distance when I squeezed one eye up against them. Nor was it the great open area I'd been imagining as we were led up the four flights of steps from our corridor. It can't have measured much more than twenty foot by twenty, which was not much bigger than our cell.

It took no more than half a minute to complete a lap and as we began our walk round and round the short perimeter, like zoo animals, Zubi explained that there were dozens of similar exercise shacks strung out along the roof and that each one was used by the cells directly below. Our area, for instance, was used by our cell, 310, and at other times of the day by the inmates of the other four cells directly below it: 110, 210, 410, and 510. I could hear dozens of voices on either side, and people clearing their throats and noses and gobbing repeatedly. All along the roof prisoners banged their fists on the metal walls, creating a hellish din. When our neighbours realized we were there, they immediately began to shout and hammer on our corrugated walls, and the clamour was all the more disconcerting for coming from people we couldn't even see. Zubi shouted back to them in Russian, and by the way he spoke it was clear that he was fielding questions.

'What do they want? What are they saying?' I asked Zubi.

'They want you, my friend. You're a celebrity. They're asking "Who's the English boy? What the hell's he in for? What's he like? Is he bad?" English boys just don't end up here. You're a novelty.'

'A prison novelty! Great. So I'm the English idiot with 500 dollars in his wallet who somehow couldn't buy his way out of some minor hassle at the airport.'

'That's what I've been telling them, man, but they just don't believe that. They think you're one bad mother-fucker who committed such a heinous crime that you couldn't even bribe your way out of it!' he laughed. 'They think you're a big player in the crime world – and I'd go along with that if I were you. It'll win you a bit of respect.'

For an hour we walked, like zombies, round and round the exercise area with nothing to do but listen to the demonic sound of other prisoners shouting and shaking their decrepit, rusting enclosures. I felt very mildly exercised but it was something of a relief when the hour was up and we filed back downstairs.

Back in the cell, Ranjit gave me three empty Russian exercise books and a biro and I promised that I'd pay him back when the Embassy or my family came to deliver my parcel of provisions. 'I hope not, my friend,' he replied. 'I should be out of here by then.'

For an hour or two I lay on my bunk, writing up my diary, filling the pages with depressing thoughts and wild fears and desperate expressions of love for Lucy and remorse for the grief I'd caused everyone. The act of taking all these feelings out of my head and my heart and putting them down on paper somehow relieved their intensity.

I'd only been in the cell for about twenty-four hours – and it was a great cell compared to the previous one – but I had begun to feel the first but very real sensations of claustrophobia, the very physical discomfort of not being free to go where I wanted, when I wanted, of being trapped, stripped of the basic comforts I took for granted at home. But the worst bit was being separated from the people I loved. The trauma of the arrest, the panic about how to react to the rapidly unfolding events, the lack of sleep, Zubi's crash course in prison life, the rush of new experiences ... together they'd overwhelmed any other feelings competing for my attention. But lying on my bed, staring at the slats of the bunk above, my wrist aching from writing so much so quickly, the loneliness, the boredom, the frustration began to take hold of me.

As I lay there behind my sheet, paralysed with misery, I could make out a dull muttering coming from the direction of Zubi's bunk. It had been going on a few minutes and I thought little of it, assuming he and Ranjit were having a quiet chat, perhaps about Ranjit's impending court appearance. When I emerged from my bunk to have a smoke, however, Ranjit was sitting at the table going through his papers and Pasha was sitting on his bed, in the lotus position as ever, staring into the middle distance. But the murmur from behind Zubi's bunk drape continued.

I looked at Ranjit and then at Zubi's bunk, and Ranjit smiled at me. Embarrassed, I took this to mean that Zubi was answering a call of nature and pleasuring himself, but after about five minutes, Zubi pulled back his screen and said: 'English boy, come over here. We need to chat.'

I was nervous as I leant back against the wall with my legs sticking out under the drape, fearing that he was about to show me his private stash of porn mags so that I could take them away for my own half hour of fun. I had noticed that when Zubi wasn't talking about prison, he liked to talk about sex. It was all pussy this, and pussy that, and Christ if only I'd seen some of the beautiful pussy he'd had the pleasure of bedding down the years ... The way he talked about girls made me feel a little priggish and uptight and I found myself unable to join in the banter. It was the only thing that irritated me about him. In all other respects he was my saviour. But girlie mags were not, it turned out, the purpose of our meeting.

'Look, English boy, if we're going to get you out of here, you need to start making a few calls, and doing some deals.'

'How am I going to do that? You're not allowed phone calls, are you?' I replied, nonplussed, but relieved that he hadn't handed me a copy of a hardcore Russian girlie mag.

'I think I know I can trust you,' he said.

And from under his leg, he produced a mobile phone.

'What the fuck?!' I blurted.

Zubi could see the excitement burst across my face as I took it from his outstretched hand and examined it. He hadn't been wanking in there, he'd been talking to his wife or his daughter or his lawyers! He was in contact with the outside world.

'This crappy little pay-as-you-go phone is worth about ten dollars on the outside. In here, my friend, it's gold dust. It's our lifeline to the world beyond. It's our prized asset and we need to defend it and care for it, like our lives depend on it. If they find this, we'll be in for a big-time beating and probably a spell in Razburg.'

I was so overjoyed at the thought of being able to call home that I barely listened as he explained that the main body of the phone was kept behind a loose brick just outside the open barred window, the battery behind a brick by his bunk and the charger beneath the tiled threshold of the door. Zubi's wife had brought the phone to him in the cells below the courthouse after a hearing. She hid it in a bowl of salad, then paid off the courtroom guard with 100 dollars.

'How did you get it back into Piet?' I asked.

'Up my arse – and I tell you it took one helluva push to get it out. The charger came a few days later with a food delivery, hidden inside a packet of noodles. This is the deal, English boy. We only use it after midnight, once the guards outside have disappeared for a couple of hours' sleep. You can make as many calls as you like, as long as I say it's safe, but your people in England have to pay to keep it topped up and I get to use it as much as I like too. It's gonna cost them some big dollars, but that's the price you pay. It's always on vibrate mode, for obvious reasons, and after tonight you should get your people to call you, otherwise it'll cost your folks, or your girl, a small fortune calling England from Russia. Now phone your Mum and let her know Zubi's looking after you,' he said.

Zubi handed me a shred of paper with the mobile's number written on it, slapped me on the shoulder and then left me on the bunk. My heart started racing and I began to feel big emotions welling up as I punched in the code and my home number – it's been the same for thirty years. o, o, 4, 4, 2, o, 8, 8, 5, 7 ... One ring, two rings, three rings, four rings ...

'Hello.' It was Mum, and her voice sounded weak and sad.

'Mum, it's me. Tig!' I said, struggling to keep my voice to a whisper, tears pouring down my cheeks. I wanted to bellow with joy.

'Tig! My boy! My boy! It's him, John. It's Tig. He's on the phone! Oh, my God, I can't believe it. How's my little boy? How's my boy? ...'

Scarcely one full, rational sentence passed between us in the five minutes that followed; both of us were crying and choking so much and telling each other how much we loved each other and talking at a hundred miles an hour about the first things that came into our heads. I couldn't stop apologizing for what had happened, but when Dad took the phone he cut me off and said: 'Don't

78

waste your energy apologizing, son. It's happened. Water under the bridge. Don't beat yourself up. Besides, there'll be plenty of people inside to do that for you!' he said with a forced laugh. 'Now we're all going to get focused on getting you out of there as soon as possible. Don't worry, we're on it. You just stay strong and stay out of trouble and your family will get you out of this business. You be cool, my boy. Just don't bend over in the showers . . .'

I gave Dad the mobile number and he made a joke about it being a 'cell phone', but I knew all the building-site banter was just bravado to keep my spirits up and make me feel everything was cool and that they weren't really too worried for me. I knew what he was really feeling and thinking. They were all going to come out and see me as soon as possible, he promised – Mum, Dad, Lucy and Rob – but first of all they were busy trying to mobilize lawyers and the British Embassy and raise a fighting fund to pay legal fees and travel expenses and so on.

I was still buzzing when I called Lucy straight after-wards. There was no reply at her mum's at Leyton and I immediately tried her mobile. It rang just once before she picked up.

'Babe, it's me.'

'Oh my God, Tig! I've been beside myself, my love. Where are you? What's going on? Are you all right? Are you safe? When are you coming home? When are you getting bail? . . .'

'I'm not getting bail, Babe. It's going to trial . . .'

'What? Trial? When?'

I took a deep breath, closed my eyes, and after a pause

79

I replied: 'It should all be over in a couple of months, my love . . .'

'A couple of months! But what about the house, what about your job? What about you . . .?'

Zubi began waving at me, pointing to the door.

'Luce, I'll call you as soon as I can. I've got to . . .'

Zubi angrily snatched the phone off me and stuffed it under his mattress, saying: 'Quick, go to your own bunk. I can hear guards.'

7

It was a hot night and sleep was difficult. The lights were kept on all night in Piet but it was the tapping on the bloody pipes that was driving me crazy. There seemed to be a lot more communication going on than the night before, and a lot of it seemed to be coming from cells near us, because it was much louder. It sounded like an orchestra of children playing with pots and pans and kettles and cutlery, creating an almost constant background din. The mosquitoes were out in force as well, buzzing in my ears like little electric drills, and I didn't want to fall asleep in case I was bitten by one – not after what Zubi had been telling me about the TB and HIV and hepatitis and fuck knows what else that was rife throughout Russian gaols. Half the people in there were junkies who'd committed crimes to feed their habit. We were at the height of the mosquito season, and the thought of one of them sucking the blood from a junkie and then landing for another snack on me was freaking me out so much that, in spite of the heat and humidity, I put on the fleece Ranjit had given me to cover as much skin as possible. It was not long before I was sweating so much I could feel my T-shirt clinging to my flesh and eventually I couldn't stand it any longer. I swivelled off my *matras* and jumped into the room to take it off.

As I emerged from behind my sheet I was surprised to

see Ranjit standing on the top bunk with his arm stuck out of the window. Zubi was sitting on the edge of his bunk with a few small pieces of paper and a biro.

'One of the *volk*'s guys needs to borrow the phone,' he whispered, beckoning me over to where he sat. 'I think he's ordering in more drugs for the prison. Ranjit's doing the *daroga*. If you hear a guard outside, dive straight back into your bunk, or we'll be in the shit, big-time.'

The *daroga* system, Zubi explained as I sat down on his bunk, was the way the prison communicated and passed belongings between cells: fags, phones, drugs, whatever. The word means path or route or network. The tapping on the pipes was one cell talking to the ones on either side, above or below. It was like the phone ringing, and when you heard the taps you went to the window and waited to be passed the message or the item in transit. It was like something out of *The Great Escape*, and I felt a buzz of nervous excitement as Zubi continued.

Each cell, he said, had a long piece of string or cord, fashioned from the pieces of thread pulled from clothes, that was easily hidden in the stuffing of a *matras*. A sock with something heavy like a spoon in it was then attached to the end of the cord and the written message or the item being passed on was put into the sock. When the message-sender was ready, he alerted the neighbouring cells by tapping on the pipes and then swung the piece of string round and round outside his window until the prisoner leaning out of the cell window above, below or next to him grabbed hold of the sock and took out the contents. The process was repeated until the message or object had reached its destination. If you had experienced operators on the windows, Zubi claimed, it was possible to send a message from one corner or end of the building to the other in under five minutes. A searchlight scanned the wall for periods throughout the night but these guys had become experts at evading it. If you heard the jangle of keys outside, or the sound of the key in the lock, you had about five seconds to pull in the rope, leap down and get back into your bunk. The guards knew all about *daroga*, and the risks were great if you were caught. Savage beatings were the common form of punishment – for everyone except the *volk* and his inner circle.

'But what if they don't give the phone back?' I asked anxiously.

'Don't worry, it'll be back. It's a question of prison honour, a code of trust. The system wouldn't work if people didn't get back what they'd lent. Also, who's gonna pay to top it up?'

As he spoke, we heard a commotion erupt in a cell a little way down the corridor, maybe two or three doors along. Ranjit leapt off the top bunk and I hurled myself from Zubi's into my own. The sound of guards shouting, dogs barking and prisoners screaming in pain and protest reverberated down the corridor. I lay on my bunk frozen with fear at the noise of the violence, terrified that we were all in for a thrashing but more worried that our phone had been confiscated. The violence continued for five minutes before we heard the cell door slammed shut with an almighty bang, followed by the sound of the guards moving off down the corridor slowly giving way to a tense silence.

Zubi pulled back the sheet over my bunk and

whispered: 'Don't worry, English boy, that was nothing out of the ordinary. They were probably just making an example of one cell to shut the rest of the prison up. Something's going on, though, and I don't like it. It was busier tonight – you could tell from the tapping that there was a shitload of stuff being passed around. We'll get our phone back later tonight. Just wait and see. It'll go quiet for a bit and then it'll start all over again.'

Sure enough, an hour or so later the tapping started up again, at first softly and just once in a while, but slowly increasing in volume and frequency. I prayed hard for that phone to come back, willing it on its way from one cell to the next, and finally, as I began to doze off, there were three loud raps on the pipe coming from the cell to our left. I felt Ranjit sweep out of his bunk next to mine and pull himself up on to the top bunk. Within seconds he was back down, and whispered: 'Phone's home.'

In the morning, Zubi said: 'That's it! No more fucking *daroga*! It's getting too dangerous. A load of drugs has been smuggled in here in recent weeks, and I'm sick of risking my ass to distribute them round the prison for a load of junkies. What's to say they won't raid us one night and catch us with a sock full of smack that ain't even ours? Try telling that to the judge. If that happens, we don't just take a beating and have the cell broken up – we end up in the dungeon and they add more drugs offences on our charges, which means they're gonna bang our pussy asses in gaol for the next ten years.

'I see it like this: we got a cosy set-up here. Why fuck with it? There's just a handful of us. It's clean, we've got food, no one's sick, we've got TV, and most important, we've got the phone. It doesn't get any better than this in here. But it can get a whole lot worse. Trust me. Every time we play *daroga*, we risk losing it. And how the fuck do we benefit from *daroga* anyhow? The answer is we don't.'

Zubi looked around the room at the three of us. Ranjit shrugged, saying nothing. He was due in court for his trial later in the day and was banking on not coming back. He'd been in for five months and his people had thrown 20,000 dollars in bribes at the judge and prosecutor. He knew they had taken the money, now he was just hoping they'd keep their word. Pasha wasn't even listening. He was sitting cross-legged on his bunk doing the Buddhist 'Om' with his eyes closed.

'Fucking airhead!' shouted Zubi, throwing his arms up in the air and looking at me. 'It looks like it's just you and me, English boy.'

'But what about this *volk* guy?' I asked. 'Isn't this going to piss him off?'

'Fuck *volk*. We can deal with *volk*. Number one: we're foreigners and the rules don't apply to us as strictly as they do to the Russians. We got a bit of leeway there. Number two: I think I can play him off. Make up some bullshit for a while, string him along. Number three: the drugs can pass through the cells around us. It's a minor inconvenience for the *daroga* boys. Number four: we ain't the only ones with phones in this joint.

'The way I see it, there'll be some bother for a week or two, then it'll die down. They'll tap and tap and tap but we won't reply. We don't take our exercise hour on the roof for a while either, 'cos that's just more room for friction and confrontation. The only thing we gotta watch is shower day – Tuesday, which is tomorrow . . .'

Zubi shot a glance at me. He could see I was worried.

'Don't worry, you'll be just fine, English boy. They know it's not you calling the shots in the cell. They know it's Zubi, the black guy with the mouth, the only black guy in the whole goddam place! They don't like niggers in here, so if anyone's going to get it in the back it's me. You can just stand there smiling and looking pretty, English boy. Leave it to Zubi. By next Tuesday the whole fuss will have blown over.'

We said farewell to Ranjit with a hug and a slap on the back as he was led away after breakfast for his trial, dressed in his best shirt and trousers, which he had pressed by folding them under his mattress and sleeping on them. 'Divide all my belongings between you,' he said, carrying only his court papers. He was a sweet, gentle guy, Ranjit, but I hoped with all my heart that I never saw him again, at least not in the Russian prison system, because what happened to him at trial that day would give me a pretty strong idea of my own fate. If he didn't come back, the outlook looked promising for me, our cases being so similar. If he returned, I knew I was going to feel crushed because Ranjit couldn't have been in a better position to walk free: he had no criminal record, his family had paid off all the relevant people and he had an excellent legal team. If he went down, I'd be following him in a couple of months.

My own lawyer, Alfred Piskin, the grey-haired Russian guy brought in by the law firm at the bail hearing, was coming to visit me that day, and I woke up with a sense of renewed hope despite the *daroga* dramas in the night. I grew increasingly fidgety as the day wore on and still no one had come to take me down to the interview rooms on the ground floor. I wrote my diary, smoked twice as many fags as normal, washed my hair, paced around the room, and still the guard never came. At one stage, on Zubi's suggestion, I even shaved my entire body – every last inch of it – so that I didn't get any lice or nits. It was standard prison practice, he told me, and I had to do it once a week at least from now on. He asked me to shave his head for him for the same reasons. It was a weird feeling, an uncomfortably intimate act, as I smothered his scalp – a virtual stranger's – with foam and then carefully shaved off the stubbly growth, trying not to nick him.

Finally, at around five o'clock, I heard the rattle of the keys and a guard opened the door, exclaiming: 'Hague, Tig!' As he waited outside in the corridor I gathered up my court papers and slid a letter to Lucy inside my slipper, feeling my heart starting to race as I did so. As we made the long walk down endless corridors and flights of stairs to the basement, the metal gates crashing behind us, one after the other, I had a job keeping the letter from sliding out of my backless grandad slippers, given to me by Ranjit, and I had to curl my toes up really tightly to hold it in place. When we reached the metal-barred door, before we could enter the visiting area, I started shitting myself again when I was told to spread my arms and legs and lean against the wall while they gave me the pat-down, right down to my ankles, then up again. It was a nerve-racking moment even though the letter contained nothing compromising. It was just a love letter.

I was put into a dimly lit booth, one of about twenty in the holding area, which felt like an upside down coffin, or a cubicle without a toilet. It was so tight you could barely have squeezed one more body in there. It contained a narrow bench fixed to the wall and nothing else, and I sat down on it, trying not to look at all the bogeys and what looked like shit and dried blood that had been smeared down the walls and the door. I lit a fag and stared at the floor, and despite the grim surroundings I was excited about the meeting and my knees were quivering and bouncing up and down. Who knew what good news the lawyer might bring? He might even have a done deal? Perhaps Garban Icap had brought some money and pressure to bear on the authorities. They were, after all, as they liked to tell everyone, 'the world's largest derivatives broker' and presumably that meant they had a bit of political clout with an emerging economy like Russia's. Besides, it couldn't be good for their reputation to have one of their brokers languishing in a prison on trumped-up drugs charges. Surely they'd want the matter dealt with quickly.

After fifteen minutes a guard led me into a square, windowless room with a metal table and chairs fixed to the middle of the concrete floor, presumably because they were potential weapons. There was a doorbell buzzer fixed on to the table, to alert the guards, and the scene was made all the starker by the strip of bright fluorescent light above our heads. First Piskin, then Julia, the translator from the bail hearing, shook my hand. She had a friendly face with a generous smile – unlike Piskin. I arrived pent up with hope, but by the time I shook his hand an hour later I was totally deflated. Julia smiled at me for England but there was no disguising that the meeting was a depressing waste of everybody's time. We went through the events of my arrest at the airport again, and when I protested forcefully that the weight of the drug had been increased by at least ten times at the airport, speaking slowly and mechanically he replied through Julia: 'And who do you think the judge is going to believe? You, a man who admits smoking hashish, or the Customs authorities and Russian police force? Is there any evidence to prove that they have fabricated the evidence?'

At the end of the meeting I gave Julia the letter to send to Lucy and I was asked to sign a form giving permission for them to send the belongings in my suitcase back to England, or to be kept by a friend in Moscow until my trial and/or sentence was over. The only positive to be drawn from the meeting came when I asked him what he thought would happen at the trial. A suspended sentence and a fine was the most likely outcome, he said with the faintest glimmer of a smile. Especially as I would already have served a couple of months, at least, he added. That was no more than I had been expecting, but at least he hadn't raised the possibility that I might be detained even longer.

When I shook his hand I tried to hold eye contact with him – as I couldn't talk to him this seemed the most direct way of communicating with him – and I was hoping that the look on my face said: 'Please, please do your best for me. You've got to get me out of here.' After they'd left, Peter the Embassy guy came in and there was, at least, some basic satisfaction to be had from talking directly to someone in my own language. He was a nice enough guy with a winning grin and he made lots of reassuring noises about making sure I was being treated properly and that my human rights were being respected. He said – and this gave me a lift – that he had been fielding a lot of calls from family and friends back home. 'Your brother Rob doesn't mince his words, does he?' he said, and I smiled at the thought of my little brother, a big aggressive character but generous and loyal to a fault, giving it some lip down the line to the British Embassy. Good old Rob, he wouldn't let me rot in here.

At the end he asked me to write out a list of clothes and provisions that I wanted the Embassy to bring in, which they would do after receiving the funds from back home. There were strict rules and limits, he explained, on what prisoners were allowed. For instance, you weren't allowed sugar or rice or potatoes because you can make alcohol from them and you weren't allowed glass jars because they could be fashioned into weapons. My shopping list contained the following: two sheets, two pillow cases, two tracksuits, some socks, pants, T-shirts, a fleece, a water boiler, as much fresh food as possible, especially fruit and veg, noodles, coffee, onions and garlic and as many cigarettes as they could fit in the truck. Cigarettes were the main currency in Piet, Zubi had told me, because we could use them to bribe the guards and pay off the *volk*. Every few weeks all the cells were required by the *volk* to make a contribution to a general pot so that goods could be handed out to the less fortunate prisoners, the ones with absolutely nothing of their own who didn't have people on the outside to help them out. Contributing a block of smokes would win me a lot of Brownie points.

As I began to write out my wish list I felt a minor thrill that I'd soon be receiving a delivery of material comforts to help me through the coming weeks, or months, but by the time I'd completed it a heavy melancholy had descended on me. The realization had sunk in that by storing up on supplies I was effectively preparing for a long period of hibernation; I was hunkering down, building and feathering my nest for the harsh months ahead.

When I got back to the cell it was about seven o'clock and there was a cup of stone cold liquid left by the *bilander* man. Looking at it, it was impossible to tell whether it was the soup shit, or the porridge shit. Both were grey with lumps in. I threw it down the toilet hole and cooked up some noodles with onions and a few slices of the cold sausage the Russians call *kolbasa*. There was still no sign of Ranjit, which was highly promising, but Zubi explained that sometimes you didn't get back from court until almost midnight because they drove around Moscow for hours, often in bad traffic, dropping prisoners off at different gaols and detention centres. 'If he ain't back by midnight, we can start celebrating for him – and for you!' said Zubi.

Waiting for nothing to happen, *willing* nothing to happen, was an odd feeling. I lay on my bed praying for Ranjit's freedom, but really I was praying for my own. I told Zubi about my frustrating meeting with Piskin and he was up off his bunk and throwing his arms up in the air, telling me that a good lawyer with some cash in his back pocket would have had me out by now. 'Sack him! Sack him now! Zubi'll arrange a new legal team who will get you out of here, guaran-fucking-teed.'

It was difficult to know who to put my trust in: a drug dealer who sounded like he knew the system and all the underhand tricks, or a steady, dull, middle-aged lawyer with years of experience? And did I hand over up to 30,000 dollars of my family's money to a shady Russian lawyer, linked to a drugs dealer, whose only guarantee was his word? If we had money to burn, fine, but I had nothing like that in my account. There was about 1,000 quid to see us through to the end of the month, plus about 5,000 quid in savings – but that was for the deposit on the house we were trying to buy.

I was wrestling with all these dilemmas when, at around eleven o'clock, a guard pulled back the eye-slot and summoned Zubi. I sat bolt upright and listened to their brief muffled exchange. 'Ranjit's free,' smiled Zubi, as the eye-slot slid shut with a metallic clink. 'He got a suspended sentence and a fine.'

'Good on him,' I said, punching the air. I sparked up a cigarette and started pacing the room excitedly. A tremor of guilt ran over me as I realized I didn't actually give a flying toss about Ranjit. I was only happy for me.

8

I had to squeeze my towel as tight as I could so that nobody could see how much my hands were trembling as we lined up in the corridor outside the shower area in the basement. 'These are the dudes from cell 309 next door,' whispered Zubi. 'And they ain't happy. Stick close to me.'

Zubi had explained earlier that there were three rooms in the wash area, each of them occupied by one or two cells at a time with a fourth cell waiting its turn in the corridor outside. In the first room you got changed, hung your clothes up on a trolley and waited to be called into the showers. When they were turned off, you moved through into a third room where the guard had wheeled the trolley with the clothes, and the next cell was brought into the showers. And so on until the whole prison had been washed.

The guards stood outside as we filed silently into the first room, which was no bigger than our cells. Slowly, we started to undress. The floor beneath my slippers was slimy and I had to be careful not to slip as I began to peel off my T-shirt and then my tracksuit bottoms. It was cramped, though, and it was impossible not to come into contact with the people standing around me. There were two dozen bodies in the dank, airless room less than half the size of a squash court, and the stench coming off the other guys was nauseating. It was the smell of mildly rotten human beings. Clearly these guys didn't wash between showers, or brush their teeth, or clean their clothes.

Most of us had completely stripped off and were cupping our hands over our cocks waiting for the call to proceed to the showers when one character started ranting at Zubi, who was standing right next to me. The guy was early twenties, dark and hairy, with craggy teeth and wild 'fuck you' eyes. He wasn't big, but wiry and knotty. He looked like he didn't give a shit about himself, let alone anyone else. He started tugging at Zubi's shirt, while angrily remonstrating with him. Without turning to me, Zubi said in English:

'This joker says I should give him my clothes because I'm a piece of nigger shit, and he's a nice white boy. And I told him he's an ignorant cunt who can kiss my black ass.'

One of the other older Russians grabbed the arm of his cellmate and told him to cool it. Zubi didn't take his eyes off his tormentor as he unzipped his tracksuit and hung it on the rail with his T-shirt. We were all naked, standing and waiting in silence, when the young guy lunged forward and went to grab Zubi's clothes.

The room went into slow motion. It was just a sequence of images, stills almost, or a slideshow. I saw Zubi's hand thrust out and push the hairy guy in the chest. The hairy guy flew backwards, his feet flying up in front of him as he slipped and landed smack on his backside in a pile of bodies. His face curled up in rage as he scrambled to his feet and hurled himself at Zubi. I found myself trying to back away towards the wall, but there were too many bodies in the way, and there was uproar.

Except for about eight or ten guys who had squeezed up against the walls, everyone else was piling in, punching and kicking the fuck out of each other randomly. The scene would have looked almost comical to onlookers, with twenty-five cocks flapping around and everyone trying to keep their balance on the slimy floor as the fists flew. But it didn't feel in the least bit funny where I stood. The room appeared to have moved around 180 degrees and I found myself right next to Zubi in the corner, both of us thrashing out at anyone within arm's length. I was gasping for breath as the adrenaline coursed through me, but Zubi was somehow managing to throw some Russian insults with the same speed as his fists. At six foot four, two or three inches taller than me, he had a long reach and very few of them managed to lay a blow on him. I held out my upturned left hand like a traffic cop to try and stop the blows, but one fist smashed my arm out of the way and caught me above the eye. My right arm and fist, meanwhile, were going back and forth like an out-of-control steam piston, but I was making only glancing contact with the guys flailing in front of me. Only once did I make proper contact and that was right on the side of the hairy guy's head, which hurt me a lot more than it hurt him.

The fight was barely two minutes old when the guards burst through the door, holding their truncheons above their heads, and screamed for order. Almost instantly, the whole room stopped and we all stood panting, slowly dropping our fists to our sides. A fat guy with a pasty face and a mop of blond hair was on the floor, completely sparko, and half a dozen others had blood wounds on the face. Zubi had a slight swelling under his left eye and I had a trickle of blood coming from my eyebrow. Two guards lifted the unconscious guy out into the corridor while a third opened the door to the shower room, the steam bellowing out as he motioned us in with his truncheon, barking something in Russian as we filed past him. Through the haze of the showers I could see people's chests heaving quickly as they tried to recover their breath and composure. It was over now, you could tell by the atmosphere. All the tension had disappeared as fast as the water down the big drain in the middle of the floor, and as I stood with my face under the stream of hot water, I heard Zubi's voice chuckling through the steam: 'What did I tell you, English boy? Bunch of pussies, eh?'

I was set for a meeting with my lawyers the following day, and I'd needed to speak to everyone back in England to find out what was going on at their end and tell them what to do next – in accordance with Zubi's advice. I'd needed to let them know that I had next to no faith in Piskin and that we needed to be looking at all the alternatives. I also wanted to press them to start raising a 'bribery fund' to buy our way out. Zubi was insistent that hard cash was the only way I could guarantee walking free, partly because that's the way the system worked but especially because I'd been naïve enough to admit my guilt. To a Russian court faced with a congested backlog, my case looked cut-and-dried, as Zubi kept pointing out. 'What kind of mother-fuck is going to believe the self-confessed drug-taker's claims that the authorities exaggerated the amount he was carrying and then trumped up the charges to get him on smuggling? Answer: no one, English boy. I'm afraid it's good night, Vienna, see you in seven years, English boy, unless you get the wallet out and start doling out all them dollars you earn back in London.'

Zubi was constantly pressing me to take control of the situation, to start running the show from the inside and not to let the case drift with the state lawyer, who was going to pick up the same size cheque whether he gave a shit about me and my case or not. The only way I could do that was with the mobile phone, but disaster struck that evening when Zubi plugged the charger into the socket and, literally, it went up in a puff of smoke – along with all the hopes I'd been building up of negotiating my escape from the inside. It was a crushing moment. My one cause for hope, my one source of comfort, my one means of power, my one way of communicating with the outside world – they all disappeared in one heart-stopping instant.

I was now completely cut off from outside help, abandoned to the mercy of fate and the whims of the Russian judicial system. There had been a great deal of low moments in the previous week, but that was the lowest. Even Zubi, a spring of positive thinking so far, appeared at a loss. He put his head in his hands, muttering: 'Fuck! Fuck! Fuck!' Angrily, he wrapped the cord around the plug, leapt on to the top bunk in a single bound and, sticking his right arm through the bars, hurled it as far as he could into the darkness of the giant courtyard below. A couple of seconds later I heard it crack on the paving stones.

'Right, let's get a new charger, English boy,' he said, bounding back down. 'It's gonna take time and it's gonna be risky but we'll get one. Don't you worry. Zubi'll work his magic. I'm gonna start working on *bilander* man from breakfast tomorrow, but we'll need to promise him a shitload of stuff, maybe 400 cigarettes plus coffee, and then we gonna have to be double careful because from then on, they'll be turning our cell over every other day to find the phone. After a few days, *bilander* man will tell the guards 'cos he knows full well we'll come begging and bribing for another. He'll take us for everything we got.'

The eye-slot was pulled open and Pasha was summoned to the door with what sounded like a rebuke. The exchange that took place was short, but when he turned round, all the colour had drained from his face. It was a pale, impassive face at the rosiest of times, but there was an obvious look of shock or dread written across it right at that moment.

Zubi asked him what was up, in Russian.

'Krastna Prestnya,' Pasha replied, looking at the floor. Zubi stood up slowly, put an arm round him, and spoke to him reassuringly in Russian. Pasha rolled up his *matras* and then, as he began to pack up his *sumka*, Zubi said to me quietly: 'It's the prison they put you in before they send you down to Zone 22, one of the gulags, in the middle of fucking nowhere. You don't want to go to Zone 22.'

Within half an hour Pasha was gone.

9

There was no such thing as a 'good night's sleep' in Piet Central, with all the tapping, the lights being on, the heat, the mosquitoes and the flies – not to mention the constant worrying – but the following morning I woke up about as refreshed and happy as a man could hope to be in there. The porridge shit went straight down the toilet hole and I brewed up a double-strength coffee with two sachets of Nescafé. I was too excited to eat. After a full body and hair wash with a big bowl of hot water, I put on the shirt and trousers I'd been arrested in, which were nice and clean, if a little crumpled after a night being pressed under my *matras*. I tidied my hair with the comb that had arrived with the provisions, took out a couple of packets of fags for what was likely to be a stressful day and made sure all my court papers were in good order. Zubi was very quiet for once as I got ready to leave, and I figured he was a bit sad at the prospect of living there by himself until the next foreigner pitched up.

All morning I paced the cell in my clean clothes, waiting for the guard to come, and every time I heard footsteps outside my heart leapt, only for the sound of the steps to fade slowly down the corridor. It was a hot day and I had to keep cooling my face and head with water, but it was as much my mounting impatience and my inability to sit or lie down as it was the heat that was making me sweat and fret. As the afternoon wore on, and still nothing happened, urgency turned to desperation. In the morning Zubi had done his best to reassure me that everything was going to be just fine; in the early afternoon he was telling me that it was probably just a backlog at the court system and that either they'd still come, or it'd be the next day.

By the time the *bilander* man had made his final delivery of slop at around five o'clock, all hope had passed and Zubi was sitting next to me, saying: 'Be cool, English boy. You gotta get used to this shit. In here, no one is gonna come and apologize and explain what's going on. You just gotta sit on your ass and stew until your time comes around. It ain't like working for Garban I-Crap or whatever it is your fancy company's called, where people email or text you to say sorry for missing the meeting. You're just a piece of shit stuck in the system waiting to get cleared out. Don't worry, man, Zubi's gonna get you out of here.'

Friday turned out to be an exact repeat, the only difference being that I had barely slept and woke up in a foul mood that only got worse as the day wore on. No one came from dawn to dark, except the *bilander* man, and I went to bed dumb with despair but with my head racing with evil thoughts and fears, knowing I would have to wait at least another two full days before I went to court or was told what the fuck was going on. What was Piskin thinking? 'Oh, fuck Tig Hague, Mr Hec-tic from London. He's just a stupid pothead, we'll let him know what's going on next week, or when I can be fucking arsed!'

What the fuck were lawyers for? Or the fucking

Embassy, for that matter? They'd probably buggered off to their dachas in the country for the weekend. Well, la-di-fucking-da, thank you very much, you useless twats . . .

These were my thoughts as I lay on my bed, tossing and turning in the heat, the sweat clinging to my clothes in the airless humidity of the cell, listening to that infernal bloody tapping on the pipes, swiping away the mosquitoes. I must have fallen asleep at least for a short time because I woke up lying on my back, with tears running out of the corners of my eyes, furiously scratching two clumps of mozzie bites on my neck and my forehead. The sound of another mosquito in my ear made me jump out of my bunk.

And then I lost it.

I started smacking my face and my neck, shouting: 'Fucking cunts! Fucking cunts! I can't stand this fucking shithole any longer!' I kicked the bunks, punched the walls, threw my *matras* across the room, hurled the bowls and cups off the table, anything that I could reach I sent flying, all the time swearing and ranting. My body was quivering. Zubi looked shocked, even a little scared. He stood by his bunk, saying nothing, just holding out his upturned hands as if to say, 'That's cool, bro, you do your thing!' letting me slowly burn myself out. Then he slowly walked towards me and gently sat me down on my bunk. I pressed my hands to my face to try to stop them shaking.

Piskin turned up at the prison on Monday with the air of a man just going about his daily business, like he had nothing of any consequence to tell me. He was looking distinguished in his grey suit, crisp shirt and conservative dark tie. I felt like a pikey in my tracksuit bottoms, supermarket T-shirt and old man's checked slippers. I was sick all Saturday, didn't eat all weekend, and the cumulative lack of sleep had left me feeling shattered. Leaning back in my chair with one leg crossed over my knee, a Marlboro Red burning between my fingers, I stared at Piskin coldly as he rifled through the notes from his briefcase in silence for a couple of minutes. I kept my mouth shut, but there was a lot of noise going on in my head. I had a lot to say to my so-called 'lawyer'. I began to understand why they nail the furniture down in these places. The tension in the room was excellent, just as I wanted it to be, and my bloodshot, baggy eyes fixed him with a glare that must have felt like a laser in the side of his head. That's what we needed right across the board in my case: ratchet up the fucking tension, knock some heads together, kick some useless lawyer arse, start banging the phones ... and we were going to start right then. No more fucking about.

I broke the silence, but the tension remained.

'Excuse me for interrupting, Mr Piskin, but if it's not too much bother perhaps you could let me know how my bail appeal went on Thursday? Was it successful?'

The question and answer passed back through the translator Julia, who made a long, sympathetic face and said: 'No, I'm sorry, Mr Hague, it was not successful. It is very rare for someone in your position, accused of smuggling drugs into Russia, to be granted bail.'

Piskin continued to organize his papers, jotting notes

here and there in the margins. There was no urgency in his movements or manner. He seemed relaxed and at ease with himself and the situation. Not like me, the crazy, unshaven guy in the tracksuit, scratching his neck and scalp like a monkey.

'Is that so? Well, that's a bit of a shame, isn't it? Perhaps Mr Piskin could see fit to explain why the hell he did not think it appropriate, in his capacity as my lawyer, my only bloody representative in this sorry mess, to come and tell me that the judge had not deemed me a suitable applicant for bail.' I put the question quietly but firmly.

Piskin looked up at Julia and calmly delivered a couple of sentences to her. He'd been in court all day Thursday and Friday, the answer came back, and the prison authorities don't relay messages between lawyers and prisoners.

'So when's my trial?'

Answer: some time at the end of September or maybe October. Depends on the schedule.

'Will you tell Mr Piskin that I'd like to start looking at placing some money in the hands of the relevant characters in my case, so we can resolve this as soon as possible?' I whispered this leaning forward over the table, because I was sure the room was bugged. To make certain Julia knew I meant 'bribery' and not regular legal fees, I gave her a couple of winks as I said it. She was only a young girl, obviously new to the world of criminal law, and she looked a little embarrassed as she relayed the message in hushed tones to the blank-faced, balding man to her right.

'Mr Piskin does not think that will be necessary,' came the relayed response. 'He says he has had years of experience of the Russian criminal system, dealing in similar cases, and that his firm is one of the most respected in Moscow. He says that he would be very surprised, once all the evidence and character references have been collated, if you were not to walk from your trial a free man.'

'You can tell him from me I'd be bloody gobsmacked if I didn't,' I snapped back.

Piskin looked up at me and made a sympathetic face. 'He says he likes the English humour,' said Julia.

So that was that. No more legal arguments or appeals. It was official. I was to be detained at the leisure of the Russian State until my trial at some unspecified date in the autumn, and until such time I would stew in my cell and go quietly insane – all expenses met by the Russian taxpayer – while my mum, dad and girlfriend would worry themselves sick and devote themselves to raising tens of thousands of pounds in legal fees, air flights, hotels and provisions from savings and donations. And all over a fucking pinhead of hash with the same intoxicating properties as a couple of lagers.

'This is ludicrous! It's crazy!' I said, bringing my fist down on the metal table, startling them both. 'Just say I hadn't been fitted up and it was true that I was carrying 28.9 grams, an ounce – that's the size of a bloody conker! That's not smuggling, that's worth 70 quid! The guy in *Midnight Express* had two fucking kilos of the stuff strapped to his chest! That's about 100 times more than I'm alleged to have been smuggling – SMUGGLING! – and that geezer got four years, and that was in Turkey, a virtual police state back in the 1970s. Does nobody see how ridiculous this whole situation has become? It's a storm in a fucking teacup!'

I realized I was getting heated and starting to swear a lot more than normal and I leant forward to Julia to apologize: 'Look, I'm sorry to get so het up but this has all got way, way out of control and proportion. It's just a nightmare. It's horrible in here. I don't deserve to be in here. I've been brought up to believe that if you do something wrong, you stand up and take your punishment like a man. But I've also been brought up to believe that a punishment should fit the crime, and I'm sorry, but banging me up for two or three months for a poxy bit of pot is just not right. So when I get angry, what I'm trying to say is that I need people to start taking some positive action and initiative, to go to the office and start earning their money. I can't do anything for myself rotting up there in my cell, and this whole thing is starting to cause my mum, and my girlfriend and a lot of people a lot of grief. Please just tell Mr Piskin to pull his finger out and at least start *showing* me that he gives a flying shit about me and my case,' I added, stabbing my cigarette at the ceiling.

I could tell that Julia didn't translate everything that I said but I did hear the words *'Midnight Express'*. Piskin replied through her: 'Mr Piskin is sorry for you and your family, and he understands the stress you are going through but what is done is done and we now have to be patient and wait for the trial until we can resolve your problem.'

I slumped forward in my chair and ground out the dog-end of my fag with the heel of my slipper.

*

I once read, or heard, a soldier describing war as long periods of boredom, of sitting around doing nothing, interspersed with bursts of intense, often terrifying activity; but all the time you're sitting around doing nothing, bored by the monotony, the fear of those terrifying bursts was constantly eating away at the nerves. That pretty well summed up my experiences in cell 310, Piet Central. Ninety-five per cent of the time it was mind-numbing routine mixed with an underlying fear about what might suddenly happen next. Day after day, I smoked, I sat, I washed, I slept (or tried to) – I lay on my bunk dreaming of Lucy and dreaming of my freedom and dreaming of all the things we were going to do together when I was out. I ate noodles, I wrote up my diary, I talked to Zubi, I watched Russian game shows on the crappy telly on the floor, I brushed my teeth, I shaved my body, I shaved Zubi's head, I swatted flies and mosquitoes, I paced the cell, I went for my weekly shower, and once in a while, to break the monotony, we'd take the walk up on the roof . . . But all the time, the fear was eating away at my guts. It was the fear of what would happen at the trial, the fear I would end up in a gulag for seven years, the fear that Lucy would leave me, the fear that Mum or Dad would die while I was inside, the fear I was going to lose my job and never get another one in the City, the fear I was going to get sick or stabbed or buggered, the fear I was going to go mad . . .

And then something terrible would happen. Like the day the *shmon* came.

It happened two days after the *bilander* man had

brought us our mobile charger, quickly shoving it through the hatch with our black soda bread. It had taken him ten nerve-shredding days to get it and we gave him ten packets of Marlboro Reds in payment, which is serious currency in Piet, as big as a backhander gets. When he was gone Zubi and I danced around the cell, whooping for joy and punching the air. But, Zubi warned, the charger came at a high price, and it was only a matter of time before the *bilander* man spilled the beans and the bad cops came looking for the phone.

It was the afternoon of Tuesday 5 August, and Zubi and I had just seen David Beckham score his first goal for Real Madrid since joining them from Manchester United, a superb twenty-five-yard free kick against FC Tokyo in a pre-season friendly. I jumped out of my chair in celebration, but almost instantly Zubi turned the volume off the telly and put his ear to the door.

'Listen,' he said, his eyes bulging. We stood rooted to the spot and the smoke from my fag floated upwards in a virtually straight line through the muggy air. Out of the corner of my eye I could see the Real players mobbing Beckham as he stood with arms aloft, saluting the fanatical crowd. It was a muffled sound, coming from the other end of the corridor, but there was no mistaking what it was: a *shmon* cell raid, or 'bad boy searching' as Zubi called it. Slowly, every few minutes, the uproar grew that little bit louder and the shouts of the guards, the screams of the inmates and the barking of the dogs became that much more distinct as the riot cops moved from one cell to the next. The rate of their approach suggested that they were cherry-picking particular cells. Piet was so big it would take them all day to trash the whole place.

'It's just a show of strength,' said Zubi. 'Piet may be a Black Zone, largely controlled by the *volk*, not the FSB, but that doesn't mean they won't come in and smash the place to pieces and crack a few skulls from time to time, confiscating as many drugs, phones and weapons as they can along the way.'

There was nothing we could do but wait and pray that we were not one of the chosen ones that day. The loud crash of the barred metal gate nearest to our cell made us both stand up at once from our bunks. It was the first time I had seen Zubi show any fear and I watched him gulp in some air.

'As soon as they open the door, put your arms over your head and just fucking run into the corridor. Don't say anything, don't look at them, just get out, don't get cornered . . .'

'Run? To where? In my grandad slippers?'

'Just get out of the cell, 'cos you'll get battered to fuck if you stay in here. We're at the end of the corridor and these guys have got a taste for blood now.'

It was all going off in cell 309 now. Heavy furniture – the bunks presumably – was being shunted across the floor and there was pandemonium out in the corridor as the prisoners piled out, yelling in pain and protest. There were at least two dogs, barking and yelping. Zubi motioned urgently for me to come and stand next to him a couple of yards from the door. My body was trying to pull me the other way into the far corner, but I went. The food hatch crashed down violently and in the space it left was a black balaclava, two eyes and a mouth.

The mouth spoke.

'We're next,' said Zubi out of the side of his mouth. 'They want the phone. Brace yourself.'

The sound of them coming was the worst bit. We heard 309's door slam shut and the tramp of boots heading in our direction, and then the sound of the big metal key in the door. The door opened inwards and we both jumped back as two Alsatians, one after the other, rushed into the room, dragging their handlers behind them. Six men poured in after them, all in combat uniform and balaclavas, with black boots laced up their calves and short riot sticks above their heads. I felt the force of a truncheon crack against my shoulder-blade as I turned away, followed by several more on my right arm, which was wrapped over my head. 'Run! Run! Run!' shouted Zubi and the next thing I knew I was standing in the corridor, panting like a long-distance runner, with my arms spread against the wall. I looked straight down at the floor but to either side of us, out of the corner of my eye, I could see riot cops holding sub-machine guns across their stomachs with their fingers on the triggers.

I could tell by the noise that the cell was being completely turned upside down and in my head I was saying, over and over: 'Not the phone! Not the phone! Please not the phone!' I'd gladly have taken a proper beating rather than lose my one lifeline to the world outside. After a few minutes, the cops strode out, one of them shouting at us in Russian. I felt the nozzle of a sub-machine gun in my ribs, urging me back into the cell, and as I got to the door

I felt the sharp heel of a combat boot dig into my lower back and propel me violently back into the room. Behind me, I heard Zubi cry out in pain as he hurtled in and the door was slammed shut.

I found myself kneeling on the floor, breathing rapidly and stretching my back to ease the pain at the bottom of my spine and across my shoulders. Food packets lay strewn across the room, some with their contents spilling out on to the floor. Both our mattresses and pillows had been ripped open and their Hoover-bag stuffing was all over the bunks and the hanging sheets they'd ripped down. Our small box of washing powder had been emptied out on to the floor near the toilet area. Within a minute the corridor was silent again, and as soon as they were gone, Zubi rushed to the tiles by the door and lifted them up.

'Charger's here!' he said, holding it up as if showing me the proof.

He darted to his bunk, pulled out the phone battery from behind the brick and then leapt on to the top bunk next to mine, squeezing his body up against the bars as he stretched his arm out along the wall. He brought the brick in and put it in his other hand, then stuck his arm out again, and his anxious face instantly dissolved into a giant grin.

'Fucking idiots couldn't find no pussy in a whorehouse!' he said, lowering himself back down and slapping me painfully on my sore shoulder. 'There are just two problems, though, English boy. They know we've got a phone and they'll keep coming back to look for it. And if that fails, then they'll send in the *kaziol*.'

'What the fuck's a *kaziol*?'

'It means goat in English; in Russian prisons it means informer. Then we'll be properly screwed.'

10

Dad and Rob were coming to Moscow the following week for a string of meetings with lawyers and people from the Embassy, so I spoke to them every night, facing the wall on my bunk and whispering quickly into the mobile. We were trying to formulate a plan of some sort and make a decision about what lawyers to go with as quickly as we could, before the cops came and discovered the phone, or lumped one of their informers in our midst. The calls home, even with Mum and Lucy, became very pragmatic, mainly because I had to be quick in case the guards came crashing in. I was so paranoid that we were being bugged somehow that we started talking in a weird kind of code, a mixture of English slang, abbreviations, acronyms and garbled, twisted idioms that only we as a family and as Londoners might fully understand. The judge became the 'J', the lawyer 'L' or 'muppet', the Prosecutor the 'P', money was 'spondoolies' or 'wedge' or 'bangers and mash', the cockney for cash . . . There was no time for tearful or loving chats. It was always straight down to business and it was only later as I lay on my bunk that I wished I'd said something kind, or thoughtful, like asking how their day went. But it was all about me.

It was impossible to know what to do, but we had to act pretty quickly so that our legal team had as much time as possible to prepare for the trial. Did we stick with the uninspiring but experienced Piskin? Did we go with Zubi's crew, who sounded dodgy but who, he promised until he was blue in the face, would definitely get me off? Or did we go with one of the firms that Dad and Rob had contacted from London? None of us were familiar with the Russian criminal code or judicial system, although Zubi made out he was a professor who'd spent a career specializing in the subjects. The more I got to know Zubi the more I realized he was one of those guys who was always right about everything, who never conceded that someone else might have a better idea or plan. Zubi always knew best, and it was starting to get on my nerves. I grew increasingly sceptical about his judgement on how my family and I should handle my case, and it was depressing to feel my confidence in the man who had held me together for a month slowly starting to ebb away. The flipside to that was good, though, or so I kept telling myself, because it meant I was slowly getting a grip on the situation, growing ever more confident and stronger in my own judgement and less dependent on Zubi. I was no longer the little lost boy I'd been on arrival.

I woke up excited the day Dad and Rob were scheduled to visit me. It was Tuesday 12 August and they'd been in town since Sunday, trying to put my legal team together. I was desperate to see them, not least to hear if there had been a breakthrough or developments. I was led down to the ground floor and given the pat-down with my arms and legs spread before I was buzzed through to the visiting area. This consisted of two rows of cubicles facing each other, with a gap of about a foot separating the visitor's from the prisoner's. The booths on either side were fronted with thick glass or Perspex and you communicated with each other through an old-style telephone with a smelly mouthpiece. I squeezed into my chair with my knees rammed right up against the wall underneath the shelf and sparked up a Marlboro Red. I was drawing heavily and smoking quickly as I waited, straining my face against the window to see if I could catch a glimpse of any activity at either end of the booths, but all I could see was lots of hands pressed up against the glass, reaching out to touch their loved ones.

Then the short, stocky, white-haired figure of my dad appeared in the booth opposite, beaming a big grin from ear to ear. For some reason, right then, I remembered one of his favourite little sayings: 'I may be five foot five, son, but that's big enough to join the fire brigade!'

He picked up the phone and in his thick London accent said: 'How's my little lad then? Who's been a naughty boy, eh? I tell you what, son, when I get you out of here I'm gonna kick that fucking arse of yours all the way back to London.' I started laughing and then crying a bit, not blubbing, because I wasn't at all sad. They were just tears of relief and delight. My dad was there in Piet Central! Sitting right in front of me!

For ten minutes he made me laugh, and I knew it was a bit of a show and that inside he didn't feel so funny. We had to be very careful not to say anything about the mobile phone upstairs, because I was convinced our meetings would be taped and monitored, but I asked him how the lawyer situation was looking. He gave me the thumbs-up sign and said: 'It's all in hand. Don't you worry. We're on it. We've got two guys on board, an

Artur something and an Arseny something, who were recommended by one of your Russian clients. We met them in a bar last night and they seem like the real deal. We even cracked a bottle of champers and raised a glass to your impending acquittal. Don't you worry about it, worrying's our job. You just keep your head down and stay strong. Right, my boy, I'm going to let that Herbert brother come in and talk to you. I can hear him climbing the walls outside. You look after yourself and just remember that we're not going to rest until you're out of this dump. I'm going in for a hip operation at the end of September so I won't make it out for the trial. I'll see you at home, my lad, where you belong. We'll have a joint party to welcome you and my new hip. And when I say "joint", son, I mean "shared"!'

He gave me a little salute and a big grin, and then he was gone.

Rob's face peeked round the corner sideways, about halfway up the doorway, before he squeezed himself into the booth, pointing at me and laughing. 'Look at the state of you!' he said, picking up the receiver. 'Fuck me, is that what they make you wear in here? You look like a fashion model for a car boot sale. It's Sue Ryder – the autumn collection! You look like shit, my friend. Are they not feeding you in here?' Like Dad, he carried on giving it the comic bravado and I wept with laughter on the other side of the glass. I was crying so much I could barely smoke my fag. It was the first time I'd laughed properly in over four weeks, and it was just what I needed. A bit of boys' banter and piss-taking, with all the bigger emotions we were feeling kept well out of sight.

I was almost more nervous than excited when Mum and Lucy came to visit almost three weeks later on Tuesday 2 September, because I was going to find it difficult to hold it together. If one of us broke, I knew we'd all go to pieces, and that wasn't how I wanted it. I didn't want them to leave that booth and fly home to England with an image of misery imprinted on their minds. Visiting times were always in the afternoon and I spent the better part of nine hours fidgeting and fretting in the cell before the guard finally came to lead me downstairs. I wanted to make myself look as nice as possible, so I washed and combed my hair, shaved as close as I could, and brushed my teeth. I put on the smartest of my two tracksuits and my laceless Pumas, which I'd been allowed to keep when they took the rest of my personal belongings away. They were the flashest pair of trainers in the entire prison, and I didn't wear them often for fear of drawing attention to myself. But this was a very special occasion and I felt just that little bit more self-confident as we made our way down the corridors and stairwells to the visiting area.

I'd been sitting restlessly in the glass booth for twenty minutes or so, wondering if something had gone wrong and the girls had been unable to make it, when I saw Lucy sweep past the open door in the visitor's booth opposite. I stood up and started shouting, 'Luce! Luce! I'm in here!' But of course she couldn't hear me. Mum suddenly appeared in the doorway and our faces lit up simultaneously. We both began waving frantically and doing thumbs-up signs. Mum motioned Lucy to come back, and in she bounced looking more beautiful and radiant than I'd ever seen her with her gorgeous curly brown hair tumbling over her shoulders. There was barely enough room, but both of them managed to squeeze into the tiny space, like two girls having their photos taken in a high street picture booth. It was like being in a silent movie for the first minute or so, as we all grinned and waved and stared inanely and pressed our palms up against the glass panes in front of us. The joy of the moment washed over me like a hot shower.

The two of them passed the phone piece back and forth to each other, and we were all talking so fast we were barely listening to what the other person was saying. The point of the exercise was just to connect, to communicate, to make contact, to hear each other's voices, to express and feel our love. The words that passed between us were virtually irrelevant. We might as well have been talking in Serbo-Croat. The thirty minutes we were allowed shot by and I couldn't believe it when the female guard stuck her head around the door and shouted, '*Dva minuta!*' ('Two minutes!'). Mum, who never does long goodbyes, said: 'I love you. I think of you all the time. Be strong. We'll get you home soon. It won't be long now.' She kissed her fingers and pressed them up against the window and then walked straight out without looking back. I was glad it was like that, and not a painfully drawn-out tearful affair. It was the same with Lucy. We both managed to avoid blubbing as we said our goodbyes, blowing each other kisses and pressing our hands against the glass. As I backed my way out of the booth into the corridor, trying to hold her in my sight for as long as possible, I carried on blowing kisses and mouthing, 'Love you, Babes, love you!' Then I turned around and there, right next to me, was a line of prisoners waiting to go back to the holding cells. My cheeks burned with instant embarrassment, and I went straight back into 'prisoner' mode, putting on a frown and trying to look hard.

We were led into the corridor of holding booths round the corner and I continued to stand, trying to avoid coming into contact with the filthy walls. Normally it was quiet in that area and all you could hear was the odd shuffling of shoes on the floor or the flare of a match being struck. But there was a bit of a commotion on this occasion and I heard locks rattling, doors opening and prisoners talking and laughing. Suddenly my own door was pulled open and I found a short thick-set man with a hairy chest grinning at me and holding up the shoelace with which he had just unlocked my door. There were half a dozen prisoners milling around in the corridor, but I didn't want to leave my booth. What was the point? What was there to do? But the others seemed to think it was just hilarious to have escaped from their cells, and they walked about like naughty schoolboys while I stood in my open doorway, making a weak show of joining in the fun.

The self-appointed 'booth-breaker' was unable to open the door opposite mine and the guy inside started asking for a cigarette to be handed over the door. Among the group in the corridor was a very tall and skinny young guy, at least six foot four, wearing only a T-shirt, boxer shorts and a pair of slippers. He took out a cigarette and stood on tiptoe as he reached up to pass it over the top of the door. As he turned his back to me I recoiled into my booth and looked away. The seat of his shorts and the backs of his legs were caked in dry shit, right down to his knees, and as he stretched his arm up, his T-shirt rose up his back to reveal dozens of livid red boils and weeping sores, each the size of coins, some leaking pus and blood. I could see black and yellow bruises all along the inside of his lower arm where he'd been injecting himself.

After we returned to the cell the guards delivered the provisions Mum and Lucy had brought in, and in among all the food and the fags were a few items of clothing from home, including my favourite motheaten, paint-splattered fleece. I pressed it into my face and breathed in the lovely, familiar aroma of Mum's washing powder and conditioner. It smelt of home and of my childhood and of happier times. As I pulled it over my head I resolved not to wash it until I was back in England.

It would be an exaggeration to say that the week that followed was a happy one, but it was probably the least troubled of the seven weeks I'd been detained. That was mainly because, though my trial date still hadn't been set, I knew it couldn't be too much longer. I was just counting down the days. The end was moving ever closer. What's more, seeing Mum, Dad, Rob and Lucy had given me a massive boost. Until their visit, and in spite of having the mobile phone, I'd felt cut off from my world, marooned on a small island of misery with no hope of escape or rescue. But seeing them in the flesh gave me the strength and hope to get through the final few weeks. Life in the cell was boring, but boring was better than unbearable, which is what it would have been in any other cell in Piet. The *shmon* riot cops paid us two more flying visits, smashing the cell to smithereens, just as they had done the first time, and leaving Zubi and me with some impressive bruises across our arms and shoulders. But the raids lasted no more than five minutes, and they never found any of our phone equipment. If it's possible to get used to the experience of being truncheoned by screaming men in balaclavas, then we did.

My health, too, was just about holding up, although I'd lost roughly a stone in weight. I'd had no excess fat to lose when I arrived in Moscow, so when the equivalent of fourteen bags of sugar disappeared, I became very bony and gaunt. I must have looked more unhealthy than I was feeling. I was taking no exercise, smoking about twenty fags a day, and I'd experienced more stress in those seven weeks than I had done in my entire life. I was living off noodles, biscuits and coffee, with the odd slice of onion and sausage, and the occasional piece of fruit, finding its way into my system from time to time. For a few days after a food delivery, we had a bag of oranges and/or apples, but we ate them quickly before they perished and we'd then go two or three weeks without anything fresh. The slop provided by the prison had virtually no nutritional value whatsoever and I very rarely ate it. The porridge-style gruel we were given in the morning and the slice of black soda bread we got with the soup at lunch and supper were the healthiest options, but the soups were really no more than warm water with a handful of miserable strands of meat or over-boiled cabbage floating around on the surface. Occasionally you might spot a few bits of diced carrot or some other root vegetable in the murk, but that was rare. It was little wonder there was so much illness in Piet when the authorities were providing the prisoners with just enough nutrition to keep them alive but absolutely nothing more. Zubi and I were among the lucky few who had people on the outside keeping us stocked up with half-decent produce. Compared to the Russians in their overcrowded, squalid cells, Zubi and I were leading a life of prison luxury.

But that all changed on the morning of Tuesday 9 September.

11

It was as if they had finally had enough of us, the two foreigners on Easy Street, with a clean cell all to ourselves, a cupboard full of food and fags, and a mobile phone they knew we had but couldn't find. We were lying on our bunks, waiting for the morning cell check, when two of the more senior guards entered the room and started gesticulating and half-shouting at us. I jumped to attention and stared at them without the faintest clue what they were saying, but aware that something serious was afoot. These officers never carried out the cell checks and Zubi wasn't coming back at them with his usual stream of banter and wisecracks.

The door slammed shut and Zubi put his head in his hands. 'They're moving us to Razburg! The fucking dungeon!' he said, exhaling loudly. 'That is not fucking good, my friend. That's where they put the bad boys. Start packing quickly and cram in as much as you can because they won't let you come back to pick up what you can't carry. Hurry, because as soon as they come back, we go, whether we're ready or not.'

I grabbed my favourite clothes and as much of the food and toiletries as I could squeeze into my *sumka* and suitcase, then rolled up my *matras* with my eating utensils inside. Zubi's first act was to grab the three components of the mobile phone and bury them deep inside his *matras*. Between us we managed to pack up about three-quarters of the food in the cupboards. We sat down on our bunks, breathing hard and fast, and exchanged apprehensive glances. Within a few minutes the door was opened and a guard barked at us to leave. Usually the guards ambled along the corridor without any sense of urgency and the prisoners just shuffled along behind them, but on this occasion they marched us away at speed. I was in my backless slippers with my *matras* under one arm, a suitcase in one hand and an overflowing *sumka* in the other. I was struggling to carry it all, not because it was very heavy but because it was awkward. Two packets of noodles and a bottle of shampoo spilled out of the *sumka* as I tried to rearrange the way I was holding the bags while trying to keep pace with the guard in front, with the one to my rear prodding me with his truncheon if I slowed up. By the time we reached the bottom of the eighth flight of stairs the muscles in my upper body were quivering under the strain.

We headed down the corridor, through a final series of metal gates and doors. Through the open doors of the offices and guards' rooms to my right, I could see small barred windows high up on the walls that looked out on to a courtyard at 'street level'. As we hurried past I caught fleeting glimpses of car wheels and the legs of prison employees as far as the knees, which gave me hope that we might still be able to get a mobile signal in our new cell. The corridor was long, like all the others in Piet, but the ceiling was much lower, which gave it the feel of a bunker. It was also damp, poorly lit and most of the pale green paint had started to come away from the walls. But what struck me the most was the quiet of the place, the stillness. There was no tapping, no muffled voices coming from behind the doors we passed, no sound of human activity. It was dead space.

We turned right, into a small alcove off the main corridor with two cell doors on either side, and the guard unlocked and opened the first door on the left to reveal a very small room. I followed Zubi in and the door crashed shut behind us. Even with the low-wattage light bulb hanging from the centre of the low ceiling it took a few seconds for my eyes to adjust to the murkiness, but it was obvious why they called it 'the dungeon'. The room was no more than eight feet long by eight wide by eight high, a cube of gloom, with two bunk beds on the wall opposite the door and two to the left that joined each other in the right angle of the walls. To the left, between the door and the head of the bunk opposite, was a hole in the ground and above it a small stained, chipped basin with a cold tap that was leaking and whistling. There was just enough room for Zubi and I to stand up next to each other, though we were uncomfortably close, but there was no space for our bags, which we had to lift on to one of the lower bunks. Zubi took the top bunk opposite the door because it was slightly longer than the other, and on the wall above it there was a small slatted ventilation opening, which he immediately inspected. 'That should get us a mobile signal,' he said, sitting on the bunk with his legs dangling over the side and bending his head forward to avoid hitting the ceiling. We sat in silence for a while, sighing loudly, not needing to articulate our despair. I lit a cigarette and almost immediately stubbed it out on the damp stone floor. For twenty minutes we lay on our backs on the top bunks staring at the ceiling less than two feet above us, until the silence was broken by the sound of the door being opened.

In walked a chubby man with bouffant blond hair, a pasty complexion and dark bags under his eyes, early thirties going on early fifties – an ugly, unhealthy version of the cricketer Shane Warne. He placed his *matras* and *sumka* on the bunk below and muttered some kind of greeting to us before breaking out in a coughing fit. I grunted back, making little effort to disguise my disappointment at his arrival. I realized I'd seen him before. During the fight in the showers with cell 309 he had been the one knocked unconscious when it all kicked off. Zubi started a conversation with him, which was hard going because the guy couldn't stop wheezing and spluttering. In between sentences he cleared his nose and throat and spat noisily into the toilet hole next to where he was standing.

'Man, this is quickly going from bad to worse to Hell itself,' Zubi said to me in English. 'I know for a fact that this fat piece of shit's a fucking grass. They've put him in here to spy on us and find our phone.'

Edik was a repulsive piece of work and I loathed him like I've never loathed anyone, even though we were unable to communicate with each other and barely a dozen words ever passed between us. He was an informer, a scumbag scab, a '*kazjol*', the lowest form of life in a prison, whose vile presence in that tiny hole of a room denied me my contact with home and the world beyond.

For five weeks I spent twenty-three out of twenty-four hours of every day doing nothing but lying on my top bunk – and there was barely a conscious moment during that time when I didn't want to swing my leg round and kick that fucking animal in his fat, gormless face.

He told Zubi he was in for fraud and that he had a trial pending, but his story and the slippery way he conducted himself didn't add up to that. Zubi was convinced he had committed some kind of sex crime and that he had cut some deal with the authorities whereby he agreed to work as an informer inside Piet in return for a reduced sentence. The guards used to keep him supplied with cheap alcohol and foul-smelling, fatty cuts of pork, both of which he claimed his wife paid for on the outside. He was also allowed to leave the cell several times a week – where he went, God only knows – and his relationship with the guards was suspiciously cosy and easy-going. There was something not quite right about him and even I, with no Russian, could tell that.

Our basic rights, by contrast, were denied to us. We were never asked if we wanted to take our daily walk up on the roof, and for the first two weeks we weren't even allowed a shower. Some days they never even brought us any food. For fifteen days we never left that hole in the ground, which was so small you couldn't even pace up and down to walk off some frustration and get the circulation going. In the open area below the bunks, you could take only two steps in any direction before you walked into a wall, a door, a bunk or a toilet hole. The only times I stood up were (a) when I cooked myself some noodles or a coffee, using Zubi's hand-held element, (b) when I used the toilet, or washed, and (c) when a guard opened the door and we all had to stand to attention. When that happened, two of us had to stand back to back because there wasn't enough room for us all to line up shoulder to shoulder. And when one of us was cooking or washing or using the toilet, the other two had to retreat to their bunks to create some space.

The rest of the time I lay on my bunk and slept and day-dreamed and read my court papers over and over again, trying to perfect what I'd tell the court during my cross-examination. And all the while, not three feet from where I lay and breathed, Edik chain-smoked and coughed and spat and shat and masturbated and cooked pork fat over his little electric cooker. He had some kind of problem with his bowels from the day he arrived. At least three or four times a day he squatted over the hole in the ground and farted and strained and splattered the floor with diarrhoea, then wiped his arse with his hand, running it underneath the tap between wipes. Every time Zubi and I saw him pull down his tracksuit bottoms, we rolled over to face the wall and pulled our heads inside our T-shirts while wrapping our arms over our heads to block out the horrendous noise and smell. I never once saw him brush his teeth, or go to the showers. In short, Edik was an unhygienic chain-smoker with diarrhoea, a bronchial disorder and the manners and charm of a sewer pig.

The room was so thick with his cigarette fumes that after a few days I gave up smoking. I didn't need my own cigarettes because, in that tightly confined airless space, it was passive smoking bordering on the active. I was worried about my health too; falling ill was a very real possibility in the squalid, smoky, damp conditions. The most exercise I got was climbing on and off my bunk, and my main source of nutrition came from a packet of cheap Russian noodles.

Within a few days of our arrival, perhaps a week, a heavy melancholy descended on me. It was different and altogether bigger and more alarming than plain sadness or frustration or anger. It felt almost physical as it seeped into every corner of my soul and body, squeezing out the rising sense of hope I had begun to feel in the days and weeks since my family and Lucy had come to visit. For hour upon hour I lay on my back staring listlessly at the ceiling, and soon the smallest task began to feel like the mightiest effort, even getting off my bunk to boil up some noodles or holding a conversation with Zubi that involved me producing more than two sentences. I was weighed down, almost crushed, by lethargy and misery – and once again, I was indebted to Zubi for keeping me afloat. He, too, was suffering the blues, but his innate exuberance refused to be killed off completely and every now and then, maybe once a day, he'd burst into colourful life.

'Right, English boy!' he'd suddenly shout, bounding down from his bunk. 'It's about time you shaved my head again 'cos I ain't catching the insects hiding in that fat fucker's pubes. Isn't that right, Edik? You're a fat, disgusting animal covered in insects and when I'm out of here I'm gonna hunt you down and stab you through the fucking heart!' he added, smiling at Edik as he abused him.

Zubi made me laugh at least a couple of times a day, and that was enough to snap me out of my gloom for a short while. There were two other good moments in the week: first, when Edik left for one of his alleged interviews with his lawyers, which used to happen every two or three days, and, second, when we bribed the guards to let us use the showers, which we managed to do twice a week after the first fortnight. I managed to call home three times, once to speak to Lucy and twice to Mum and Dad, but the conversations were rushed and unsatisfying and I was no happier – and none the wiser about my case – as I hurriedly stuffed the phone back inside Zubi's *matras* after only a few minutes in case Edik or a guard returned.

When Edik was gone I also tried to use the toilet, because I couldn't bear having to squat down right next to him with his face no more than a couple of feet from mine. (Zubi, though, liked to shit right next to him, especially when he was cooking up his pork fat.) It was while he was gone, too, that I took the chance to shave my body to prevent it becoming infested with lice. I tried to shave as often as possible, every two or three days if I could, because the longer I left it the harder it was to remove the hair and the more likely it became that I'd cut myself. And I really didn't want an open wound in that filthy hellish pit, no matter how small. But I didn't want to be stark bollock naked, trimming my privates or my arse, with that grim little ogre sitting an arm's length away.

It wasn't long before my health started to give way. A week or so after we'd been transferred I picked up a chest infection, presumably from Edik, which began mildly enough but became increasingly painful as it burrowed deeper into my lungs. It got to the point where it was agony to cough and Zubi, fearing I might have developed tuberculosis, started badgering the guards to get them to arrange an appointment with a prison doctor. TB was rife throughout the Russian prison system, and if I was found to be suffering from it I would be removed from Piet and placed in a hospital prison with fellow sufferers. I was taken to the medical area for an X-ray and then for five days I lay in the cell nervously awaiting the news. Finally, one of the guards came to tell Zubi to inform me that the results were negative and that I was suffering nothing worse than a severe chest infection and didn't need treatment.

If putting Edik in to live with us in that disgusting little cell was intended as a punishment, it certainly worked. Together with the squalor and the denial of our basic rights, his presence made our detention a form of torture. Living in those conditions amounted to a slow, insidious, relentless assault on our mental well-being or health, and by the time I was taken out to go to court, the edges of my sanity were starting to crumble and crack.

Of all Edik's revolting habits, the one that wound me up more than any other was his practice of getting up in the dead of night and cooking up his pork fat. *Sala*, as it is called in Russian, is a slab of rubbery fat with a meagre strip of meat along the bottom, like a massive, uncooked pork scratching. It is the cheapest cut of the animal but it has one virtue in that being mainly fat it takes ages to go off, and Edik was able to keep shopping bags full of the stuff. At least once a day he used to assemble the makeshift cooker by bending a metal coil into a circle and attaching two wires to the ancient electricity socket in the wall. When the coil turned red with heat, Edik removed four tiles from above the toilet area and built a stand on which to rest his pan. As soon as he started frying the pork, greasy fumes rose up into the already fetid, smoky atmosphere, but the worst part was watching and listening to him eating it. He reminded me of a dog with a bone, the way he sat on the edge of his bunk noisily tearing off strips of the slimy fat, licking his fingers and wiping his mouth on his sleeves, quietly moaning and growling with satisfaction.

One night, during the third week in Razburg, towards the end of September, I'd dozed so much during that day that I was still wide awake in the small hours, rolling around in frustration, my head full of the dark fears that the night always brought. It was always hot in Razburg, partly because there was no proper ventilation, but mainly because there were three human beings living in a room the size of a bathroom, and when Edik fired up his mini-cooker, it got hotter still. Ten minutes earlier, I had listened to him carrying out his other favourite pastime when he rolled over to face the wall and pleasured himself into a tissue, making no effort to conceal his joy and excitement as he reached his climax. You don't want to hear anyone masturbating, but with Edik, half-man half-animal, the sound was especially hideous.

I watched him rise from his bed, adjust his grimy tracksuit bottoms and drop his soiled tissue into the open bucket for used toilet paper next to the hole in the ground. Immediately he plugged in his cooker, tore off a strip of *sala* from a plastic bag and chopped half an onion in among the sizzling pig flesh. I was lying on my side, staring with repugnance and hatred, and I watched him flick a cigarette into his mouth and leave it hanging there as he sat on his bunk and began flipping his piece of fat.

The fumes were getting ever thicker and more acrid, and the anger started to well up from my stomach. Before I knew what I was doing, in a single bound I was off my bunk and screaming in his face. He knocked over his pot of pig and bashed his shoulder on Zubi's bunk above as he jumped to his feet and backed away into the corner, cowering. With both fists clenched out at my side, I was bending forward over the cooker between us, a tirade of ranting abuse rushing from my mouth: 'You fucking filthy fucking low-down fucking animal! You're ruining my life, you fat fucking nobcunt! Turn that fucking cooker off you fucking disgusting pikey cunt, scab, goat bastard, mother-fucker or I'm going to shove that lump of pig fat right up your fat fucking arse . . .'

I felt Zubi's hand on my shoulder, reaching down from the bunk and trying to pull me away as Edik whimpered, in English, 'Sorry, sorry, sorry . . .' I raised my right fist above my head and gritted my teeth at him, making him flinch and lower himself further down the wall. 'You make me fucking sick,' was all I could say before climbing back on to my bunk, coughing violently and shaking all over.

It was at that moment that I realized quite how far my head had gone. I was turning into some kind of animal, or at least into a much lower form of human life than the one that had boarded the plane at Heathrow two and a half months earlier. My only encouragement was that the longer I'd spent in Piet, the less likely they were to hand me a custodial sentence at my trial, and my only comforts were the dreams, both conscious and not, of being reunited with Lucy. I'd never thought I could love her more than I did when I had left England, but my longing for her became almost unbearable.

I had to stay strong for two more weeks before my nightmare was over once and for all. My trial had finally been scheduled to take place on 9 October.

12

'Tomorrow you go home, eh?' said the guard as he took off my handcuffs and led me through a side door into the dock of the empty courtroom. To my left was the judge's bench, raised a couple of feet from the ground, and behind it there was a wooden carving, depicting Russia's coat of arms – a two-headed eagle in gold on a bright red background. The Russian tricolour, three horizontal stripes of white, blue and red, hung on the wall next to it. The lawyer's tables were straight ahead of me and to my right there were half a dozen benches for family and friends. I sat in silence for ten minutes, trying to steady my nervous, irregular breathing while going through my well-rehearsed explanations for a final time.

The doors at the rear of the room were opened by a court official and slowly the room began to fill with the dozen or so people connected to my case. Nick, the British Embassy official who had taken over my brief from Pete Smith, was the first through the door, followed by Piskin and Arseny, my old client who had brought in Artur, the legal 'fixer'. Arseny winked and gave me the thumbs-up sign, and I waved back, but Piskin didn't look over as he walked to the table closest to me and unloaded papers from his fat briefcase. I was barely aware of him anyhow, because my eyes were drawn to Mum and Lucy as they came in with big warm, apprehensive smiles wrapped across their faces. I wanted to hop the railings and run over to them, or shout out, but all we could do was sit and blow kisses and make silly, upbeat faces and hand signals at each other.

A state-appointed translator came and sat next to the dock, positioning herself close to the railings. The prosecuting lawyer, a young man with poor skin and tinted, yellow-lensed aviator-style glasses, sat at his table and arranged his documents. The court clerk and recorder took their seats close to the judge's bench and a guard or a policeman took his position by the rear door. The room was silent but for the shuffling of papers and feet and my occasional, phlegmy coughing.

The judge appeared through a side door opposite me and strode purposefully to her seat behind the bench as we all stood in respect. It was the same judge who had sat at my bail hearing, and she wasted no time in starting the proceedings. I had imagined that my trial would be a painstakingly slow affair, but this judge was clearly trying to move the action along at a brisk pace, snapping at Piskin, the prosecutor and the clerk from the moment we sat down. I didn't understand a word they were saying, of course, but I could tell from the snippets of translation returning to me and by the rate of exchanges taking place that she was in no mood for dallying. I was encouraged by her sense of urgency because it chimed with my own feelings over the past three months: Come on, let's get a bit of snap into this case and put this whole trivial affair behind us and move on! Zubi had told me that she was the same judge who'd released Ranjit and that gave me even greater confidence as she nodded at the clerk to get the trial under way.

I was asked to stand and give my name and date of birth and then the clerk read out the charges against me. I had just sat back down when the judge, via the translator, asked me if I had received a particular document to sign. I had no idea what document she meant and I looked helplessly at the translator, not knowing which one of them wasn't making herself understood. The judge repeated the question, but I still didn't know what she was talking about and I launched into one of my pre-prepared answers about what had happened at the airport and the pressure I'd felt under, in the absence of a lawyer, to sign the Russian document they had put before me. She listened to about ten seconds of Julia's translation before cutting her off with a wave of the hand and motioning to the prosecutor to start.

As the prosecutor opened his case and one sentence fell upon the next in rapid succession, it was obvious it was going to be hard to keep pace with what was being said. The translator was hunched forward listening to the proceedings and every half a minute or so she leant back and fired a burst of translation through the railings. I was only getting a fraction of the action, no more than a brief, loose summary of what was being said.

The small Gollum-like Customs official who had stopped me at the airport was the first witness to be called, and he kept his head down as he walked to the front of the room and read out his statement, occasionally interrupted by the prosecutor and the judge — and just once, very briefly, by Piskin. It was difficult to know exactly what he was saying, but three of his assertions were blatantly untrue. First, he said I had tried to run for the exit in the Customs hall before he called me back. Second, he said that all the clothes in my suitcase were grey, including the jeans in which he had found the hashish. (My suit and socks were the only grey items.) Third, he said the piece of hash was very large and that there were lots of packets of rolling papers.

I started shaking my head and muttering under my breath, 'Not true! Not true!' and I tried to attract Piskin's attention to get him to interrupt and challenge, but he just carried on, looking straight ahead or jotting down notes in his pad. I presumed he was respecting Russian court procedure, biding his time and waiting for his opportunity to hit back. Infuriated by the Customs officer's lies, half-truths and exaggerations, I frowned over at Lucy and shrugged my shoulders, a sense of disquiet growing in me by the minute. When the Customs officer said that the lump of hash was 'very large', I put my hand up and looked at the judge but nobody paid me any attention and after ten seconds or so I sheepishly put it down.

The prosecutor continued to lay out his case, reading out the statements I had signed at the airport and at the police station the day after my arrest. The translator, constantly umming and aahing and tripping over her choice of words, relayed, at a generous guess, roughly 25 per cent of what was being said. I started getting restless, leaning back and forth in my chair in exasperation, shuffling my feet, biting my nails, running my hands through my hair, exchanging concerned glances with Lucy and Mum. My experiences, my fate, my life were the subject of the exchanges going back and forth across the room but I barely had a clue what was being said. It was as though I was watching a show about my life in a language I didn't understand, a foreign film without subtitles.

After twenty minutes the judge invited me to stand and the prosecutor walked over to begin questioning me. I had learned my lines to perfection, but they were no use now as the very ugly young man, whose eyes I couldn't see behind his tinted glasses, started to unload a quick-fire series of questions at me, barely giving me time to compose my thoughts before piling in with a follow-up question. It made it even harder that I was having to pause to try to understand exactly what the translator meant when she passed on his questions. I kept trying to impose my own order on the cross-examination by going back to the beginning and describing in simple, plain language what had really happened. But after five minutes I was struggling for the right words and starting to panic; and the more I panicked the more confused my thoughts became. All eyes in the courtroom were turned to me as I flailed around in my head trying to get my answers right, but I was aware, as I spoke, that everything I was saying was going to be mashed up in translation anyhow. From time to time, I caught sight of Mum and Lucy's desperate faces, creased up in anxiety and sympathy, as I tripped over my words, sounding anything but polished and convincing.

I had been waiting for three months for this chance to put the record straight, imagining that when the moment came I would get to my feet and, with a rhetorical flourish, would lay out the truth, simply and eloquently. I would speak without bitterness or anxiety as the court hung on my every convincing word and at the end of it, common sense and decency would win the day and I'd be sent on my way with a fine and perhaps an apology for my long detention and the way I had been treated.

But in the event I was seized by confusion and panic, and once my garbled answers had passed through my shredding machine of a translator, I must have come across like an incoherent fool who didn't know his own mind.

My mouth was dry and my stomach knotted when the judge cut off the prosecutor and asked me to explain the contradictions between the statements I had made at the airport and the following day, and the one submitted by Piskin several weeks later. She was presenting me with a golden opportunity to recover some ground, and I took a deep breath to try to compose myself before slowly and deliberately rolling out my explanation, so that the translator would understand every last word. I told her how I'd been made to sign documents in Russian that I didn't understand, how I had been denied a lawyer or an official from the British Embassy, how I had felt intimidated and confused, how the airport authorities had grossly exaggerated the weight of the piece of hashish, and how sorry and stupid I had been not to check my clothes and luggage properly before coming to Moscow.

My performance was a slight improvement but, with the translator stammering her way through a few scraps of my testimony, there was barely any point in me saying anything at all. To compensate, I tried to communicate with the judge using facial expressions and hand gestures, hoping they'd tell her more than the abridged, emotionless, faltering version she was getting from the girl. When I was told to sit down, and the court broke for a forty-minute recess, I sat with my head in my hands for a few moments, convinced I had blown my big moment. I was put back in my cuffs and as the guard led me round the corner and back along the corridor I could see Lucy approaching from the other direction. As we crossed I quickly leant towards her and whispered, 'I love you,' but as I turned my head the guard nudged me in the back to move me on. He didn't understand that she was the reason I got up in the morning.

Lucy was the first to give evidence when the trial resumed, and my heart went out to her as she walked to the front of the court. She looked beautiful in her brown woollen top and jeans and her boots that clicked as she walked across the courtroom floor. She stood near the judge's bench with her hands out in front of her, like a schoolgirl called to the front of the class to explain her conduct. The prosecutor rose to begin his cross-examination and I could see Lucy's left leg shaking violently as he began to ask her about the suitcase she had allegedly packed for me on the eve of my flight. The prosecutor tore into her, asking her repeatedly to list every item she had put into the case. Every time she paused the prosecutor harried her for an answer. I closed my eyes and put my head in my hands, muttering, 'Stay cool, Babe, just stay cool, in your own time ...' but she was clearly flustered. It wasn't helping that she didn't know whether she should be addressing the court translator, the prosecutor or the judge, and ended up looking from one to the other. I could see the growing desperation on her face as she shifted from one foot to the other and fidgeted with her hands and cuffs under the prosecutor's aggressive line of questioning, and I had to restrain every instinct in my body from leaping the barrier and ripping his fucking head off his shoulders.

The main issue of her cross-examination was the colour of the trousers in which the piece of hash was discovered, with Lucy contradicting the Customs officer's statement by saying, correctly, that they were light blue, not grey. The prosecutor accused her of lying, and she started cracking up, and there followed a horrible pause in the proceedings where the only noise in the courtroom was the sound of her sobbing and choking. It was at that moment that I remembered I had the very pair of jeans downstairs in my holding booth, and I leapt to my feet, shouting, 'I've got them, I've got them. They're downstairs!'

Arseny shouted from the public benches, 'Go get them!' and for a brief moment there was an electric tension in the courtroom. I looked at Piskin, waiting for him to say something, but he remained stock still, staring vacantly ahead of him, and the judge motioned to me to sit down. What the hell was Piskin playing at? He might as well have stayed at home. Except for two or three brief exchanges with the judge about procedure, he'd sat through my trial in total silence! He didn't challenge the integrity of my original statement, he didn't cross-examine Lucy. He didn't even cross-examine me!

This eruption of excitement over the trousers signalled

the end of Lucy's cross-examination and she turned and gave me a loving, apologetic smile as she returned to her seat, wiping the tears from her face. Piskin stood up and started reading out some character references from people in the UK and clients in Russia, but after a couple of minutes the judge cut him off and he just sat down. We'd paid him thousands and thousands of dollars, to do next to nothing. The judge proceeded to sum up the evidence and then asked the prosecutor what the State recommended as a sentence. He stood up and said: 'The State recommends five years for smuggling, and two for possession and acquisition.' I'd known that was coming, but it didn't make it any less painful when I heard Mum let out a cry and I watched her get up and disappear through the main door into the corridor, choking on her tears as she shuffled down the aisle. The judge said she would give her verdict in five days' time, on Tuesday 14 October, and banged her gavel on the bench to signal the end of the trial.

When the guard put my handcuffs back on he did it gently, and I was surprised that he was looking at me sympathetically, sighing quietly and shaking his head. His face said: 'Well, you fucked that one up, eh, buddy?' I tried to hold myself together as he led me back along the corridor through a blur of figures. I looked straight ahead, focusing on the wall at the end, but in my peripheral vision I could see Piskin, the prosecutor and the translator milling around by the main door to the court. As I approached Piskin, he looked over his shoulder at me and I leant forward, about twelve inches from his face, and said: 'Thanks very much, Alfred. You're a legal legend.

Fucking brilliant.' The guard kept me moving, and as we walked round the corner Lucy was standing near the door to the booths, tears pouring down her cheeks. Neither of us spoke. She blew me a kiss. I tried to return one but realized my hands were cuffed and she laughed as I disappeared down the stairs.

As soon as I was back in the privacy of my booth below stairs I broke down, my head swarming with one grim vision of the future piling on top of another. Seven years! I'll be thirty-eight – thirty-five if I get parole – by the time I get out. There's no way Lucy will wait for me that long ... Was that blown kiss a farewell? ... I'll never get a professional job again ... or a mortgage ... or a credit card ... I'll be an ex-con ... I'll get TB or HIV and die in a Russian camp in the middle of fucking nowhere ... I'll never see my family again ...

I was heaving and sobbing and moaning when Zubi, also in court that day, suddenly burst in, saying, 'What's wrong? What's up? English boy, what happened?' He put his arm around me and soon he started crying too.

'I fucked it up, Zubi, I fucked it up! I'm going down! My life is fucked!'

'Me too, man. Me too.'

I put my head on his chest and we sobbed like babies.

The journey to court the following Tuesday was a nightmare. One of the prisoners shat himself, filling the crowded truck with a nauseating stench that not even the cigarette smoke of thirty men could overpower. But the worst problem was sitting right opposite me in the form of a junkie, already delirious with drugs, who was drifting in and out of consciousness while trying to inject himself with a further hit. My legs were interlocked with his and he was so floppy that his head kept lurching forward as the truck kangarooed its way through the Moscow morning rush hour. In one hand he held a filthy syringe, loaded with God knows what, and every minute or so he'd make a feeble effort to stick it into his other arm. But he was away with the fairies and never succeeded. It crossed my mind that he was trying to top himself before he got to court. For an hour I didn't dare take my eyes off him in case he fell forward and stabbed me with the syringe, and several times I had to gently lift his hand and put it back on his lap when it slid too close for comfort. After the first courtroom drop, when a couple of dozen prisoners were shipped out, the four of us sitting closest to the junkie lifted him down to the far end of the truck, letting his syringe fall to the floor, and then we all sat as far away as possible in case he puked.

Mum and Lucy cried throughout the ten-minute verdict hearing. I sat impassively until I was asked to stand. The verdict came to me in staccato bursts of pidgin English through the railings . . .

'Your sentencing is five years . . . You are four years for smuggling drugs and one years for the possessing . . . In Russia law, two sentences are being together, it is because four years, six months . . . You are in the Russian prison for four years and six months . . .'

The judge brought her hammer down with a sharp rap, and as she rose from her chair and the rest of the courtroom followed suit, I sat down with a thud while she disappeared through the door. I looked around for

Mum and Lucy but they had gone. Out in the corridor, I saw Mum from behind, sitting at the top of the main steps and leaning against the wall, her back and her head heaving up and down.

'Mum! Mum!'

13

Christmas time, December 2003

I woke up with a jolt as the guard jabbed his riot stick into my ribs. '*Anglichanin, Mordoviya,*' he muttered down at me, barely opening his mouth. I sat up on my elbow, my head heavy with sleep, as he stepped among the prostate bodies, prodding an African, a Kurd and a Vietnamese with his stick. '*Mordoviya!*' he mumbled at each of them. It was pitch black outside, and though the sun didn't rise until about nine o'clock and I could only guess at the precise time, my body was telling me that it was still the dead of night. The four of us were slow to move and after a few moments the guard shattered the sleepy silence, bellowing in Russian, '*Idi! Idi!*' ('Go! Go!') I was in no hurry to go to Mordovia, but I leapt to my feet. 'The Great Fuck-All' was what Zubi called the backwater province, famous for nothing but its prison camps. That's all there was in Mordovia, just the 'Zones', or the gulags as some Russians still called them. Prison camps and snow and forests of pine and birch. In the middle of fucking nowhere, roughly 500 miles or, weather permitting, a long day's drive from Moscow.

Shortly after my trial they had transferred me from Piet Central to Krastna Prestnya, the transfer prison for convicts being moved to the Zones. My appeal failed a few weeks later in spite of hiring a new – supposedly hot-shot – lawyer, who tried to get me off on a technicality. The judge reduced my sentence by a year, but that was no consolation or victory. Three years? Four years? What's the bloody difference? Since then, I had done little but lie on my mattress – on the floor for the first week before graduating to a bunk – and wait to be taken away, keeping my head down and trying my best to avoid contact with my new cellmates. We were a motley collection of foreigners in cell 208. There were half a dozen sullen Chinese, some Vietnamese, a scattering of Africans, silent Afghans praying to Allah, a violent Bulgarian drunkard, a Hungarian *kaziol*, a few Kurds and two hard-nosed Turks who ran the cell – and me, the English boy with all the cigarettes and the noodles and the fancy trainers.

The only guy I wanted to talk to in there was a middle-aged Nigerian called Philip, a very small, insecure, religious character with lively, intelligent eyes and un-naturally massive lips. He was not a well man: his eyes were yellow and he wheezed and coughed like a chronic asthmatic. On my arrival in the cell, he came and sat next to me and I gave him my sob story, but I felt a little ashamed when he began to spout his own woes. He had absolutely no one and nothing to comfort him: no money, no support from his embassy, no family or friends on the outside. Like most of the Africans, Philip had been convicted for selling drugs – he'd been sentenced to twelve years and, like many of his black brothers, he had seen the error of his ways and become deeply religious. He had been to Mordovia once before for a previous offence and was terrified about going back. More than anyone else

Philip had filled me with dread about being moved to Mordovia, with his tales of how the guards worked him to the bone and were quick to hand out the beatings. But it was the malnutrition and health threats in Zone 22 that worried him the most, and in those few weeks before he was put on the convicts' train, I shared all my food with him and gave him as much of it as I could to take to Mordovia to build up his strength.

When he left, two weeks before me, he hugged me and said: 'Thank you, thank you. I won't forget your kindness. God will reward you.'

Zubi had arrived a few days earlier, and it was a relief to see his friendly face in that grim, overcrowded cell. But in the space of a few weeks poor old Zubi had become a shadow of the person I'd met six months earlier. The judge had given him ten years, and he dragged his disappointment round like a ball and chain, visibly crushed by the length of his sentence. The fighting talk was gone, the shoulders were stooped, and he barely had the will to argue with Kadri, the Turkish *smatriashi*, or his hairy little right-hand man with the wonky eyes. He was appealing but he wasn't optimistic about the outcome.

I gave him a pat on his shoulder as he slumbered, whispering: 'See you in the Great Fuck-All, big man!'

Zubi pulled me closer and said: 'Remember this, the motto of the Zones: *Ne veri, ne boisia, ne prosi*. Don't trust, don't be scared, don't ask. *Bon voyage*, English boy. Watch your back now,' he smiled.

The other three had only a small *sumka* each, while I was carrying a large one as well as two shopping bags and my ostentatiously plush black Samsonite suitcase. Mum had bought me a whole wardrobe's worth of winter clothing to take to Mordovia, where the temperature sometimes fell to thirty, even forty, degrees below, and it was a struggle to carry it all across the room without bumping into the bodies sprawled out in various postures on the floor. I took special care not to knock into one of the five Chinese guys, recently added to the cell following their conviction for the brutal murder of two Russian men on the border. They were hard, miserable little fuckers when they arrived, but after they were handed life sentences, they really didn't give a flying shit who they upset. If they got into a fight, or stepped out of line, what more did they have to lose?

The truck reversed violently and I had to cling on to the bench and press my feet down on the floor as the driver brought it to a juddering halt. The doors were thrown open and a few yards in front of us there was an old railway carriage with bars on the windows. A guard in combat gear and a black balaclava waved his sub-machine gun at us and then at the door and we followed him up the short steps into the carriage corridor. With a flick of his head he told us to enter one of the small compartments strung out along the length of the train. It was roughly the size of one of the first class apartments on the old British Rail trains and it was empty except for four wooden bunk shelves, two on each side, bracketed on to the walls. The four of us squeezed into the tight space, but we had so much luggage between us that we ended up stepping and falling over each other's bags as we tried to manoeuvre ourselves round the restricted area. Leaving my bags on the floor I pulled myself up to one of the top shelves, lay down and stared at the ceiling about eighteen inches from my face.

Judging by the fading light it must have been mid-afternoon, but I had no real idea how long we'd been waiting when the old train finally started to move, shunting clumsily back and forth. For an hour or so I gripped the side of the bunk and wedged my knees against the ceiling to stop myself rolling out on to the bags below as the engines pulled and tugged, first in one direction then the other. The train's heating was on full blast and I soon began to feel my sweaty underclothes clinging to my chest and back, so I got down from my bunk in order to take off a couple of layers. It was difficult to keep my balance against the shunting as I got undressed, and I kept lurching over from side to side and hanging on to the shelves, but after one especially powerful jolt I shot forward and cracked my forehead against the wooden shelf on the other side. Blood flooded over my eyes and nose, but as I grabbed one of the bars of the window to steady myself, almost immediately I felt the butt of the guard's machine gun slam against my fingers and I fell backwards on to the bags in agony. The young Vietnamese guy gave me a handful of toilet paper from his *sumka* to soak up the blood, and all three of them helped me back up to my bunk. 'Thank you, thank you, *spasiba*, *spasiba*,' I said, but they just nodded impassively, like they were only doing their duty to a fellow prisoner in difficulty.

I had been drifting in and out of sleep for hours when I heard a growing commotion in the corridor as the train ground and spluttered to a halt. The guards were walking down the carriage hollering orders, while banging the walls and unlocking the compartment doors. A balaclava-ed face shouted through the bars of our door and I didn't have to understand what he was saying to know that he wanted us to get off the train. And fast. We grabbed our bags and hurried out to join the dozens of other prisoners piling out of the compartments and carriages on to an icy, brightly lit platform. A row of policemen, standing with their legs apart, were lined up facing the train with their backs against a high mesh fence. The barking of their dogs shattered the crisp, still air.

Suddenly we were all frantically scrambling through a large gate and towards some kind of fenced-off precinct a few hundred yards from the train station. Weighed down by my luggage, and with my injured left hand throbbing as I gripped the handles of my *sumka*, I was soon struggling to keep up on the ice-bound tarmac. We were being run like buffalo into the precinct, with the dogs and guards yelping and snapping at our heels, and my heart was pounding with effort and fear. In my stumbling attempt to keep up, I lost my footing, somersaulted over my *sumka* and landed on the compacted ice, sprawling and panting. As I got to my feet I felt the heel of a boot dig into the bottom of my back and I collapsed back on to the ice with clothes spilling out of my *sumka*. The policeman was screaming at me to get a move on, while his snarling Alsatian strained on its leash at his side. Inside the precinct I joined a line of roughly forty prisoners strung out in the snow, facing about half that number of policemen. We were all panting hard from the sudden burst of exertion and a long cloud of steam floated away above our heads into the almost blinding brightness of the floodlights.

All fell quiet except for the occasional bark of a dog, and one of the guards shouted something in Russian and pointed over to his right with his baton. Roughly a dozen prisoners, including a Nigerian from my cell in Prestnya, stepped forward and walked over to form a separate line.

I elbowed the Chinese guy to my right and asked him what was going on by shrugging my shoulders and holding out my hands.

'Plisoners with the HIV,' he replied. 'They go AIDS plison.'

They were taken away to a waiting truck and the rest of us were escorted inside a large depot building, where we were locked in a holding pen.

We spent three nights and two days behind the meshed walls of the cage, hunched in balls on the stone floor to try to keep out the freezing cold that seeped in through the concrete walls and hung in the air of the cavernous warehouse. Twice a day the guards let us out to stretch our legs around the compound for half an hour at a time, and we were given the regulation three crappy meals a day (more 'porridge' and 'soup'). No one seemed to know why we were being held there, and as the hours and then the days slid by, we became a restless mob ready to erupt. The place was called Portma, that's all anyone knew. By the second day all forty or fifty of us were pacing round the cage and some began to cling to and shake the mesh fences, shouting whenever a guard appeared to try to find out what the fuck was going on.

At the end of the second day a furious fight broke out between the Chinese and the Middle Eastern guys. I didn't see how it began because I was hunched up with my face on my knees, trying to sleep, but in a split second, there was uproar. The rest of us pinned ourselves against the fencing as the two rival groups punched, kicked and spat at each other in a wild frenzy. The furore alerted the guards outside the warehouse and within two minutes they were running through the main door, pulling their truncheons from their belts. The dog-handlers waited outside the cage while the truncheon boys, about a dozen of them in total, set to work on the brawlers, thrashing them on to the floor or up against the fences. They covered their heads and screamed under the blows and when the guards marched out, half of them lay on the floor curled up or rolling around in pain.

On the morning of the third day we were led back to the train and we set off once again, chugging and spluttering deeper and deeper into the flat, snowbound plains of central Russia, my heart growing heavier with every mile we advanced. I had barely slept for three days and the world outside had a dream-like, almost hallucinogenic quality about it as it rolled past the steamy window. For hour after hour, fields of snow and mile upon mile of forest rolled past the barred window under a blanket of low grey cloud. After a while, we passed the first of several Zones and I pressed my nose to the condensation on the window for a closer look. They seemed more like army bases than conventional gaols, with their observation posts in each corner, barbed wire fences running around the outside and pairs of guards in combat gear on patrol. Through a gate or a fence I caught the odd, fleeting glimpse of prisoners in dark uniforms and hats standing in columns like a ragdoll army or walking up and down the exercise yard, their arms pulled against their chests as they huddled up against the biting cold. I couldn't hear anything over the noise of the puffing and grunting of the old train, but it looked like a silent, still world out there, as if life had ground to a frozen halt.

Around each prison was a scattering of old wooden houses nestled back among the pines, smoke wafting vertically from the chimneys into the windless air; dogs and chickens scratched around in the snow but, except for the odd moving car and an old woman in a headscarf carrying a basket of sticks on her back, there was no other sign of human activity. The cars were decades old, but they were the only sign of modern life. I could see there was little point trying to run away from the Zones because if I managed to avoid being shot by one of the snipers in the watchtowers, or mauled by a pack of guard dogs, I'd just get lost in the forests or freeze to death in the snowbound plains.

I was to spend a week at a hospital prison undergoing a series of medical examinations before being taken to my Zone. One of my Russian clients had generously paid for the visit to make sure I hadn't picked up tuberculosis or any other hideous illness in the Moscow prisons. My cough had never gone away, even when I quit smoking while in Razburg, and the fear that I had picked up TB constantly nagged away at me. I was the only person to get off the train at the hospital, a huge sprawling community of drab buildings, and it was eerily quiet as a guard led me across the compacted ice and into the warmth of the crumbling red-brick reception centre.

An orderly led me along a series of corridors and corners and into a large ward housing roughly two dozen other patients. Naïvely, I had imagined that the hospital would be a clean, peaceful, organized place where I could enjoy some rest and privacy and some half-decent food before beginning my sentence proper in the strict regime of the foreigners' Zone. But it was a dispiriting sight that greeted me when the orderly pushed open the door and walked me down the aisle between the two lines of beds. It was like a cross between an army field hospital and a lunatic asylum, *The Longest Day* meets *One Flew Over the Cuckoo's Nest*. All but a few of the inmates had shaved heads or short-cropped hair; roughly half were missing either a limb or an eye, or were nursing serious wounds, and the rest looked straight sick and were lying motionless or shuffling slowly among the beds.

As I stowed my bags under my bed, a man missing an eye and half a leg hopped towards me, grinning and holding out his hand. 'Marlboro?' he asked. I gave him a Marlboro and he hopped back down the ward to smoke it on his bed. Within a minute a dozen men were swarming around my bed, smiling and patting me and holding out their hands or putting them together in prayer. I doled out the remaining cigarettes in the packet and opened a packet of sweet biscuits for everyone to share.

It was more like a Victorian freak show than a hospital ward and I quickly became fed up with the begging. I had far more provisions than the other patients, but I didn't want to exhaust them all before the Embassy visited me in the Zone. (I'd been warned that in deepest winter visits were sometimes delayed owing to the weather.) At first I tried not to look at them when they came and pleaded for food and fags, and I stared at the ceiling, hoping they'd get the message and go away, but after a while I began to lose my patience at their insistence, and I snapped 'No!' and waved them away with my hand. 'No' and '*Nyet*' were virtually the only words I uttered in that room for a week.

The food was better than the prison slop, but only marginally, and none of it was fresh as I'd been hoping for. It had been almost a month since I'd finished the fruit and vegetables Mum had left me before flying home, and my body was starting to crave them with the same intensity I usually crave nicotine. I lay on my bed dreaming of apples and oranges as well as piping hot cups of tea and strong coffee, pints of lager and glasses of red wine. Except when I was led away for my daily test, I did precisely nothing in the hospital other than lie on my bed and sleep, write up my diary and daydream – mainly about Lucy and the life we'd lead together when I got out. They weren't fantastic, outlandish dreams, like living in a mansion or holidaying in Barbados or eating out in swanky restaurants, but modest and homely, like reading the weekend papers in bed, cooking up a meal or watching a DVD wrapped in each other's bodies.

I played a game trying to guess what she would be doing at a particular time of day: perhaps making herself tea, taking a bath, chatting with her friends on the phone, and when I pictured her it was like I was there in the room with her, like a ghost or a fly on the wall, unable to communicate, but in her presence all the same. I tried to imagine her happy, or at least putting on a brave face and not crying all the time, but then I got a vision of her curled up on the sofa watching the telly, by herself, and a wave of despair rolled over me like a heavy weight. I hated myself for condemning her to such a miserable existence and I yearned to make it up to her. I kept writing it in my diaries: 'I'm going to make you the happiest girl on the planet.'

When night fell, thoughts of home were replaced by fears of what lay in store for me in the Zone. I tried not to think about it during the day, but at night I woke up every few hours, wriggling and wrestling with the demons from the deep of my unconscious mind. In six months, I had yet to hear a good story about Mordovia.

Once a day I left the ward to go for some form of medical examination – a chest X-ray, a blood test, a urine test, a stool test, an eyesight examination, or just a general stick-your-tongue-out-say-aah check-up. No one ever came to fetch me – I had to go down to reception each morning and through a mixture of pidgin Russian, basic English and hand signals discover when and where I was meant to be going for that day's test. So on chest X-ray day, the receptionist pointed to his chest, coughed, showed me on his watch the time it took place and then, scrawling a map on a piece of scrap paper, showed me how to get there. At the appropriate time, I'd set off into the vast network of roads and buildings looking for the right clinic. All the signs were in Russian, and although I had learnt the Cyrillic alphabet and some basic words, phrases and numbers, I had no chance of understanding the names of the various medical departments. I was forced to engage in a further exchange of hand signals in order to find my way – generally with unhelpful officials and guards who despised the sight of me and just grunted a one-word answer and pointed in a vaguely northerly direction.

I wandered around and got lost every day, tramping through the snow, sliding on the icy roads and gesticulating with men in uniforms, and as I did so it dawned on me that I hadn't enjoyed such freedom since leaving Heathrow six months earlier. And until my arrival there, I hadn't felt the sky over my head or the weather on my skin for longer than a minute, or however long it took to walk from the prison wagon to the courthouse. To be outside was a modest thrill, a mini-adventure, but when the time came for me to return to the train station, I said goodbye to no one and marched as fast as my two heavy bags would allow to the platform to join two dozen others waiting for the signal to climb aboard. Next stop Zone 22.

For hour after hour I sat on my *sumka*, wiping away the condensation on the window and staring out at the grey skies merging into the flat, snowbound horizon as the old train hauled its cargo of criminals through the nothingness that is Mordovia. Every hour or so the train spluttered into one of a dozen prison camps, or Zones, and disgorged a handful of prisoners on to the caged platform where the guards and their dogs were waiting for them. With mounting apprehension, I watched their dark figures being led away inside the prison walls beyond.

There are as many Zones in Mordovia as there are types of criminals: Zones for lifers, Zones for women, Zones for violent sex offenders, Zones for corrupt officials, Zones for psychopaths, Zones for those sentenced to hard labour, Zones for your regular bog-standard petty criminals. I was going to Zone 22, or the 'Forgotten Zone' as they called it back in Moscow. It's for foreigners, and they called it 'forgotten' because it was bottom of the list of priorities for the Russian judicial system. Prisoners languished in there for months, even years, after their *udo* (parole) date. They weren't just criminals; they were foreigners. Who cared? Fuck 'em.

Each Zone looked just like the one before, a makeshift fort made from wood, mesh fencing and barbed wire with sniper towers at each corner. As the train slowed and bumped to a stop along yet another platform, I didn't know that we had reached Zone 22 until the train guard stuck his face to the bars of the door and barked, 'Hague, Tig!' Quickly I gathered up my *sumka* and suitcase and jumped out of the wagon door on to a caged platform where four guards and their Alsatians were waiting to lead us away. The frozen air seized me like an electric current and for a moment I couldn't move. Never in my life had I felt cold like it, and it was all the more shocking for having spent ten hours in an overheated train compartment. Men were emerging from all eight carriages along the platform and, though no one told us to do so, we all gravitated towards each other like iron filings to a magnet, forming a scruffy line in front of the guards.

From the caged platform we filed through the set of huge metal gates and into the Zone itself. It was almost dark but, squinting, I was able to make out a series of low wooden buildings in the middle of the compound, a scattering of other buildings and four watchtowers, one at each corner. It looked a little like the POW camp in *The Great Escape*, only more run-down. If only the cheery figure of Dickie Attenborough had been there to greet me, bounding across the snow with his outstretched hand. 'Jolly good show, Hague. Let's get you a nice warm cuppa. We'll tunnel you out of here by Easter.' I could have done with seeing a friendly face right at that moment, because I was absolutely shitting myself.

There were about ten of us from the train and we were steered by a line of guards down a corridor of high wire-mesh fences and into a large holding pen, where we lined up facing a row of guards and prison officials. To a man all of us were stepping from foot to foot and blowing into our cupped hands to try to keep warm. When it was my turn, I picked up my bags and presented myself to the most official-looking character in the middle of the guards facing us, just as the others before me had done.

'Name, conviction, sentence?' he snapped, in Russian, without looking up from his clipboard.

'Hague, Tig, acquisition and possession of illegal contraband, three years and six months.'

14

The prison guard pointed to a little black man, in a dark prison uniform with a homemade baseball cap, standing just outside the pen. '*Idi! Idi!*' ('Go! Go!') he shouted, waving me away with a flourish of his hand. I left the pen and immediately started following the man across the compound, dragging my bags behind me across the compacted snow. When we were out of earshot of the holding pen, he leant towards me and whispered, 'I'm Alan.' As we walked towards the bottom of the compound I could see the outline of dark figures, their faces shrouded in steaming breath, moving around in smaller pens outside three long, low shed-like buildings to my left. They had their heads down as they paced up and down, up and down, up and down. Only the odd bark of a distant dog broke the silence. '*Atrads*. For sleeping,' Alan whispered, nodding towards the buildings. 'Atrad 1 for prisoners in normal *obshi* regime, Atrad 2 for sick prisoners, Atrad 3 for long-sentence and bad prisoners in *stroggi* regime.' Each pen contained a small pagoda-style structure with a roof and open sides. I could make out the small bright orange lights of four cigarettes burning in the shadows. 'For smoking,' whispered Alan.

To our right, directly facing the accommodation blocks, there was some kind of administration office, and as we walked into the light streaming from its long bay window, four guards stared out at us with grim, impassive faces. Their heads turned and followed us as we disappeared from view.

The fur-lined boots Mum had bought me in Moscow crunched into the crisp fresh snow blanketing the ground, accentuating the silence that clung to the Zone. We headed across a further open space towards another row of huts lying at right angles to the ones we'd just walked through. 'One for the cooking, one for the eating, one for the books,' Alan said. Pointing to a small red-brick building to our left, he added: 'For praying for the Almighty's Salvation and for the forgiveness of our sinning.'

We were moving towards a building at the bottom left-hand corner of the Zone, close to the perimeter fence. There was a dull mechanical hum coming from inside that grew louder as we approached. Smoke and steam belched from two chimneys in its corrugated iron roof. A huge heap of coal, higher and wider than the building itself and draped in snow, was piled up against the side wall. As Alan slowly pushed open the heavy metal door with his shoulder, a cloud of steam gushed out into the cold, still air and a great roar of industrial machinery ruptured the silence. It was pitch black inside. Alan beckoned me to follow him, but I couldn't move. I swallowed back a surge of nausea and steadied myself against the wall.

My instinct told me not to go, but Alan was frantically signalling to me to hurry up. He was saying something too, but I couldn't hear a word above the noise of the churning machinery. The door closed behind me and

I could see nothing, not even Alan. The growl of the machines suffocated all other noises and a powerful stench of oil and coal filled my lungs. A drip of condensation landed on the back of my neck and made me jump. Slowly my eyes adjusted a little to the darkness and I could see Alan holding open another door leading into a dark corridor. Again, he beckoned me to follow, but I didn't move an inch. Alan came back and seized me by the arm.

The door closed behind us. The darkness was total again. Alan, still holding my arm, slowly led me forward. The noise ahead of us grew louder and louder. I was breathing rapidly. We came to a stop and I was aware only of the pounding of the machines that I heard and felt but could not see.

I saw the whites of eyes and the glint of teeth. I started to walk backwards, when close by and booming above the noise, I heard a heavy African accent say: 'Relax, my friend. Don't be scared. We are the same as you. Prisoners. No guards, no Russians here. It's cool.' My eyes were adjusting fast and four Africans came into focus. Someone turned on a dim, flickering lamp mounted on the wall. One of them got up from a chair and walked towards me, his huge frame towering over mine. He smiled as he put an arm around my shoulder and said: 'First, the barber shave your head. Then you have the hottest shower. Then we talk. We will be your friends. We protect you. Have no fear. My name is Julian, this is Boodoo John, this is Hulk and this is Eke Jude.'

Julian shook my hand and gently led me by the arm into a small adjoining room, where a Middle Eastern man with greying temples was sitting smoking a cigarette. He stood up, inviting me to sit on his stool, wrapped a large oily cloth around my shoulders and turned on his electric shaver. Two of the Africans were standing in the doorway, grinning. 'He make you look like a sheep in the spring,' one of them said. The sensation of the shaver touching the back of my neck made me shudder and then, with the first of a dozen firm sweeps of my scalp, my thick black hair began to tumble down my face and shoulders. I stood up and rubbed the thin coat of soft bristles and tried to wipe the hair from my face.

'Welcome to Zone 22,' said the barber, with a toothy grin.

Like all new arrivals in Zone 22, I was to spend my first two weeks in 'quarantine', a small room inside the administration building where the prison governors and officials had their offices. The room was across the corridor from the observation area where the guards had watched me being walked down to the boiler room, and as Alan led me into the building after my shower, one of them summoned us with a shout. I followed Alan into the room and half a dozen guards turned round and looked me up and down with a mixture of curiosity and contempt. Three were slumped in their chairs, and a couple leant against the wall by the window with half an eye on the three prisoners' quarters fifty yards across the compound. Fixed into the wall to my right was what looked like an old telephone switchboard with dozens of sockets, wires and receivers. Across the other side of the room was a small kitchen area where a sixth guard, fat and middle-aged, was stirring a mug of something while eyeing me with the same disdainful sneer as his colleagues. He pointed at me and shouted. I had no idea what he was saying. He shouted again and started quickly walking towards me.

'Take your hat off! Take your hat off!' whispered Alan at my side, and I noticed that he was holding his own hat in front of him as he looked at the floor. I quickly whipped mine off as the guard approached and stood so close to me that his belly was almost touching mine. He snarled something in Russian and I could only hold his stare for a few moments before I looked down at my boots and muttered my apologies: *Izvini, nachalnik! Izvini, nachalnik!* ('Sorry, boss! Sorry, boss!')

He put his hands into my coat pockets, took out my packet of Marlboro and walked round the room offering them to his colleagues. He pulled one out with his teeth, slid the packet into his shirt pocket and then lit up, blowing the smoke up towards the ceiling. He let out a sigh of satisfaction and walked back towards me with a smile, saying in English: 'Nice English boy! Nice English boy!' Almost immediately his face lunged towards mine and I recoiled as he shouted, *'Idi, anglichanin! Idi, anglichanin!'* and pushed me violently towards the door. As I spun round I felt the toe of his boot against my backside and I crashed out into the corridor with the sound of mocking laughter in the background.

I was still breathless with shock as Alan led me into quarantine, a small drab room ten yards further down the corridor facing out the back of the building. There were three sets of double bunks, two on the left-hand wall and one in front of me on the right. At the far end there was a small window looking out towards the prison wall, with only a shed and what looked like a long washing-line in between. Two Mongolians with round weather-beaten faces and sad eyes, and a slightly camp Vietnamese boy, nodded a welcome from the two bottom bunks on the left where they sat. The younger Mongolian stood up and introduced himself as 'Baska'. I shook his hand and, gulping for breath, said: 'Tig.' The other Mongolian, a skinny man with almost luminously yellow-brown skin, stood up and said: 'Greecia.' The Vietnamese boy just looked up shyly and said: 'Fam.' Alan left and returned a few moments later with my bags. He said goodbye and I sat down on my bunk, at Baska's invitation. Greecia started to brew some tea and slowly a very basic kind of conversation developed. Baska did most of the talking, in a mixture of broken English and prison Russian, and I nodded and ummed, smiling when he smiled and frowning when he frowned.

Baska pointed at me and asked: '*Statya*?'

I put my fingers to my lips and mimed smoking a joint, aware of the absurdity of my predicament as I did so. It was insane that that was the reason why I was sitting, shaven-headed, in that little room in the middle of the frozen Russian wilderness, trying to hold a conversation with a man from Mongolia.

'You?' I asked, pointing back at him. Baska smacked his fist into his open palm three times, then clenched both fists and held them out in front of him to show that he had won the fight. He nodded towards Greecia, putting one hand over his mouth as he pulled his head back and ran the fingers of his other hand along his neck in a cutting motion. Fam stood up and lifted an imaginary wallet from his back pocket.

'Fam, *peederaz*, Moscow,' said Baska, simulating a blow-job with his hand and mouth. 'He no like, much fighting. In Zone 22, more sex problem. He go quarantine for his safe sleeping.'

Fam smiled in agreement, but I looked away, embarrassed and unnerved by the images of his abuse that sprung into my mind.

'Greecia and me go quarantine, fighting Chan. We always the fighting Chan. Chan, bad Chinese, bad man ...' Baska pointed to a lump on the bridge of his nose as evidence of their encounter.

Six months in the Russian prison system had taught me that language is just one way of communicating; slowly I was able to piece together a rough picture of the life in store for me in the camp as Baska explained about life inside Zone 22, using hand gestures, mime and scribbles in the back of the cheap school textbook I was using as a diary to fill in when speech failed. The main message that kept coming through was that the guards ('*nachalnik*') in Zone 22 were as great a threat as the most violent inmates. Baska stood up and mimicked the beatings they handed out, taking Greecia by the shoulder and bringing down a flurry of imaginary blows on his back. He described the threat of solitary confinement by making Fam go and stand in the corner away from the rest of us.

I listened to Baska with growing dread for a couple of hours, saying little in reply but concentrating till my head hurt, and it was almost a relief when one of the guards came to turn off the light and I slumped back on my mattress and wrapped myself in the rough blanket. I was desperate for sleep but I lay awake in the blackest of moods, listening to the wind that had started to whistle around the building and the sound of muffled laughter coming from the guards' room along the corridor. Through the small window I saw the snow swirling around the silhouette of the sniper in his tower, and beyond the prison walls, lit up by the Zone floodlights, I saw the tops of waving trees and the lumpy outline of clouds on the horizon. I tried to work out which way was west and I thought of London, 2,000 miles away, where my former colleagues at Garban Icap joined the tens of thousands of other City workers flooding out into the streets and down into tube stations or into the noisy bars and pubs, ordering a round of drinks, hailing taxis, rushing home to be with their families and loved ones ... To think I ever used to moan about that daily commute, the delayed trains, the packed tubes, the stress of my job, the queue for a sandwich, the cost of a pint. And all these thoughts led my mind in the same direction – to Lucy. I could picture myself stepping in from work and into her arms as I walked in the door at her mum's in Leytonstone, or at my mum's in New Eltham, squeezing her close and never once imagining that we'd ever be separated for more than the few days of a business trip. I felt the tears running down my temples as I stared up at the wooden ceiling above my bunk and tried to imagine what she would be doing right then, at that very time of day when we used to be reunited after work and settle down for a bowl of pasta, a glass of wine and an evening in front of the telly, saying and thinking little, just happy in each other's company. But then I disappeared from the image, and it was just her left in my mind, curled up by herself on the sofa, her face taut with worry about what was happening to me in my strange little world at the other end of Europe.

15

The shock of the cold made me withdraw into the doorway as Alan led me out of the office building to go and collect my prison uniform and utensils from the storeroom, down by the boiler room where I'd been taken the night before. I was wearing a thermal shirt and underwear, long johns, two T-shirts, a thick fleece, a heavily padded black jacket, a thick woollen scarf, a bobble hat and a pair of gloves (all in regulation prison black). My face was the only exposed part of my body and the blast of frozen air slapped my cheeks and stabbed my nose as I stepped through the door into the blinding low sunlight and a bustle of early morning activity. I had slept poorly and woken early, struggling to free myself from a horrible nightmare that seemed to go on for ever. I dreamt that Lucy was pregnant and she needed me to come to her aid, but no matter how hard I tried to reach her, I never got there. I took a bus, a taxi and a train, but they all went the wrong way or stopped moving or broke down. I walked, I ran, I crawled but still I couldn't get to her. Lucy started to cry out louder and louder, her face riven with pain, and I grew increasingly frantic but I was powerless to help. It was so vivid that it felt like a real experience and I was still feeling shaken up by it when Alan came to collect me.

We stood at the door, waiting for three columns of

roughly 100 black-uniformed prisoners to trudge past, up towards the main gate where they waited to be escorted through to the factory beyond. They weren't quite marching in step, but they had the air of a defeated army about them as they tramped wearily by, heads down, in silence. A dozen others were busy clearing the concourse and road of overnight snow and ice, noisily scraping the tarmac with giant snow shovels; snipers looked down from the four observation posts with their rifles slung over their backs, blowing and rubbing their hands; two handlers and their dogs were patrolling the bottom wall of the Zone while other guards, most in combat gear but some in olive green uniforms, wandered to and from the camp's scattering of wooden buildings. The Zone was surrounded by high concrete walls but right at the far end of the factory area the perimeter was made up of two parallel mesh fences, topped with barbed wire, through which I could see the landscape beyond: a stretch of flat marshland extending to the horizon, a sheet of white punctuated by clusters of pine and birch trees.

I was looking around, trying to take in my new surroundings, when a sudden clatter of hooves and the grinding of wagon wheels made us spin round. Trotting down the main thoroughfare from the gates, between the office building and the *atrads*, was a horse and cart being driven by a prisoner of Middle Eastern appearance. He was standing at the front of the open flatbed wagon like a charioteer as he drew alongside us, gently pulling back on the reins to bring the two great horses to a stop. On the back of the cart was a large silver churn, a few lumpy brown sacks of what looked like potatoes or onions and a handful of cardboard boxes. As he chucked a sack over his shoulder and disappeared through the door of the kitchen, I couldn't help but stare at his nose, which was the largest I'd ever seen on a human being.

We walked on towards the bottom of the Zone, where the African boys were busy shovelling coal into large metal buckets, watched by a guard leaning up against the side of the building, lazily drawing on his cigarette. It looked like punishing work, even for men of their colossal build, and a cloud of steamy breath enveloped their heads as they scooped up the black lumps and slid them noisily into the containers. I presumed it was the presence of the guard that made them less friendly towards me than they had been the night before. They winked or nodded or smiled, but no one said anything and they carried on working as Alan and I approached and entered the storeroom.

I re-emerged five minutes later, the owner of one metal bowl, one metal cup, one spoon, one horsehair mattress, one rough sheet, one horsehair blanket, one small hard pillow, one pair of thin socks and one pair of the largest, worst cut underpants I'd ever seen. My uniform consisted of a black smock shirt with an inch-wide green stripe across the back and over the pocket on the left breast, a pair of baggy black polyester trousers, a black peaked cap made of cardboard and different cuts of dyed black cloth, and a very thin pair of black shoes stitched together with a variety of different materials.

'Most prisoners are very poor and wear the prison shoes, made in another Zone,' said Alan. 'They are bad shoes, very, very cold for the feet. You can wear your own black hat and shoes, but if they are expensive, like Reeboks or Nikes, be careful – in a week you can bet the guards will be wearing them at home.'

We walked back up towards the office building and I looked down nervously at my fur-lined walking boots, which the Embassy had bought me with money from Mum and Dad.

The rest of the Zone had already eaten their breakfast in the dining area, but Alan delivered our porridge and sweet black tea to us in quarantine and we ate it on our knees. Three hours later, he delivered lunch: a slice of black soda bread with a kind of soup containing marginally more evidence of vegetables than the shit we had had in Moscow. There was greater nutritional value and taste to be found in a cardboard box, but at least it didn't make me retch.

Before supper, Alan arrived to escort me to my first head-count, known as *preverka,* when the whole prison assembled on the concourse between the *atrads* and the office building. *Preverka* took place three times a day before meals, and I could tell by the way Baska and the others, at the blast of a siren, had scrambled out of bed and rushed from the room for the first one of the day, pulling on their clothes as they went, that getting there on time was a matter of the greatest urgency. Now that I'd been issued with my uniform, I could officially join the black ranks and I jumped from my bunk, in synch with the others, when the first of the three long blasts of the siren erupted through the public address system. The second blast followed two minutes later, and I was still tying up my boots when Baska tugged me as if to say 'Get a move on,' pointing to his eyes to tell me that I should watch what he did as I leapt up and we rushed down the corridor and out into the frozen darkness.

Across the compound from us, lit up by the glare of the floodlights, prisoners were pouring from the three *atrads* into the exercise pens and through the metal gates, buttoning up jackets or hopping on one foot as they pulled a shoe or boot on to the other. From the air they would have looked like a colony of ants streaming out of their nest after some kind of trauma below ground, and I saw the stress etched in people's faces as well as in their frantic movements as they took up their positions. In spite of the commotion of movement, a powerful silence hung over the gathering crowd. Whenever there was a break in the flow of prisoners, the mesh gates of the exercise pens swung shut with a metallic bang. The gates were opened by a guard operating a buzzer in the observation room behind him, and I watched the anxiety on the faces of the last prisoners to emerge as they clawed at the mesh and waved anxiously at the window to be let out. After a few moments the gates were buzzed open and a couple of guards chuckled to themselves as the stragglers sprinted into columns and rows, facing the buildings from which they had just emerged.

Slowly the tramping of boots on the icy ground came to a stop, and 300 prisoners, dressed in black from head to foot, stood stock still under a thick flurry of snowflakes, looking directly ahead of them. I was standing right in the middle of a group of roughly 100 men from Atrad 1, where I was to be housed after my spell in quarantine. Half the faces around me were black African and the rest a mixture of Middle Eastern characters, Chinese and what I guessed were Afghans, North Africans, Vietnamese and maybe half a dozen white Europeans or Westerners. And they were all staring at me. I looked at the ground, half embarrassed, half freaked out by the attention I was drawing. I heard the wooden door of the office building behind us swing open on its creaking hinges and slam shut, followed immediately by the sound of footsteps crunching through the snow.

All of a sudden, there was a commotion over in Atrad 3 and all our heads turned to the right, like soldiers on parade. I saw a young Vietnamese guy bursting out of the building and flinging himself against the pen gate. He was signalling crazily to be let out while at the same time bending down to tie up his laces. A guard marched down to the gate and started bawling at the lad, who was pleading and apologizing, putting his hands together in prayer and screwing up his face in contrition. When the entry buzzer sounded, the boy fell forward through the gate. The guard seized him by the collar and pulled him, still apologizing, past the lines of other prisoners and round into the offices.

The other guard walked up and down the rows, inspecting the inmates, stopping from time to time to give someone the eyeball. A pair of dark glasses sat above his bulbous nose and droopy moustache, his pot belly hung over his trousers and he tucked his thumbs into the belt carrying his truncheon, mace spray and handcuffs. His gunmetal-blue fur hat with the ears up, perched awkwardly on top of his big fat round head, gave him a faintly comic-book appearance. I closed my eyes and was able to hear only the crunch of slow footsteps. He was counting to himself as he walked among us and when he got to the end he just sauntered away, up the steps and into the offices without a word. At the sound of the door shutting we began to melt away into the falling snow back to our sleeping quarters, and I was immediately surrounded by a dozen or so of the prisoners, slapping me on the back and whispering: 'Hey, English boy ... Englishman ... how are you, friend? ... you eat with me ... UK is best ... you want cigarette ... Tony Blair great king ... we share food, OK, you my friend in Atrad 1? ...'

Alan and I walked into the office building and I saw the young Vietnamese guy standing nervously in the corridor outside one of the governors' doors. He was biting his thumbnail and cursing to himself as he waited, legs apart, staring down at the floor. We sat on our bunks and Baska exhaled and shook his head sympathetically.

After a short while, we heard the door of the governor's office open and close, and we all looked up as the Vietnamese boy passed by the open door, moaning as he rubbed his hands over his face and disappeared out into the night.

'Boy, now more time for him in Mordovia. Six month time!' said Baska, with anger in his voice. 'No *udo*! Many prisoner get no *udo*! No go home to family. No to freedom. Six month more in Mordovia for be bad. Always the six month more. You careful no be bad, Englishman. Six more month.'

I knew '*udo*' was the Russian word for parole and it was difficult to say what was more shocking and depressing: the fact that no one got out of there at the time of their scheduled parole date, or how terrifyingly easy it was to have an extra six months slapped on to the end of your sentence. Freedom in Zone 22 was not a date fixed in the calendar, like a birthday, but a moveable feast that could be delayed indefinitely.

16

Fam left quarantine on my second day, but Baska and Greecia were to remain until the end of the week and they passed on as much prison wisdom as possible. I was an eager student and I concentrated hard to understand what they were trying to teach me. Baska showed me practical details like how to make my bed, the Zone way, with the top of the sheet turned down on the blanket, all creases smoothed out, the pillow perfectly straight, and my towel folded into a triangle next to the pillow. When I practised and failed to get it exactly right, he became angry with me and started gesticulating and raising his voice. He showed me how I must stand up as soon as a guard or governor walked into a room, take off my hat and look at the ground humbly, never making eye contact unless ordered to do so.

We left the room only to attend *preverka* before each meal, and to use the toilet hole in the room next door, but on the fourth morning Baska gestured that I should put on my outdoor clothes and boots, saying over and over, '*Divzhenya! Divzhenya!*' and pointing to his eyes to indicate that I was to watch what he did. He took a handful of cigarettes out of their packet, kept two for himself and put the rest in my pocket. I followed him out into the corridor and into the reception area by the front door of the building, where a fresh-faced young guard with corn-coloured hair sat at a desk reading a newspaper. On the back I could see a picture of an ice-hockey player wheeling away from goal with his stick held aloft in celebration. A cup of steaming black coffee sat in front of him and Baska placed the two cigarettes next to it, neither of them acknowledging the exchange. Baska mumbled something in Russian and the guard nodded, slipping the cigarettes into his pocket at the same time.

'*Divzhenya! Divzhenya!*' Baska smiled at me as the door slammed shut behind us and we strode across the concourse between half a dozen road-scrapers who were keeping it free of snow by piling it on to the great heaps using giant wooden shovels rimmed with metal, known as '*lapats*'. The sound of metal on tarmac had the same effect on me as nails down a blackboard, and I grimaced as we headed the 100 yards down to the kitchen, which adjoined the dining area. '*Divzhenya! Divzhenya!*' Baska repeated, as he walked into the kitchen. An African man was washing dishes while a Vietnamese chopped potatoes at the table in the middle. A Middle-Eastern-looking character with a receding black hairline, sharp nose and mess of craggy teeth turned round from the stove, where he was stirring a giant metal vat of soup with a long wooden spoon. The vast majority of prisoners I'd seen were slim or positively skinny, but the cook was fat and his belly hung out over his dirty apron.

Baska introduced him as 'Mehmet', and he nodded at me without smiling as he wiped his hands on the apron before flicking his head back at Baska, as if to say: 'Yeah, so what do you want?' Baska reached into my coat and took out four cigarettes, saying something in Russian as he handed them over. The cook winked as he slipped the Marlboro into his shirt pocket and turned to the table to pick up part of an animal carcass stripped of everything but some tendons. With one violent swipe of his meat cleaver he chopped off a piece of bony gristle, picked a potato from the hessian sack on the floor and presented them both to Baska, who shoved them into his deep jacket pocket. The pair nodded at each other, and Baska and I turned and left the room.

'*Divzhenya! Divzhenya!*' said Baska, smiling from ear to ear. We strode back to the office building, blowing into our hands and shivering against the cold. When our soup arrived for lunch, Baska poured it into his metal bowl, added the potato and the bone and heated up the mixture with the heating element they otherwise used to make tea. Fifteen minutes later it was ready and he poured some into my mug, looking the very picture of pride as he handed it over. '*Divzhenya! Divzhenya!*' he laughed. I thought *divzhenya* was another word for *bilander*, meaning soup, but the penny dropped when Baska held out a couple of cigarettes in one hand and the bone in the other. 'For food, you give cigarettes or coffee. To go kitchen, give cigarettes or food for guard. To no go factory for day, you give doctor much, much cigarettes, chocolate, coffee ... Understand *divzhenya*?' he said. 'All *stashoi*, all prisoner are do *divzhenya*. Every day!'

Mehmet was 'very bad man', Baska stressed, grimacing and shaking his head. 'You careful with Mehmet. He trouble. Guards like Mehmet. He give guards food, he give guards meat for the prisoners.'

'Why he Mordovia?' I asked.

Baska put down his soup. 'He sex with young woman, and kill with knife many times.' To make sure I got the point he pointed to his balls, made a violent thrusting movement and then acted out a frenzied attack. I looked into my soup and felt sick.

While he was talking, two faces, one Chinese, one black African, had appeared in the doorway, but they stared not at him but at me, without embarrassment, for half a minute before disappearing down the corridor. All week, a parade of prisoners who'd come to the admin building to see one of the officials had been sticking their heads through the quarantine door to check me out. All the guards had done it too. It didn't bother me at first, but the more they came the more uneasy I felt. Some waved and smiled, some did a thumbs-up sign, but most just stared without expression, which I found even more unsettling. I didn't know whether to smile, turn away or to try to look hard and scary whenever a face appeared at the door. When I shrugged my shoulders at Baska and said, 'Why? What they doing?' he threw his hands up in the air as if I was stupid and said: 'You English! You English!'

Greecia's English was virtually non-existent and he spoke very little (the only English word I heard him utter was 'tea'), but he was an extraordinary-looking man and I found it difficult not to stare at him, as the others stared at me. There was barely an ounce of flesh on him and his yellow-brown skin, which looked like it had been stained or painted, clung to his face like cellophane. He ate next to nothing and gave away most of the food brought to us by Alan. From what I could tell, the only things to pass his lips were cigarette smoke and incredibly strong tea known as *cheffir*. On the day the two of them were to return to the *atrads*, I accepted his offer of a cup of *cheffir* as a kind of farewell present. The pair were housed in Atrad 3, which was for those sentenced to the more severe *stroggi* regime. I was to be moved to Atrad 1 (*obshi* or 'normal'), which was only 100 yards away at the other end of the building, but they were separate worlds and we would never have the chance to eat and drink and talk together as we had done that week.

I watched Greecia place six heaped teaspoons of black tea into a small cup, which he covered with boiling water and left to infuse. Half an hour later he handed me a cup of thick black tar and, just as he had done, I bolted it in one gulp. Almost instantly my head began to spin and I could barely stand up to hand back the cup and take the little boiled sweet you were meant to suck straight afterwards to take away the foul bitterness of the tea. It was the biggest caffeine hit I'd ever experienced. I was rushing.

'Greecia big love the *cheffir*,' Baska said with a laugh. 'Greecia always *divzhenya* for the tea.'

It was no wonder they were always fighting Chan and getting into trouble, drinking that stuff. It gave me such a rush that for half an hour I was unable to sit back down on my bunk, and much to their amusement, I had to walk up and down the small room before I calmed down. When they packed up their *sumkas* and Alan came to escort them back to their living quarters, I was still sitting on my bunk, wild-eyed and taking deep, slow breaths in an effort to slow my racing heart. I stood up to shake their hands as they left. 'Thank you! Thank you! *Spasiba, spasiba*,' I said, also nodding my gratitude.

'Good luck for Mordovia, Englishman,' replied Baska, patting me on the shoulder. 'Careful *udo*, careful guard.'

The quarantine room looked especially drab and bare after the Mongolians had left, and the five empty beds and the silence seemed to be mocking me in my isolation as I lay or sat on my bunk, at a loss over what to do with myself. What to do? That was the nagging question that the loneliness asked. From time to time, I got up and walked to the window or touched my toes or shadow-boxed around the room, just for something to do. I screwed up small pieces of paper into balls and used them to throw at various targets around the room, quickly pick-ing them up afterwards in case a guard came in and saw the mess. I put my hands behind my head and made dreamy plans about my life with Lucy back in England after my release, but the optimism was always driven out by a swarm of doubts and fears. How was I going to get a job with a criminal conviction? What would we do for money? Was my working life over barely before it had started? Alan came to deliver my meals three times a day, but the only other human contact I experienced for forty-eight hours came during the jostling, nerve-jangling chaos of *preverka*. Quite why it was taking so long to process me through the Zone system was a mystery.

On the morning of the third day by myself, I was sitting on the lower bunk, glumly tossing my set of paper balls into my metal mug, when the sound of a man gently clearing his throat made me turn around with a start. A small black guy was leaning in the doorway. He was wearing a silk shirt, designer trousers and smart leather shoes, all in black like the rest of the prisoners, but these were clearly his own clothes. He had a very slim, baby-like face but he was good-looking. He was standing with his hands in his pocket and his hat tilted to one side, holding out a shallow cardboard box.

'Fancy a game of chess?' he said with a smile.

'I'm Papi,' he said, putting out his hand for me to shake before sitting down on the bunk opposite, leaning back on his elbows and crossing his legs like he owned the place.

'*Parlez-vous français?*'

'*Oui, bien sûr.*'

Our conversation continued in fluent French as Papi laid out the chessboard on the floor between us.

'So how come you're not at work with the rest of the Zone?' I asked.

'You probably think I'm some kind of informer sent to spy on you, eh?' he replied with a grin. He handed me a note with Russian handwriting and a signature, adding: 'Sick note from the doctor. She says I've got a severe chest infection!' Papi laughed and rocked back on the bunk. 'Truth is I just gave her 100 Marlboro and three Toblerones. Cigarettes, chocolate and coffee – they'll be your best friend in here. You should start loading up on them. There's not one guard, governor or official in the whole Zone who's above a bribe. These guys earn less in a month than an Englishman or a Frenchman earns in a day or two. They'll do anything for a packet of Marlboro or a jar of Nescafé!'

Papi put the cardboard box between us and started setting up the white pieces as I reached in for the blacks.

'Most prisoners in here are so damned poor they've got nothing but a few boiled sweets, a bit of black tea and the cheapest of the cheap Russian cigarettes. But you, an Englishman, with a good embassy behind you ... Man, you might even get out of here on time! If you got money, you got power and influence. At the moment, I'm the richest dude in the joint because my *smelnik* – that's your eating partner you share your provisions with – was a Danish guy called Erik. When he left a couple of weeks ago he left me a suitcase and a big *sumka* full of gear – bags and bags of food and cigarettes that his embassy had brought down by the vanload. The Danish Embassy are the best! I've been a virtual free man inside the Zone ever since he left. I haven't been to that hellhole of a factory for two weeks. I just hang out doing a few light chores around the camp, like sweeping the corridor in the office building and emptying the waste paper bins. It's not going to last, so I'm just enjoying the break while I can ... as soon as the supplies run out, the fuckers will start giving me a hard time again; get their own back on me, for playing Mister Big. They don't like any of the prisoners but they like black prisoners even less and most of all they hate black guys throwing money around!'

Papi leant down and moved the pawn in front of his queen two squares forward. Talking! What a joy it was to be able to have a conversation with someone and understand every word they said. And an intelligent, amusing person at that! Not since I'd left Zubi and Philip back in Moscow, almost three weeks earlier, had I enjoyed the pleasure of a conversation that didn't involve hand gestures, monosyllabic grunts and endless repetitions amid a general fog of misunderstanding.

For the next four days Papi breezed into the room after breakfast with his chessboard and a supply of luxuries like chocolates, tinned fruit and peanuts. It turned out that we shared a birthday and he started calling me '*mon jumeau*' ('my twin'). He had an English wife and two young kids, who'd gone back to London after his arrest for drug dealing, and on the last day before I was to be transferred to the *atrads* he showed me photos of their London house and his family. The house was a brown-brick, terraced two-up two-down with a little walled garden out the front, strikingly similar to the type that Lucy and I had been trying to buy, and the sight of it sent a shock of sadness shooting through me, transporting me for an instant back to my former life.

'The last time I saw my kids, the younger one was just learning to talk. The next time I see them they'll be teenagers,' he said, brushing away a tear. He was trying to make me feel better, but it only made us both sadder.

We sat in silence for a few minutes, staring at the half-empty chessboard. I pretended I was contemplating my next move, but my mind was thousands of miles away. I was back in London, waking up alongside Lucy. It was about seven o'clock UK time. After a while I took one of Papi's pawns with a knight.

'Check,' smiled Papi, immediately diagonally sliding his bishop into line with my king. 'Get out of that one! All I can say, my friend, is I hope you play the Zone 22 game better than you play chess, 'cos otherwise you're going to be cooling your ass in here for longer than you think. Getting out of this hole is the hardest game you'll ever play. Want me to explain the rules?'

'Tell me everything you know.'

be pushing you up in line. You forget that you think
I think, can't this lady's the hardest time you have.
We. You're the man in here.'

'Tel me' nothing, you too.

17

'I'll give you the bad news first. There are guys in here
who should've been released months, even years ago; the
system's fucked and there's a huge backlog. And do you
think they give a shit? Do they fuck. They couldn't care
if you died in here an old man. You're just scum in a black
uniform, a head to be counted, an arse to be kicked.
They're not going to help you out of here, the system
alone's not going to get you out of here ... but, and it's a
big "but", *you* can get yourself out of here. You just have
to learn the game and then play it with skill, cunning and
ruthlessness. Half the Zone's playing it – everyone except
the long-termers – so you've got competition. But if
you've got money, you've got power. You can be a front-
runner. You've got as good a chance as anyone. This is
what you've got to do.'

We had stopped playing chess and were now leaning
towards each other over the board. The smile had gone
from his baby face, and he was looking at me intently.

'The first thing you need to do is attach yourself to a
"cop", one of the top officials in the Zone sitting a few
yards away from us along the corridor,' he said, pointing
his thumb over his shoulder. 'For a price, they can exert
influence over the progress of your parole, or dig you out
of trouble if a guard starts giving you a hard time and
slaps you with an extra six months for whatever minor

offence you've committed – like standing in the wrong place, or not taking your hat off and standing up fast enough when he enters the room.'

He was growing ever more passionate as he spoke, using his hands to stress his points: 'Most of these guards are as bored and frustrated and miserable and poor as we are, and when you finally get out of here, just remember these sad bastards will still be here. They're in for life. The prison's all they've got, and they like to entertain themselves and feel a bit bigger about themselves by playing God with our lives. They don't want *you* to get out of here. They resent the fact *you*'ll be free and they'll still be stuck here in this shithole. Besides, you're a free lunch to them, an endless supply of Western cigarettes and coffee and chocolate – stuff they could never afford on their wages. So they're going to try and keep you here as long as possible. It's Zone 22's catch 22 – the more you give them to secure your route out of here, the more they're going to want to keep you in.'

He paused and took a slug of water from his metal mug.

'This is where the embassy comes in. Most of the guys in here never get visited by their embassy, or even acknowledged, but the Brits have got a good embassy. The Western embassies look after their people, and they can do more for you than just bring or send down food parcels and check on your human rights – but it's up to you to motivate them. When the time comes to make your move, you've got to get them to jack up the pressure on the authorities from the outside. You've both got to push at the same time; you showering your cop, your governor, with goods, while your embassy starts waving the big stick at them back in Moscow.'

'What kind of goods?'

'Small. Small but expensive. Stuff you can conceal in your clothes. The whole Zone's taking bribes or handing them out, but everyone has to pretend it's not going on. It's one of the golden rules of the game. So the shopping list you give your family to give to your embassy should include exquisite Western items such as pens, watches, chocolate, cigars, real coffee, jewellery – anything a poor backwater Russian would consider luxurious. The guards and lesser officials can be persuaded to grant small favours – like using the library – with cheaper bribes such as cigarettes, a few slices of salami, or a couple of tea-spoons of instant coffee wrapped up in a piece of paper. Good-quality cigarettes are your chief currency in here.'

'So which governor should I target?' I asked eagerly, scribbling abbreviated notes in the back of my diary as Papi talked.

'There's no point,' Papi continued, 'in trying to win over the head governor because he has little to do with the day-to-day running of the prison and you rarely see him. Besides, I've already seen three governors come and go in five years, and there's no point concentrating all your efforts on a man who's going to move on before your parole date comes up. You want to choose one of the four others, who are all permanent fixtures in the Zone. They live in the little wooden houses just beyond the walls of the camp. They grew up here, and they'll die here. They're not going anywhere. Each has their own merits and weak points and it boils down to a question of what you want most: an easier life in the Zone, or the quickest possible escape out of it . . .'

'The latter, any day.'

'The second-in-command is a bastard known as Regime. It's a name he gave himself in order to impress his authoritarian manner on the prisoners. He's good for clearing problems inside the camp, such as ensuring that a "black mark" – the extra six months they hit you with – is erased from the records. But your best bet for securing your release from the Zone is the third-in-command, a man known as Zanpolit. He's in charge of the legal affairs of the prisoners and has good contacts and influence at the region's main courthouse. A third option is the FSB officer, known as the "*koom*", who, like Regime, is useful if you want an easier life in the Zone. Zone 22 is a Black Zone run by the FSB, and part of the way they assure control of the prison is through a "grass" or spy network that involves prisoners reporting back to the *koom* on any misbehaviour or skulduggery going on in the *atrads*. The *koom* runs the network, but most of his spies are the poorest guys in the Zone. They can't afford goods as bribes, so they use information instead.

'The fourth alternative is the prison doctor, a plump, middle-aged woman with peroxide blonde hair who puts her make-up on with a bucket and spade. Most of the prison's in love with Olga Dimitrova because . . .' And Papi broke out in a huge grin. 'She's got a lovely big bum – a good cushion for pushin'!! She also hands out sick notes for the right price.'

'Why don't I try and get friendly with all of them?'

'No, don't go that route,' he said with emphasis.

'There's no point trying to work all four of them because you'd spread yourself too thin and waste valuable resources. There's a physical limit to how much stuff you can store in here, and you need half that for your own food supplies. Also, they like to feel special, so concentrate all your efforts over the coming months on one individual; and if it's the quickest route out of here you want, there's only one choice. It has to be Zanpolit. He's the guy who goes to court every month with a list of guys up for parole. The only way your name's going to get on that list once your parole date has passed is if Zanpolit writes it on. He's your man. You may have come across him already. He's the young guy who thinks he's a bit of a smooth operator.'

I knew the one he meant because I'd seen him a few times sweeping past the quarantine door to his office. He was tall and slim, maybe early thirties, and he had his hair slicked back over his head with oil or gel – an image which, by Mordovian standards, was bordering on radically cool. With his thigh-length leather coat, he was a bit of a natty geezer who stood out from the others.

'So how do I work him?'

'OK. First of all, every time you want to come to the office, you have to bribe the guard on duty with a couple of smokes or a teaspoon of coffee. The first time you visit Zanpolit, give him a generous gift, maybe three packets of Western cigarettes and a jar of coffee. That way, he'll know you'd like to recruit his services. Then, for the first six months, find an excuse to go see him every two or three weeks, each time bringing him a gift, such as a bar of chocolate for his wife, or another packet of cigs. If you have an important request, like making sure a parole document is lodged with the court – often they sit in trays or filing cabinets for weeks or months – take him something fancy like a decent lighter or a good pen.

'There's no point plying him with goods for the first half of your sentence because you're not going to get out early and all you're doing is raising the bar of his expectations. Just slowly build up a solid relationship with him. A gift here, a gift there, and then, when winter comes, a few months before your parole date, start making your moves on him. Increase the visits, as well as the quality or quantity of your gifts. Around then you need to start stockpiling goods so that you have enough to start showering him with stuff two, even three times a week, piling up the moral pressure on him to make sure your parole application is somewhere near the top of the list that will be submitted to the local judge that month.'

Parole for me meant a half-sentence, because the trial judge had handed me the more favourable *obshi* regime and strictly, my release date was 15 February 2005, roughly fifteen months from the day of my arrival in the Zone. But more realistically, given the delays and congestion in the system, and assuming I avoided black marks, I was looking at June or July.

'You got to be ruthless and push your way to the front of the queue, whatever that takes, and fuck whoever you have to push out of the way to get there,' Papi said. 'It's everyone for themselves in here. Don't listen to anyone's sob stories. There are guys in here without a penny to their names and no support on the outside, who are months and years beyond their parole date. They're constantly forced to the back of the queue by the richer prisoners like you, who are able to bribe their way to the front. But you can't worry about them. It's just their tough shit. If you want to be a good Christian about it and wait your turn, well, that's your business. But if you want to get home within a few months of your parole date, you've got to use your elbows.'

All week I'd been convinced that, from the moment I'd stepped off the train and trudged under the sniper towers into the Zone, I had surrendered all control over my own fate. I just had to sit and wait, keep my head down and be a good boy, avoid trouble and pray for a prompt release. I had gone into passive mode. Lucy, my family and the British Embassy would carry on trying to exert some influence on the outside to ensure my freedom – in more optimistic moments, I even hoped they might get me out a little earlier – but Papi showed me that I could have a sense of purpose in Zone 22, an ongoing challenge to occupy me and focus my mind. The thrilling realization dawned on me that I still had some power over my own destiny. When he was gone, I clenched both my fists and punched the air.

18

It was late afternoon, already pitch black, an hour or so before the prisoners came back from the factory, and the Zone was very quiet when Alan and Ahmed came to move me out of quarantine into my living quarters – the *atrads*. Ahmed was a tall wiry Moroccan with cropped dark hair and a scar running on the diagonal over his nose, from one side of his face to the other. Papi had warned me not to get on the wrong side of him because the threat of solitary confinement or a sentence extension never stopped him from fighting someone who crossed him. An aggressive drunk, serving ten years for stabbing someone to death in a Moscow knife fight, Ahmed had been put in charge of Atrad 1, because he was a reliable informer and the authorities knew that the other prisoners – or most of them at least – were scared of him. He wasn't strictly a *smatriashi* because the prison was not a Red Zone; he was more a kind of head prefect, a union rep or an office manager who supervised the day-to-day running of the *atrad* and the settling of minor disputes between inmates. That was his job in the Zone, and he had earned it after five years' hard graft in the factory.

It was probably just the scar, but I felt the man's simmering menace as we shook hands and looked into each other's eyes. Even his toothy smile failed to wipe away the sense of danger that hung on him like a cloak.

'An Englishman in Zone 22, eh? We are honoured,' he said, offering me his hand.

The two of them helped carry my bags across the concourse, and after we'd been buzzed through the gate by the guard in the observation window behind us, they led me across the small dirt exercise yard and up three wooden steps into a small hall area. Atrads 1 and 2 each housed roughly 120 prisoners, while Atrad 3, in exactly the same amount of space, had double that number.

At least fifty pairs of threadbare slippers and trainers were stacked on top of each other along the walls inside the door, and all three of us removed our outdoor shoes and changed into our 'indoor' ones. Alan put his finger to his lips and whispered: 'The night shift prisoners and the sick guys are still asleep in bed.' Inside the room to the left were rows of cupboards and lockers. 'For your food and cigarettes,' Alan whispered, as we turned right into a dormitory and a maze of double bunks, stacked head to toe along the walls and in columns across the middle, with no more than a foot between each one. It was like the lower deck of an old ship of the line, only with wooden bunks instead of hammocks. All the beds were made with immaculate precision, with the sheet turned down over the rough grey blanket and a towel folded neatly below the pillow, just as Baska had shown me. Around ten of the beds were occupied as we tiptoed over the creaking floorboards, and the guys were sleeping in woolly hats and jackets. There was a window in each wall, but the one in the front was twice as big as the others, presumably so that the guards could see straight in from the observation area across the concourse. There was no decor to speak of; just bunk after bunk, wooden walls and wooden floors painted pale grey-blue. It was impossible to walk between bunks without brushing against them.

To the right, immediately on coming out of the dormitory, was the toilet area, which consisted of three sinks and two holes in the ground separated by a low wooden screen. An Afghan guy, or Uzbek maybe, was finishing a shit. His trousers were around his ankles as he crouched over the hole while washing his hand under the tap at the same time.

Next door was the kitchen area, which consisted of a small table with a bench on either side. And that was it, except for a concrete ledge on the right where a heating element was coiled up next to a socket. Alan led me along the corridor, which had two hot water pipes running across the ceiling over its entire length. A couple of towels were hanging from them, dripping on to the floor. We turned right into a second dormitory, which looked exactly the same as the other one except that it was marginally smaller and felt even more cramped. Another dozen or so guys were sound asleep, some of them snoring, and we trod as quietly as we could on the creaking, splintered floorboards. Squeezing between two rows, Alan showed me to my bunk, which was the third to the right of the door against the wall, and, in silence, we laid the sheets Mum had brought over from home, separating the filthy mattress from the rough horsehair blanket.

To the right of the dormitory as we walked out was a room that looked out towards the perimeter fence and the main gates. A small black and white television sat in the corner on a low table, and there were a dozen plastic chairs stacked up next to it. Heading back down the corridor, there was a coatroom next to the TV room, with black jackets hung on pegs above a few pairs of black shoes. Along from that, before the hall area by the door, there was an admin office where Ahmed was sitting at a table, still wrapped up in his thick coat and woolly hat, cradling a steaming mug.

'Let me help you,' he said, getting to his feet and taking my suitcase from me. 'Thanks, Alan, I'll look after Tig now.' Ahmed led me to the storage cupboards near the entrance and eagerly helped me unload my provisions into one of two large food lockers. As we stacked the noodles, biscuits, cigarettes and coffee on to the shelves, it was obvious, looking at the others' provisions, that I had a hell of a lot more than most people in there, and a wave of embarrassment washed over me. 'We can share our food if you like,' he said, the scar zig-zagging across his face as he grinned. I remembered Papi's warning that everyone in the *atrad* would try to befriend me when I arrived and that it was going to be difficult for me to work out who I could trust as a friend and confidant, and who just wanted to get their nose into my food bags. Papi's advice was that as I would probably always have enough cigarettes and basic foods of my own and wouldn't need handouts from my *smelnik*, I should choose someone who spoke good English, whose company I enjoyed and who didn't cause trouble. Ahmed spoke good English, but that's about as far as it went. I didn't want to cook and share my food with a man who scared me shitless. I mumbled a reply, trying to avoid the subject.

Back in his little office with its window overlooking the yard to the front, Ahmed sat me down and, over a cup of sweet black tea, ran through some of the basic rules of life in the *atrad*. 'No lying or sitting on your bed until bedtime at ten o'clock; smoking only in the exercise yard, whatever the weather ... Your shoes must be clean at all times ... Make your bed after breakfast ... Sundays we shower and wash our clothes ... Respect other people's property. Prisoners never steal from each other. We try and live as a family, as a team. We help each other ... If you have any trouble with another prisoner, come and see me ... And, by the way, steer clear of Papi, he's trouble. If you hang out with him, the cops will notice and associate you with him. You'll get a bad reputation. Trust me.'

Through the window I could see the other prisoners hurrying back from the factory, heads down against the falling snow and hugging their arms to their chests. Nodding his head at the figures passing through the gate into the yard, Ahmed gave me a running commentary on my new room-mates. 'That one's OK ... that one's a paedophile ... he's in for murder ... that one's a reborn Christian ... avoid him, he's mad and violent ... he's a good guy ... don't trust that one ... he's just come out of solitary and has lost his mind a little ...' When the last man came through the gate, his face barely visible as he cowered against the snow, Ahmed paused and said slowly: 'And that one, that fucker, is Chan. Be very, very careful with him. He's a loner, a very bad man. Double murderer. Always fighting. Very violent. Avoid him.'

I nodded, remembering the warnings about Chan from Baska and Greecia.

On Ahmed's suggestion I went to meet the people sharing my dormitory, stepping around half a dozen Muslims on their knees in prayer as I made my way along the corridor. I walked towards my bunk, nodding and smiling sheepishly, and one by one the Africans came over and shook my hand and welcomed me in English. Not one Asian and only a handful of Middle Eastern guys even acknowledged me. It was a relief to see the friendly faces of Julian, Boodoo John and Eke Jude in the room. Many of the Africans were devout Christians and they greeted me with a religious comment along the lines: 'May God be your guide in here ... Repent your sins and God will protect you from danger ... May the Lord deliver you from evil ...'

A huge man called Adek was one of the last to introduce himself to me, and it was then that I understood why the Africans had given me such a warm reception. 'Our brother Philip has told us all about you. You did wonderful Christian things for Philip in Moscow and he is eternally grateful to you. He is in Atrad 3 and you will not see him so much, so we gave him our word, on God's holy name, that we will look after you to the best of our abilities in here.'

'It was really nothing, but thank you,' I replied, inwardly delighted that some minor acts of kindness had bought me so much respect, as well as a promise of protection.

I returned to Ahmed's office, where the *atradnik*, the guard in charge of our quarters, was standing talking to

Ahmed. I quickly pulled off my hat, nodded and said: 'Good evening, *atradnik*.'

'Regime wants to see you in his office,' said Ahmed. 'I'll come with you and help translate.' It was clear from his grovelling demeanour as we walked into Regime's office, next door to the quarantine room, that a show of pathetic humility was in order. Like Ahmed, I took off my hat, held my hands down in front of me and looked at my shoes.

'Welcome to Mordovia,' said a voice in Russian, Ahmed translating. I looked up to see a middle-aged man of average build with a round face, piercing, severe blue eyes and the droopy, black moustache that British men used to sport in the 1970s. On his large brown desk there were several piles of documents, a lamp, an ashtray and a large old-fashioned red telephone with the rotary dial. It was just like the phone Mum and Dad used to have when I was a kid, and my eye kept being drawn to it.

'My name is Vladimir Kuznetzov, but you will call me Regime.'

He rose from his seat behind his desk and walked over to the window, where he looked out at the falling snow and the *atrads* beyond, lit up by the camp floodlights. He held his hands behind his back and rocked gently back and forth on his heels, saying nothing for over a minute. Still facing the window, he broke the silence: 'Follow the Zone rules in here, Englishman, and you and I will get along fine. Break or bend them and you will not have a happy time in here.

'Every time you hear the Zone buzzer you will

assemble in front of the *atrads* within three minutes. There is a ten-metre no-go area within the Zone perimeter fence – step into that and a sniper will shoot you …' He swung round to look at my reaction before turning back to the window and continuing: 'Ahmed will tell you that we don't have any secrets from each other in Zone 22, so if any of the other prisoners upset you, you come and talk to me, man to man. We are here to help you with your rehabilitation as a good citizen.'

Regime spun sharply on his heel and returned to his seat, putting his feet up on the long wooden desk next to the old red telephone.

'You will start work tomorrow, and now we must decide what job you are best suited to. What did you do in England before you committed your crime?'

'I worked as a broker in a bank, *nachalnik*.'

'I'm sorry to tell you that unfortunately we don't have an investment bank in the Zone for you to run, Hague Tig,' he replied, the faintest flicker of a sarcastic smile appearing on his face. 'What else can you do?'

'Well, my dad's a builder and I've learnt some basic construction skills from him.'

'Englishman, there has been one building erected here in fifty years, and I don't think we'd be able to find enough work to keep you busy for your time in here. Does your mother sew?'

'Well, yes, she can put buttons on shirts and repair tears in clothes.'

'Excellent, then you will start work in the sewing factory tomorrow morning …' And he waved us away with his hand as Ahmed was in the middle of translating.

'*Spasiba, nachalnik!*' Ahmed and I muttered as we headed for the door.

'One more thing!' snapped Regime, and we turned round. 'Now you stay out of trouble, Englishman, and I'm sure you will leave here a better man than when you arrived. We don't want him to leave like the last Englishman, do we, Ahmed?'

Silence hung in there for a few moments. I looked at Regime, who looked at Ahmed.

Ahmed said: 'He died in solitary confinement and left the Zone in a body bag on the back of the horse cart.'

19

The sound of the first long blast on the camp siren heralded the start of the day in Zone 22, and there was a collective groan across the dormitory as all fifty of us swung out of our bunks and quickly began to dress ready for morning exercises. Most of us had slept with our woolly hats and jackets on, but we needed at least two extra layers for the outside. At the second blast of the hooter we hurried half asleep down the corridor, as if running away from a fire, to the entrance by the door, which quickly became a scrum of pushing bodies as we all scrambled to put on our boots and shoes. By the third and last call, five minutes after the first, the final few were scurrying through the gate of the pen on to the concourse to join the rest of us, stamping our feet and jumping in the air in an effort to keep out the numbing cold. It was still pitch black outside and it would be another two hours before the first grey streaks of dawn began to appear in the sky.

Two guards wheeled out a big speaker and one of them put on a cassette tape that crackled like an old gramophone before the formal, old-fashioned voice of a Russian male began to talk us through our drills. It began with star jumps: '*Rass, dva! Rass, dva!* . . .' ('One, two! One, two!') said the cheery voice from the ancient speaker. I was at the far end of our group, nearest the main gates, and I looked to my right to copy what the others around me were doing. I saw roughly 350 men in black uniforms flopping about in the snow like scarecrows in a gale. A few guards walked around the group, inspecting the quality of the exercises. We touched our toes – or tried to; we reached for the sky; we leant to the left and we leant to the right; and it was so cold that I started stretching faster and faster just to keep warm. The worst drill was squat thrusts, because that meant getting down in the snow and ice. We weren't allowed to wear gloves, so by the time I got back on my feet my hands were so cold they felt like they belonged to someone else. Judging by the crackle of the tape and the age of the speaker, the recording was almost certainly a remnant of the Soviet era, and as I squatted and thrust I tried to imagine the many millions of Russians, over the decades in gulags across Mordovia and the Soviet Union, stretching and jumping and thrusting under orders from that very same, annoyingly merry, voice.

We all did the bare minimum to get by and not draw attention to ourselves, but we weren't an impressive sight. In fact, we must have looked like a comedy piss-take of a Jane Fonda video, with lots of skinny, tired, malnourished, grim-faced, wheezing lads flopping about like bored ragdolls. After fifteen minutes we shuffled a few steps closer together for *preverka* before returning to our *atrads* to get ready for the day – washing, brushing teeth and shining shoes. Not everyone was washing and brushing their teeth by any means – maybe a third of the *atrad* – but as there were only three sinks in the small toilet area it was still a bit of a scuffle. While we waited our turn, other men pushed past us to squat over the open toilet holes right next to the sinks. Their upper bodies remained visible above the low screens, and I had to look away as I brushed my teeth because just three feet from me a man was straining and farting and splattering the floor.

When I walked out of the toilet area and back to the dormitory, the corridor was a hive of surreal activity. A dozen Muslims – Afghans, Uzbeks, Turks and North Africans – were kneeling down in prayer, surrounded by as many others frantically polishing their shoes and boots, spitting and buffing them as though their lives depended on it. It was imperative for prisoners to keep their shoes meticulously clean, but not so easy for the majority, particularly in the slush of winter, who couldn't afford polish and had to make do with water and spit.

Breakfast was served in three fifteen-minute sittings between 6:45 and 7:30. As we filed out of the *atrad* at seven o'clock towards the canteen by the kitchen, the sick prisoners of Atrad 2 were coming the other way, having already had their breakfast. In the dark it was difficult to tell the difference between the two groups of shuffling black figures, hacking and wheezing into the frozen morning air, and gobbing thick mouthfuls of phlegm into the overnight snow.

'Let's hope they washed the bowls well this morning,' whispered a short white man with cropped brown hair walking next to me. 'Fuck only knows what germs those fuckers are carrying.' His English was perfect, and he winked a bright blue eye when I turned round to acknowledge his comment with a smile. 'Nice to meet you, Mr Hague. I'm Benny Baskin.'

The end of the queue for food trailed out of the dining area to the pavement outside and we stood there in silence, with our hands tucked under our armpits, shuffling slowly forward. Inside, the queue continued over a red line that had been painted on the floorboards a yard away from the wall. The serving-hatch was in the far corner from the door and once a prisoner had received his food he sat down on one of the benches at one of the three long metal tables arranged in the middle of the room. No one said a word. Two guards stood against the wall, bleary-eyed and grouchy. I collected my bowl, which was still damp from being rinsed, and held it through the hatch for Mehmet, the Turkish rapist and murderer, to drop a ladle of porridge into it. I took a piece of black soda bread and picked up a cup of sweet black tea. I turned round and immediately jerked to a stop, making my tea slop on to the floor. One of the guards was standing right in front of me. He was one of the younger ones, tall and rangy, and he was looking down his nose at me with disgust as he blocked my way. He moved his foot away to draw attention to the spilt tea that had narrowly missed his lace-up combat boot and continued to eyeball me as I edged around him and slid on to the nearest bench. His look said: 'That's your final warning, pal.'

Breakfast, like all meals, was to be eaten in silence, sitting on the benches that were fixed to the long metal tables under the gaze of the guards, but within ten minutes we were filing back out as the men of Atrad 3 were making their way in. I joined a handful of others under the smoking shelter for a cigarette, and when I pulled out my packet of Rothmans, three of them, two Vietnamese and a Turkish-looking character, immediately put out their hands. I held out my packet and all three of them lunged for it, each quickly pulling one out. Only one of the Vietnamese guys nodded his gratitude; the other two just pocketed the cigarettes and carried on smoking their cheap Russian ones. We stood drawing on our smokes, huddled against the biting wind that had picked up since *preverka*, kicking up the snow and creating mini-tornadoes of white around the camp. Five feet away in the lee of the building, Chan was down in the snow pumping out press-ups at incredible speed. He had done over a hundred when he leapt to his feet and grabbed the homemade weights bar – a metal pole with two old car tyres roped at each end – and started lifting it up and down over his head, his face grimacing with pain and effort.

At ten to eight, after we had made our beds, the work buzzer sounded and except for the night-shift workers who were traipsing back to the *atrads*, and the two dozen or so who had jobs inside the Zone, the rest of us filed up to the main gates and waited to be buzzed through into the factory compound. The men from all three *atrads* stood in separate blocks facing the gates as the guard read out the names from cards made from dozens of ripped-up cigarette packets. One by one, we were buzzed through a small side gate into the factory area, forming a black snake of bodies that slid across the snow and into the main building on the right.

My name was among the last to be called out, and I

hurried through the gates, trying to keep pace with the African guy in front so as to watch where he went and copy what he did. The factory was a long dilapidated structure that looked more like an abandoned cowshed than an industrial unit. A foot of snow lay on the corrugated roof and icicles hung from the gutters along its entire length. The walls were a dirty white, and there were bare patches where the paint had peeled away and long brown streaks from water leaking from the gutters. A row of windows ran along the top of the wall, but half of them were broken and had been filled in with pieces of cardboard and cloth.

I followed the African guy through a heavy metal door, at the end of the factory closest to the gates, and into a dismal entrance hall where a low-wattage bulb swung gently from the ceiling. A Western-looking prisoner, roughly my age, with glasses, freckles and wiry ginger hair, was standing in a doorway off to the right and he beckoned me into his office. The room was no more than fifteen feet by fifteen and it was dominated by a large square wooden table in the middle. A window on the far wall looked out at the concrete perimeter that ran around the factory area. One of the four panes was missing and had been filled with a square of cardboard that bulged in the wind. In the corner, a Vietnamese boy, no more than eighteen years old, was crouched over an old Singer-style sewing machine, his eyes straining in the dim light as he ran a piece of cloth under the needle. A second Vietnamese man, maybe five years older, was leaning against the wall by the window, with his hands in his pockets, like a teenager in a sulk.

'I'm Ergin,' said the man with red hair, offering me his hand. 'Before you asking, I'm Turkish, not Irish. I am factory manager and I show you it today and explain how it is working. This is Mafia,' he added, pointing to the older guy, who nodded back at me, trying to raise a smile. 'And that is Molloi, which is the Russian word for boy.' The teenager at the machine turned round and beamed a friendly smile, bowing his head in greeting before turning back to his work.

'Now, Hague Tig, listen to me because today you starting your work. Number one, it is important you must work well, or the system stops and we all get into the trouble. It's not difficult, but much pressure to go fast. The machines are old and bad and the factory like in England 200 years before. And you are pay one rouble a month [3 pence]. There are much injuries for the hands and arms. It is hard work and it is the same all the days. The factory is open all the day and all the night. We make the clothes, the hats, the tank nets, the anything they say to us. In winter it is frozen; in the summer, it is the mosquitoes and you are wet with sweating. Some prisoners are going crazy and they put on train for the hospital treatment in Zone 19. If they come back, they are even more crazy. My advising to you, Mr Hague, is work hard and there is no trouble. Maybe, also you try be proud of your working. I am strict with you, but I can be your friend too.'

Ergin opened the door from the entrance area on to the factory floor, revealing a scene lifted straight out of a Charles Dickens story. Stretching down to the end of the room were two columns of roughly twenty-five work stations piled high with material, separated by a long metal table, stacked along its entire length with further piles of textiles. The prisoners, with their backs to us, were already busy at work, making black jackets. 'All the Zones in Mordovia and in other regions make the uniforms for each other,' said Ergin, leaning towards me to make himself heard above the rat-a-tat-tat and hum of the machines. Some of the Africans were humming or singing to themselves as they sewed, rocking their heads from side to side. I looked in nervous amazement at the speed with which the workers took the main body of the jacket, sewed on an arm or a pocket, then passed the jacket forward and immediately started another. The room was almost as cold as outdoors, and the patched-up windows rattled in the wind as the steamy breath of the workers floated away above their heads. A prisoner with a large basket ferried the finished articles out through a door, while others paced the room distributing more jackets, arms, pockets and other items to the men at the machines.

'The system is *pick*, *sew*, *push*,' said Ergin. We walked slowly down the room, over the uneven flagstones which had been worn smooth and shiny from thousands of boots tramping back and forth over them through the decades. Each station had an old-fashioned Singer-style machine with a foot pedal, and not one of them could have been under fifty or sixty years old. Patched together with random pieces of metal, wire, string and cloth, it was a miracle the Heath-Robinson contraptions worked at all.

'You can see how bad are the machines,' continued Ergin. 'It is thanks to the Afghan maintenance man. Very skilled, clever man. In Afghanistan, he mechanic. When machine is broke his job fix quickly. He always have machine to working. Sometime he taking the screws and wires from other machines; sometime he giving guard many cigarettes to buy pieces from shop in town. His very difficult job, most pressure. The guard they always saying to him: "Go away and fix it . . . Now!"'

We had reached the end of the room when one of the prisoners at the back bellowed '*Zdrastvitay, chalnik!*' ('Welcome, sir!'), and at once all the jabbering and humming came to a stop. A guard had entered the room and the only noise came from the squeak of his rubber-soled combat boots on the shiny floor as he ambled slowly down the work stations with his hands behind his back, swinging his long truncheon from side to side, like a dog wagging his tail. He was the middle-aged man with the droopy moustache and the pot belly I had seen at my first *preverka*. 'He Maximovich, the master guard in the factory,' said Ergin, raising his eyebrows, and, as we turned away, he imitated a man swigging from a bottle and then rotated his finger around his temple.

Ergin led me through the maintenance room where the Afghan fixer, who had the round face of a Chinese or an Uzbek, was hammering away at a piece of bent metal on his workbench. The room adjoined a large delivery area where two Vietnamese guys were busy unloading piles of old clothes and material from the back of a truck and sorting through them on two huge tables. In the corner a small, greying African man was throwing bundles of finished clothes tied up with string through a large hatch.

'This is the one toilet for the whole factory ...' said Ergin, holding open a door and turning away as a stench of sewage filled the air. A single low-wattage light bulb hung from the ceiling near the door and I could only just see the other end of the room in the gloom. On the left-hand wall there was a tap and a bucket and through a square opening cut into a dividing wall I could see a hole in the middle of the floor surrounded by turds.

Gagging, I quickly followed Ergin to a room beyond the delivery area, where dozens of prisoners, most of them Vietnamese or Afghans, were bent over desks, busily carving little wooden chess pieces. In the adjoining paint-dry area, where they were applying the lacquer, Ergin handed me a couple of finished pieces from the hundreds that lined the shelves. I was struck by how intricate and attractive they were. I wasn't expecting to find beauty in Zone 22, and the fact that it was three inches high and made of wood didn't take away any of the surprise. 'The Zone want many carvers,' said Ergin. 'Much money to make from the chess pieces for the authorities and also for ...' He stopped talking and imitated someone stuffing money into their pocket. 'Many pieces go from the back door,' he added with a wink. 'One day you can try, but very difficult. Much skill you needing. Many injuries with carving knives and the tools. Look at the hands ...'

Ergin led me back to his office, off the main entrance, where he and his two Vietnamese assistants demonstrated the way in which they worked out how to design items of clothes from the pile of blue-dyed rags that lay on the floor around the central table. Molloi sat at a sewing machine producing a mock-up, while Ergin and Mafia cut out shapes from the cloth. Using cardboard cut-outs of bodies and arms and collars, they tried to work out how to complete their quota from the limited amount of cloth available. 'We need make 2,000 jackets,' said Ergin. 'Nothing to waste.'

We talked as they worked and I watched. Ergin was a serious character but there was an air of decency and fairness about him, which could not be said about the majority of people I'd come across in Zone 22. It was only in the company of Papi and the boiler-room Africans that I had felt at ease. There were a lot of hardened criminals in the prison, men like Chan and Ahmed and Mehmet, who radiated menace. Ergin was different. He had been a successful tailor in Moscow – hence the top job in the clothes factory – and although he and his family had led a comfortable, middle-class life he had been lured into some kind of fraud scam and been sentenced to eight years. During the fifteen-minute break at mid-morning, when most of the Zone braved the driving wind for a smoke, Ergin produced a creased photograph from his jacket pocket. 'My family,' he sighed. The picture showed a well-dressed woman with long dark hair tied up at the back, with her arms around two young girls. All of them were smiling. 'Now their daddy is criminal. I miss them so very bad.'

Before lunch the entire factory lined up at the gates for the second head-count of the day, and when we were released ten minutes later, my hands and face stung and my feet ached from the cold. Lunch was served in a dining area next to Ergin's office by the front door, and the room was so small that there were four sittings at the two long tables. There was a small table behind the door with a giant vat of pale, watery soup and next to it a pile of black soda bread. I helped myself and squeezed on to the end of a bench between Ergin and Baska, who nodded and smiled at me as he tried to create an extra inch or two of space. Chan was sitting directly opposite me, next to Mafia. There were four benches in all, and although they were designed to take no more than six people, I counted ten on each and there was barely any room to lift the spoon to our mouths.

The soup was lukewarm and virtually tasteless – there was the vaguest hint of potato and onion – and yet everybody was going at it as if it was the first food they had seen in days. To a man – even middle-class Ergin – they ripped the chewy bread in their teeth like wild dogs tearing meat from a carcass and with their mouths no more than three inches above their bowls spooned the soup in, like they were in a race. I was hungry too, but I knew I had noodles and *kolbasa* sausage and some biscuits back in the *atrad* and by the time I got towards the bottom of the bowl, my soup was virtually cold and everyone else had finished. Half the table were watching me as I looked up, and I realized they were waiting to see if I was going to leave any. Embarrassed that I was wasting food, I pointed to my stomach and grimaced to indicate that I wasn't feeling great. Immediately, Chan and Mafia dived forward to grab my bowl. Chan, who was marginally closer, got there first and dragged the bowl back to his place, as Mafia threw his hand up in the air and cursed at him. For a few seconds the pair stared each other down, their noses a few inches apart, until Ergin leant forward to Mafia and pointed to the door. Scowling, Mafia got up and slowly walked out of the room. Following him into the office, we watched as he paced up and down, kicking the walls and punching the air in front of him. Ergin walked over to him and put his hand on his shoulder. 'Forget Chan,' he said. 'Forget Chan.'

As they sat down to work, and I pulled up a chair alongside Ergin, he gave me the background of his two assistants. 'There are many lazy people in factory, but Mafia is one of most lazy – don't worry, they no speak English – he always leaving to the chess area to talk to his *zemliaki*, the other men from his country. I always taking him back before guard find him. I am like father to Mafia. I promise my old *smelnik*, old Vietnamese man who gone away from Zone one year before, that I am protecting Mafia. Mafia wild boy. Rebel. He do many crimes before Zone, the violence and stealing. He with Vietnam Mafia in Moscow. In here, he no care. No fear. He need father man or he die in here, in fight or in the solitary prison.

'Molloi, he seventeen years. He arrive from Zone for young boys for hurting Russian man with knife in fighting in street for his father. His father attacked by fascists, hooligans, skinheads. Molloi save father. He just fourteen. He twenty-three when leave Zone 22. His father dead now. Everybody has bad story in Zone 22. Not one happy.'

Ergin started me on one of the easier jobs in the factory, marking up where the buttons were to be sewn on the blue smock-style jackets. My station was at the far end of the factory, facing the two columns of machine operators stretching back towards the entrance. Ergin handed me a piece of chalk no longer than a cigarette butt, saying: 'Treat it like gold. Don't lose it, don't waste it. You must do 1,000 jackets with this.'

The jackets began life at the back of the factory in the form of different-shaped pieces of dyed cloth. There, the first prisoner cut the body into shape using a cardboard cut-out and passed it forward to the guy in front, who sewed on a left arm. He then passed it forward to the next person, who sewed on the right arm, and by the time it had reached me at the front, fifteen minutes later, the jacket had arms, pockets, a lining, collar and cuffs. My job couldn't have been more straightforward. There were four different sizes of jacket and, using cardboard templates with four little holes, I chalked up the spots where the buttons went (extra large had five buttons). I stood facing the two columns of machine operators with a pile of jackets to my right, and when I had chalked one up, I passed it to my left where Baska ran it through the button machine and threw it over his shoulder into the collection pile.

I had been able to see my breath all day in the factory but from about three o'clock, when the darkness began to descend, the big airy hangar of a room got progressively colder. We all started working faster and faster just to keep warm, and the pile of jackets began to pile up in front of me. When the buzzer sounded at five o'clock to signal the end of the day and the start of the night shift, my legs and lower back ached from four hours of standing up and leaning forward over the low desk. I dropped the jacket I was holding and quickly joined all the others streaming out for check-in just inside the factory gates. On the way out, two guards patted us down and made us turn out our pockets to make sure we weren't smuggling out any knives or tools. Maximovich, the master guard, was unsteady on his feet and his breath stank of liquor as he ran his hands up and down my legs and chest.

Outside, we lined up by the gates in the stunning cold for the day's third *preverka*, stamping our feet and wriggling inside our jackets as Maximovich lurched his way up the columns with his fur hat almost falling off the side of his head. Twice he walked up and down our lines, and we all started stamping our feet harder and faster because the cold had passed from being uncomfortable to painful. We were not allowed to stand down and return to the warmth of the *atrads* until every single prisoner in the Zone had been accounted for. No one was missing on this occasion, it was just that Maximovich was drunk and had counted incorrectly. Finally, halfway through his third count, he gave up, waved us all away with a loud grunt and stumbled off back towards the factory door.

It was difficult to avoid the conclusion that *preverka* was more than just a way of imposing some order on us, a drip-drip discipline to instil some respect for authority in us wayward souls. It was also a subtle way of inflicting pain, at least in the frozen months of winter. To stand outside doing nothing for more than five minutes in temperatures plunging to 30 degrees below was an ordeal; for more than ten minutes it was agony, and for more than fifteen minutes it became positively dangerous, especially for the poorer prisoners among us who had crap, thin clothing and shockingly inadequate prison-issue foot-wear. Ten minutes after returning to the *atrad* after work, still frozen solid from the count outside the factory, the first blast of the siren sent us rushing to put our outdoor shoes on again for evening *preverka*.

Once again we lined up five deep and about twenty-five long in front of the *atrad* and waited for the noise of the wooden door to the pen behind us, willing the guards to get up from the warmth of the observation room, put on their fucking coats and hats and get the fuck outside and start counting.

After ten minutes, there was still no sign and I heard a handful of prisoners starting to whimper as we danced from foot to foot. My fingers were so cold I took them out of my armpits and put them in my mouth. Another couple of minutes passed before the door opened and the guards slowly tramped past behind us. The guard checking Atrad 1 was counting to himself in threes: '*Tree, shrest, deyvat . . .*' as we continued to wriggle and stomp and shake our heads and do anything to stave off the cold. 'Surely that must be it now?' I heard myself say out loud. The moans of pain and the stamping on the icy tarmac were growing louder when the guard counting the men of Atrad 3 barked an order and someone scampered away down towards the boiler-room area, a black silhouette against the glare of the floodlight. Three minutes later he emerged – he looked like an African from where I was standing 150 yards away – and he was pulling another man by the elbow. The other man was half bent over and coughing violently. As the pair drew closer, his legs gave way beneath him and he slumped to his knees and then fell forward into the snow. It was little Philip, whom I'd befriended in Moscow.

20

January was a cruel month in Mordovia. It was dark for eighteen hours a day, and it was as cold as anywhere on the planet outside of the North and South Poles. There were some mornings and evenings when the temperature suddenly plunged so low that everyone, prisoners and guards alike, had to remain inside the *atrads* or the office building. The heating system in the wooden living quarters was not powerful enough to keep out the very worst of the cold, and often we had to pull on as many layers as we could and wrap ourselves in our blankets, but still we shivered and shuddered. At night I slept with my thick coat and woolly hat on. One morning we woke to discover that the Zone boiler had broken in the night – a common occurrence, apparently. The pipes inside the *atrad* went cold and all 100 of us took refuge in the TV room, trying to get as many bodies as we could into one space, to try and generate some warmth.

A few days later, during evening *preverka*, a dramatic freeze, a kind of ice storm, descended on the Zone and left us all standing in awe as if we were witnessing a biblical experience. The temperature had risen steadily during the day, and just as darkness began to fall there was a heavy shower of sleety snow that soaked our hats and coats as we stood waiting for the guards to hurry up and count us. It was then that the cold came down in a snap, an invisible but audible force rolling off the flat landscape beyond and enveloping the Zone. The branches of the trees crackled, the wood of the buildings creaked as the air tightened its icy grip and the cold hit us in the face like a stinging slap. It was beautiful and thrilling to watch and hear, but as soon as the guards disappeared inside, the rest of us made a run for the *atrads* to escape its painful clasp.

It was easy to understand why there was so much illness in the Zone. Bodies, already feeble from a poor diet and hard work, were weakened further by the perishing cold. The *atrads* were hothouses for germs, with eighty or so of us – and almost twice as many in Atrad 3 – living and sleeping, literally, cheek by jowl. Often I rolled over and woke up in the night to find the snoring, wheezing face of my Afghan neighbour less than a foot from my own, or an arm accidentally draped over my bed. A Nigerian called Uba had the bunk below me, but as he worked night shifts the only contact we had was when we passed each other heading to and from the factory. During the day, the building resounded to the sound of men hacking, sneezing, and clearing the snot from their noses and throats. All the Far Eastern guys, especially the Chinese, and most of the Arab characters, were in the habit of spitting whenever they were outside, and the ground in the exercise pen was covered with frozen smears and gobs of greeny-brown phlegm.

My chesty cough was no worse than when I had left Moscow, but, barring miracles, it was just a matter of time before one of the more severe infections that were rife throughout the Zone found its way into my system.

My great fear was that the name of that condition was going to be tuberculosis. When Philip, one of the frailer inmates, had collapsed in the snow, coughing blood, during *preverka*, TB was suspected, but after a week in his bed in Atrad 3 he started to show signs of recovery and the doctor was optimistic that what he was suffering was a very severe chest infection. While he recuperated, the devout Africans were delighted that the prayers they had been saying for him in the little red-brick chapel had been answered.

The first time I stopped feeling cold, if only for a few wonderful minutes, was six days after leaving quarantine when I joined the rest of the *atrad* for our weekly shower down in the building that housed the boiler room, a workshop for general maintenance work and the barber's room. It had been almost three weeks since I'd arrived in the Zone and enjoyed the heat of the hot shower I'd taken after having my head shaved; although I had washed as thoroughly as I could in the sink every morning and evening, the grime had started to cling to my body and whenever I put my nose inside my fleece to breathe in some warmth, the smell of my own stale body odour was truly disgusting. After twenty-odd days without a full body wash I stank like an old tramp.

I'd been looking forward to Sunday all week, partly because it was the only day off we had, and it gave me the chance to check out the library, maybe even the church, but mainly because Sunday was shower day and I was desperate to clean my body and my clothes. I had run out of fresh underwear at the start of the week and had been wearing the same pants, thermal T-shirt and socks ever since. We weren't allowed to wash our clothes in the sinks in the *atrad* because they didn't want to have dripping clothes constantly hanging from the water pipes. The only opportunity we had to wash them came in the few minutes we were allowed under the shower on Sunday.

At ten o'clock the buzzer sounded, signalling that it was time to assemble, but most of the *atrad* was already standing near the entrance ready to go. The scramble to get outside that followed was even more frantic and urgent than it was for the head-counts, which I didn't understand, and I stood there bemused as I was elbowed and jostled to the back of the mêlée and the rest pushed their way outside. Running was strictly prohibited in Zone 22, but people were close to a jog as they streamed into formation on the tarmac, lining up, as we did for *pre-verka*, three men wide and about twenty-five long, holding the plastic bags full of dirty washing that we stored in the cupboards with our provisions. On this occasion the columns had turned ninety degrees away from the *atrads* and were facing down the compound past the kitchen and dining area to the boiler building at the bottom. There had been fresh snowfalls over night, and only the concourse, which had been scraped all morning, was clear. The rest was blanketed in snow, including the pine trees and marshes that I could glimpse stretching away for miles over the top of the barbed wire.

As we began our march down, the sick boys of Atrad 2 were filing out of the door to the shower room, their wet scalps steaming so much as they returned to the cold it looked like their heads were on fire. The shower I'd enjoyed the night I arrived in the Zone was a single, makeshift installation that the Africans had built in the boiler room. I'd not been in the main shower room, but for some reason I'd been expecting to walk into the kind of shower area you find in a municipal sports centre, with benches and pegs and rows of shower-heads around the walls. Hope sprang eternal. The reality was quite different, and my heart sank as soon as I walked in – or squeezed in more like.

The room, no more than twenty-five feet by twenty-five in total, was divided into two with a changing area by the entrance and the showers beyond, and there was barely a square inch of floor to be found. The twenty or so pegs above the benches around the walls had all been taken, and everyone else was crammed into the middle of the room, trying to balance between the 100-odd bags of washing on the floor while trying to remove all their clothes and place them on top of the bags so they didn't slide on to the filthy, slimy tiles below. The bodies were so tightly packed that we had to put a hand on each other's shoulders to steady ourselves, and every time I bent over or pulled off a piece of clothing I felt my body rub up against someone else's. The smell of BO, stale piss, shit and rotting feet was overpowering, and I stopped breathing through my mouth within seconds of walking in, in case I puked up.

'And you Brits have always moaned about the Black Hole of Calcutta,' said Benny Baskin, whose face appeared a few feet away when the guy between us bent over. 'Welcome to the black hole of fucking Mordovia!' he spat.

Clutching my dirty washing and a bottle of Fresh Cherry and Cotton Timotei shampoo to my chest, I joined the crush of naked bodies pushing their way into the tiny shower area, trying to make sure my rapidly shrivelling cock didn't touch the backside of the guy in front. The Afghans, the only ones to keep their pants on, had monopolized one of the six shower-heads in the far corner. Everyone was washing their clothes as they washed themselves, but there was some kind of order behind the apparent chaos. There were four or five people standing in a circle around the other five showers fixed to the ceiling, and we took it in turns to stand under the stream of water to wet ourselves and our clothes. We then stood aside and lathered our hair, bodies and garments until it was our turn to go under the water again and rinse off. The water was beautifully hot, but nothing good came in Zone 22 without its price, and I shouldn't have been surprised that the pleasure of feeling a sensation of warmth for the first time in a week was wrecked by the horrendous smell of mildly decomposing humans and the awkwardness of getting undressed, towelled and reclothed on a greasy floor while being pressed up against a scrum of naked murderers, rapists, muggers and cut-throats.

After the steamy heat of the showers, the cold outside came as a sharp jolt as we formed up and began to march back up the Zone. I could feel the freezing air getting to work on my wet scalp and by the time I reached the relative warmth of the *atrad* the moisture had turned to an icy sleet. I gave my head a vigorous rub with the towel before throwing it, together with my wet washing, over the hot water pipe in the corridor that ran down the middle of the building. When I had finished, Boodoo John, one of the Africans from the boiler room, was standing next to me holding a folded piece of paper. I'd been getting on well with Boodoo John; he was a gentle, unassuming character who seemed out of place in the Zone. He had a sympathetic, slightly sad expression on his face as he handed over the paper and said: 'It's from Papi.'

I quickly unfolded the paper and began to read the neat handwriting, in French: 'Dear English friend, they're taking me to Zone 19 for "treatment". I will probably never see you again. If I do, I'll probably be like Cosmos so avoid me at all costs! I enjoyed our chess together. It was my best week in the Zone in five years. Be good, my friend, and be careful who you trust. Stay out of trouble, remember everything I told you, and you'll get out of here in one piece. If only I'd taken my own advice. Who knows, maybe I'll see you in London one day and you can come round to our little terraced house? Best wishes, brother, Papi.'

'Who's Cosmos?' I asked Boodoo John.

He shook his head before replying in his thick African accent: 'Used to be one of Moscow's top drug barons. Lived like a prince until they busted him live on Russian TV. They wanted to make an example of him so they sent him to Zone 19, zapped him with some volts and gave him some very uncool drugs. Now he's in Atrad 3, half-vegetable, half-maniac. He's the one with the eyes as wide as plates. Crazy Cosmos ...'

Rakim, the Turk in charge of the horses and the delivery cart, was not popular in the Zone, and it wasn't just that he looked like a cartoon cut-throat with his absolutely huge hooked nose, bushy black eyebrows, piercing cold blue eyes and bony face – a face crying out to be punched over and over again. He was a human being in the style and mould of Chan: a mean loner, who rarely spoke and never smiled. You could tell he was a wanker from 100 paces, and the fact that he was allowed to run errands outside the prison walls made him even more unpopular. What all of us would have given to be Rakim for a day and get out into the world beyond! Every day we watched him standing astride his open cart like a character from *Fiddler on the Roof*, as he trotted off through the prison gates to go to Leple village and fetch the sacks of grain and root vegetables, the urn of milk for the kitchen and the post.

As the rest of us lined up like the living dead at the main gates, waiting to be summoned for another day of deadly monotony on the factory floor, Rakim swept by and disappeared into the free world, the wind tugging at his clothes, with an extravagant flourish of the reins and a cry of encouragement for his horses. I suspected he timed his departure to coincide with our morbid march through the snow to the factory, and as the gates shut behind him and the sound of hooves and creaking wooden wheels faded into the morning air, we looked at each other, sneering, and shook our heads. He was clearly a fine horseman, but it wasn't so much his equestrian prowess he was showing off – it was his independence. And that, to the rest of us, felt like a stab in the ribs.

One morning, Rakim was tending to the horses in the stable near the sewing factory as usual while we were all back in the *atrads* waiting for a new consignment of cloth to be delivered. I was standing in the corridor staring vacantly through the window of Ahmed's office, wondering how to kill some more time, when three guards emerged from the admin building opposite and strode briskly towards the *atrad*. Usually they just ambled across alone or in pairs, so I knew something was up. We all stood up and took off our hats as they rushed through the entrance area and swept down the corridor into the dormitory. Moments later they re-emerged, with one of them holding up a medium-sized potato as if it was a trophy. It was an offence to keep food in the dormitories. We quickly put on our outdoor boots and shoes and hurried into the exercise yard, and a few minutes later we saw Rakim being frogmarched down from the stables in the factory area, back through the Zone gates and into the offices. A couple of guys chuckled to themselves, while the rest began to whisper excitedly. Rakim soon re-emerged with two guards on either side of him and immediately shouted angrily in our direction. It sounded like Turkish. The three of them turned right at the end of the building and began to walk diagonally across the compound to the far corner, towards the kennels and the solitary confinement block.

Boodoo John was standing next to me as we pressed up against the mesh fencing and watched Rakim being led away. Every ten yards or so, one of the guards shoved him in the back and he staggered forward, slipping on the compacted snow. As they approached the kitchen and canteen building, Rakim turned his head and started shouting abuse in Turkish in its direction.

'He who seeks vengeance must dig two graves: one for his enemy and one for himself,' said Boodoo John. 'The snake himself has been bitten, and he deserves his pain after the trouble he has caused others. We won't be seeing him for three months.'

'*Three months* in solitary?' I replied, in disbelief.

'Rakim will survive. He's strong and stubborn. He has learnt from his mules in Turkey. The last prisoner to get that long was not so lucky. A Vietnamese guy called Bao, who was always causing trouble. He went mad after a month and hanged himself with his bootlaces. We watched them take him out in a couple of brown sacks, one on either end, and it was Rakim who drove him out of here on the back of his cart. But Rakim will come out like he went in. Dead inside.'

I shuddered as I asked: 'How many people die in here?'

'Five have gone since I arrived four years ago. Two in solitary, two who were taken away and died in the hospital Zone, and one who died in his bunk in Atrad 2. It's a good place to die, Mordovia – you're halfway to hell already.'

I liked Boodoo John. There was a gentleness and

serenity about him that singled him out from the rest. He went to the church service but he wasn't a fanatic like Philip and some of the other Africans; he was quiet without being withdrawn; he worked hard and never complained. He wasn't well educated like Ergin or Yevgeny the brainbox librarian, but there was a basic wisdom about him. Like the other Africans, he'd found it difficult to secure work in Russia and had turned to selling drugs to try and make a living. He wasn't a scary, hardened career criminal, just an impoverished guy who had been tempted into illicit activity in order to put more food on his family's table. It's not easy being a poor foreigner in Moscow, and it's even harder if you're black.

'So what's the secret of avoiding trouble and getting out of here with body and soul intact, Boodoo John?' I asked.

He thought for a minute and said: 'Make yourself as invisible as possible. Back away from trouble. Work hard, and even the guards will respect you a little in the end. Help those you like where you can. Favours always get returned eventually. But don't *ask* any favours from anybody. Let them do you a favour. Then you know you have a friend.'

It took a few days for the Zone's jungle drums to reveal the full story of what had happened to Rakim. A raw potato was something of a luxury in Zone 22 and Rakim's *smelnik*, Mehmet the cook, had placed one under his mattress and then gone to the admin building and told the FSB *koom* that the horseman had stolen it from the kitchens. The prison officials had as little time for Rakim as his fellow prisoners and they had no hesitation in condemning him to the cooler for the maximum period. The most shocking aspect of the episode was that it was his very own *smelnik* who had ratted on him. It was appropriate that two of the most malicious characters in the Zone ended up as eating partners, but that was only because they were Turkish, not because they were natural buddies. Over the months and years they had developed a seething hatred for each other.

No one knew *exactly* what had gone on between the two, but the universal suspicion was that as both of them were up for *udo* within the year, Mehmet had killed off one of his rivals for freedom in order to boost his own chances of getting out. The *udo* hearings in the local court came round every six weeks or so, and it was rare for more than a dozen to walk free at the same time. By stabbing Rakim in the back, Mehmet had climbed an extra rung or two up the ladder while sending his former *smelnik* towards the back of the queue with an additional six months nailed on to his sentence. As a 'fuck-you', it was a pretty impressive piece of work and I could only applaud his ingenuity in dispatching one of the nastier characters in the Zone. But it was disturbing all the same, and I realized I'd have to sharpen up and keep my wits about me at all times.

The one guy you were meant to trust in Zone 22 was your *smelnik*. By sharing your food and provisions with each other, you shared each other's kindness and confidence. That was an unwritten rule: you don't break the trust of the man with whom you break your bread. The incident with Rakim showed that even the sacred relationship between *smelniks* was not above violation.

Boodoo John gave me a gentle pat on the back and disappeared into the *atrad* as I headed for the smoking shelter and lit up a Marlboro. Ahmed was there and he smiled as I approached. We stood in silence for a while, hunched against the bitter wind, drawing on our cupped cigarettes.

'So who's it going to be?' he hissed in a conspiratorial whisper. 'Your *smelnik*, I mean.'

It was the third time Ahmed had asked me to be his eating partner in three weeks. A dozen others had made advances too, and it was starting to get embarrassing.

'I don't know, Ahmed, I still haven't decided. Maybe I'll just carry on eating by myself . . .'

He stepped a little closer and a cloud of steam and acrid smoke from his cheap cigarette shrouded his face as he spoke. 'I don't have much food to share with you, but I'm powerful in the *atrad*. I can make life easier for you. The guards like me,' he grinned, making his long scar zig-zag across his face. 'Forget the Africans. They cannot help you in here. I can protect you better.'

He was whispering so quietly I had to lean forward to catch what he was saying. That was how everyone spoke in the Zone. Only rarely did I hear an exchange take place in a normal voice at a normal volume. We spoke in pairs, muttering in hushed tones. You saw conversations, but never heard them. There was no 'socializing', no sitting around the kitchen table recounting tales of our former lives or discussing events in the Zone. Some of the Africans could be noisy on occasion, erupting into laughter or bantering with each other in the factory, but for the most part a sullen, suspicious silence hung over the camp.

This was partly to avoid drawing the attention of the guards, who didn't like the sight or sound of prisoners enjoying themselves or engaging in ordinary human activities such as communicating freely. But mainly it was because nobody trusted anyone else, except their *smelnik* and a handful of others with whom they'd built up a relationship over the years. Half the Zone were informers. The experience with Edik in Moscow, Papi's insights into the ways of Zone 22 and the almost tangible air of conspiracy that pervaded the Zone like a fog had put me on red alert from the moment I'd arrived in the *atrads*. Only among the boiler-room Africans, who tended to stick together as a group rather than splinter into pairs of *smelniks*, did I feel comfortable. Otherwise, I trod warily and avoided contact with the others as best I could. It was information on a strictly need-to-know basis. '*Be careful who you trust*,' that was what Papi said, and he'd repeated it in his note.

I smiled at Ahmed, trying to muster some feelings of brotherhood towards him, but it was difficult to warm to a man with a face like a butcher's chopping board. I knew he had close links with the officials across the way, but whether that was an asset for me or a risk I just couldn't decide. I looked around the exercise yard at the half-dozen other pairs of prisoners leaning towards each other so that no one else could hear what they were saying. Ahmed was no different from the others who'd come grinning and slapping me on the back and warning me who I could and couldn't trust and telling me what a great guy I was and how England was the best country in the world and that David Beckham was the greatest footballer ... He just wanted a share of my spoils, and I couldn't blame him for trying when he had barely any provisions of his own.

'Ahmed, I know I can trust you and I think you're a good guy,' I said, shuffling my foot in the snow and squirming inside. 'I promise I'll give you cigarettes and food when I have some spare, but ...' And the sentence trailed away.

'I understand,' he said, stubbing his cigarette out under his foot. 'One day you'll realize I'm a better man than I look.'

I wanted to call him back and try to explain myself better but he was away up the three steps to the door in a bound. I flicked my butt towards the *atrad* and it bounced off the wall in a spray of orange sparks. I spun round to see if a guard had witnessed what I'd done, then quickly went over and picked the stub up and put it in the bucket provided. As I walked back inside I saw Boodoo John directly ahead in the kitchen, preparing a bowl of *foo-foo*, a Russian version of a Nigerian dish, made with soggy soda bread instead of the traditional yams.

'I know you said I shouldn't ask favours of other prisoners, and I'll make this my first and last. Will you be my *smelnik*?'

Boodoo John put down his bowl and said: 'I won't be able to offer you any food, or coffee or cigarettes, but what I can offer you is my confidence and my loyalty. It would make me very happy to be your *smelnik*. Thank you, brother.'

*

I wasn't bothered that Boodoo John didn't have much food to share with me, because my supplies had been replenished a couple of weeks after I'd been transferred to the *atrad* in an incredible act of generosity by Alexi, one of my former Russian clients. Alexi, a great kindly bear of a man who'd looked after Mum, Dad and Lucy when they'd come to Moscow, had made the twenty-four-hour round trip from Moscow in terrible weather to bring me a second box of staple provisions and cigarettes. He'd bought all 200 pounds' worth of it with his own money, not to mention the petrol, but I never got to see him and thank him because the bastards in the offices said he had failed to make a visitor's appointment, and he had to get straight back in his car and make the long journey home through the night.

The mercy run came just at the right time, because my reserves of food and cigarettes were almost exhausted. I'd been expecting a visit from the British Embassy, but the severe weather had discouraged them from risking the journey. Unknown to me, though, Alexi had braved the conditions to get some supplies to me, and within minutes of it arriving that afternoon the news had swept around the factory. Whenever I looked up from chalking the buttons, there was always at least one guy on the sewing machines smiling at me, and when we filed out of the building at the end of the shift I was escorted by a small posse of grinning, backslapping wellwishers, eager to remind me what a nice, kind Englishman I was and what a brilliant country I came from.

After supper I went to the office to sign for the delivery, and the entire contents of the three foot by three

236

foot cardboard box had been laid out on a table in the reception area. My eyes lit up at the sight of them as I stepped out of the swirling snow and pulled the door shut. There were fifteen packs of noodles, 800 cigarettes, six jars of Nescafé, six tins of a pea and sweetcorn mixture, six tins of peaches, four *kolbasa* salamis, four bulbs of garlic, a bag of apples, a bag of oranges, six bars of chocolate, some Bic razors, a tin of shaving foam, a bottle of shampoo and a bar of soap, some biros and exercise books. A stout, middle-aged woman called Raisa Petrovna, who acted as the prison liaison officer and had a reputation for being the only kind official in the administration, pushed a document across her desk for me to sign. As I leant forward and took the pen from her she looked me in the eye intently and, smiling, opened the top drawer of her desk and left it there. I turned round to the table, picked up a bar of Lindt Milk Chocolate and slid it into the drawer, which she immediately closed.

I had just finished packing up the box and was heading towards the door when the sound of clicking fingers made me turn round. The guard who'd kicked me up the arse on my first night was standing in the doorway of the corridor with an unlit cigarette hanging off his lip, slowly curling his index finger back and forth as if to say, 'Not so fast, my sneaky little Englishman.' Regarded as the most severe and vindictive of the guards, he was known as the Undertaker because he always volunteered to deal with the body of anyone who died in the Zone. I went to put the box down on the table, but immediately he blurted out, '*Nyet! Nyet! Nyet!*' I followed him the few yards down the corridor and left into the observation room, where three other guards were standing near the big bay window at the front, facing me as I walked in carrying my box. The Undertaker indicated that I should put the box down on the table by the wall, then dispatched me to the corridor with a dismissive wave of his hand. As I stood outside the door, in the Zone pose of legs wide apart, hands out in front, staring at the floor, I could hear the Undertaker and his friends ransacking the box, making muttering noises of surprise and delight. After a few minutes, the Undertaker barked, 'Hague Tig,' and I re-entered the room to see all of them with their backs to me, looking out of the window. What remained of Alexi's shopping, which was roughly half of it, was scattered across a table. 'Filthy thieving fucking pigs!' I muttered under my breath, as I started shoving the remains back into the box as fast as I could. The Undertaker swung round from the window and grunted something in Russian, which I read as, 'What did you say, you little shit?' He was glaring at me with hatred and disgust in his eyes.

Panicking, I replied in a quiet, grovelling voice: 'Sorry, sorry. Nothing. *Spasiba, nachalnik* . . .'

Back in the *atrad*, a dozen of the poorer inmates were waiting in a small crowd by the cupboards near the entrance. Ahmed was there too, ready to open the food lockers, and when I started stacking the food on to the shelves, they pushed forward, holding out their hands and saying: '*Di menya!*' which means 'Give it to me!' It sounds blunt, even rude, in translation, but that was just the common phrase used in Russian prisons and I'd become accustomed to it. Looking on to the shelves behind me they could see all the piles of packets, bags and tins and I didn't have the heart to turn them away – they didn't have so much as a plain biscuit between them. I began to hand out small items to anyone who appeared: I opened an orange and broke it into segments, I split open a garlic bulb and passed out a couple of cloves, some biscuits ... all meagre offerings in themselves, but each prompting a gush of grovelling thanks, as if I'd handed them each a Harrods' Christmas hamper.

'*Spasiba! Spasiba!* Mr English ... Englishman very kind man ... God love you ... *Anglichanin* is Robin Hood, yes?'

All day, every day, people begged for cigarettes, which they often used to keep to use as bribes for the guards, but it was the food that they wanted above all else and I was taken aback by the shameless insistence of the beggars. The three small prison meals failed to provide the energy we needed, especially with the cold and the labour forcing our bodies to burn up the calories at a rate of knots. Everyone in Zone 22, to varying degrees, was malnourished, and as a general rule the longer a prisoner had served, the bonier, paler and gaunter he became. The beggars that evening were among the least healthy-looking characters in the *atrad*.

After a week of handouts, half my provisions had gone and I was in danger of running out before the Embassy came down. I had just come from the locker area, where I'd spent ten minutes doling out more bits and pieces, and I was cutting up some *kolbasa* to put in with the noodles I was making for Boodoo John and myself, when a queue of five or six people formed at the table. The Vietnamese guy at the front was staring at me, holding out his hand, like it was automatic now that I just gave him some of my supper.

'For fuck's sake, this is getting out of hand!' I sighed, turning to Boodoo John at the end of the table. 'They expect it now. What do you think I should do? There's going to be nothing left in a few days at this rate.'

Boodoo John shrugged and said: 'Just tell them to go away. They know the score in here. It's your food, not theirs.'

I turned round to the small mob that had now gathered round me and, holding out my hands in front of me, said: 'No! *Nyet!* No more! Finished! Caput! Food over!' Immediately, they turned around and melted away without a word of complaint or a frown.

The only provisions Boodoo John had were powdered mashed potato and a couple of packets of instant soup, to which he treated himself roughly every three or four days, depending on how much he had in his locker. He made the *foo-foo* by mixing bread with some water into a paste and then once it had set he swallowed it whole, as was the custom in Nigeria. Mostly, though, we ate my noodles, and once the parcels had arrived we were able to liven them up with some kind of combination of garlic, *kolbasa* and some tinned sweetcorn and peas. In the first week we ate the apples and oranges before they went off, and saved the cans of vegetables for the following week when there was going to be nothing left but carbohydrates in the form of noodles and biscuits.

The evening after Alexi had made his visit I went to introduce myself to Zanpolit. I'd wanted to go earlier but I didn't have any coffee or other 'luxuries' to offer him.

When Ahmed opened the locker I took out one jar of Nescafé Gold, four packets of Marlboro and a bar of Lindt chocolate. I put the coffee and chocolate into my underpants and the smokes into my socks, and waited by the front window in the television room. As soon as the light in Zanpolit's office came on, I went to the *atrad* office, slipped two Marlboro and a teaspoon of coffee wrapped in a piece of foil from my cigarette packet on to the table in front of the young guard, and said, 'Zanpolit.' His spots looked especially livid under the glare of the unshaded light bulb when he looked up from his magazine – it was about guns and featured a front-page picture of a cardboard human target riddled with bullet holes, with a man in combat gear and a hunter's hat holding his automatic rifle and grinning from ear to ear. Pocketing the cigs and coffee but saying nothing, he got up and we walked to the entrance. As I headed across the exercise yard to the electric mesh gate, he leant out of the door behind me and raised his arm to the observation window. The gate buzzed open and with my trousers bulging I waddled across the tarmac, leaving a trail of boot prints on the blanket of fresh snow. There was no one in reception and so I nervously approached the doorway of the guards' room, where I could hear the muffled noise of a football match emanating from the TV.

The Undertaker was waiting for me in the doorway with his head turned to one side, wearing a face of mocking curiosity.

'Zanpolit, *spasiba*,' I said.

He looked the other way, whistling to himself as if he was waiting for something. I took out my open packet of

Marlboro from the shirt pocket inside my coat, pulled out two cigarettes and placed them in his outstretched hand. Leaning forward and putting his hand towards my face, he flicked his middle finger over his thumb, like he was trying to get rid of a fly or bogey. I took that as my cue to leave, but just as I turned to go, he pulled me by the arm and ripped open the poppers on my black jacket, revealing the bulge in my groin. He turned and shouted something to the other guards, and four of them stood up and walked over and began to laugh as the Undertaker pointed at my balls. 'English boy like the Russian man very much!' said the Undertaker, and then repeated it in Russian, triggering gales of laughter among his friends as they ambled back to their seats and my cheeks burned with anger.

I shuffled down the corridor, took a deep breath and gently rapped my knuckles on the door. At the sound of a grunt within, I pushed down the handle and walked in.

Zanpolit was sitting in a leather-bound chair behind a wooden desk cluttered with papers and files, smoothing back his gelled brown hair, which ran over the top of his shirt collar. A Russian flag dangled limply from a pole behind him, next to a framed painting of a wintry landscape. I was breathing faster than normal. Along the wall adjoining the corridor was a bank of filing cabinets. Through the three windows on the wall opposite I looked across to Atrad 1 and Atrad 2, the red night-lights clearly visible in the dormitories at the front. He held out an open hand, inviting me to approach, and I was conscious of the wet footprints I left as my boots squeaked across his red linoleum floor.

I turned away from him to extract my gifts from my underpants and the chocolate was slightly soft as I pulled it out. Along with the coffee, I placed it in his drawer while he carried on pretending to read a document. I added the four packets of Marlboro, stepped back from the desk and looked down at the floor, waiting for him to speak. After half a minute of silence I looked up. He was looking at me with his fingers entwined on his lap, and then he held out his hands at his side as if to say: 'So what can I do for you?'

'Hello, *spasiba*, Zanpolit, me Tig Hague,' I stammered nervously, pointing at myself and trying to smile.

'Uh-huh?' he replied, raising his eyebrows and holding them there. '*And*?' was what his face seemed to be saying. I had no idea what to say. My Russian wasn't good enough to start a conversation. I knew quite a few nouns, mainly words for physical objects, but my inability to communicate properly made me panicky and I started stuttering.

'Um, er, *spasiba*, er … *udo*? My *udo* good? …'

'*Udo*?' he said, sounding bemused. He pointed at his watch and, not knowing whether he meant 'Don't waste my time', or that my parole date wasn't for over twelve months, I started walking backwards to the door, nodding my head and muttering: '*Spasiba*, Zanpolit, *spasiba* …' He looked back down at his papers and I pulled open the door, desperate to escape from my embarrassment, but as I rushed through the door with my head down I stopped in my tracks. Two feet in front of me, with a guard at his side, was a black man with eyes bulging so far out of their sockets they looked as if they'd been stuck on to his face with superglue by a mad scientist. His hands were held out in front of him in handcuffs. For a few seconds I froze, unable to extract myself from the intensity of his stare. Shaking his head from side to side, he started singing in a nursery-rhyme style: 'Cosmos is going to solitary, Cosmos is going to solitary . . .'

22

It kept coming back, every time harsher, clearer, louder, more graphic, more unsettling. It disrupted my sleep and haunted me during the day, like a short video on a loop switch that rewound automatically and played itself over and over again. And the more it tormented me at night, the more it stayed with me in the day, the images burrowing themselves deeper and deeper until they had become a permanent fixture in my mind . . .

Lucy, heavily pregnant, lying on a floor, howling in pain, and crying out for me to come and rescue her. Me trying to board some form of transport but it's always too crowded to get on, or the ticket collector or cabbie won't let me in; me waiting for a bus that never comes; finally getting on the train or bus or into the car that never arrives at its destination or a plane that never lands, and Lucy carries on screaming and wailing . . .

I wrestled myself awake and lay on my back panting. My woolly hat had come off and was lying on the floor five feet below, and although my scalp was cold I was too worn out to get down from the bunk and get it. I lifted the blanket over my head and curled up into the embryo position, trying to chase away the images of Lucy in agony and fill my mind instead with happy memories and plans for the future. Judging by the groans it was getting on for five o'clock, the noisiest time of the night, an hour before we got up, when half the room began to stir. The sounds of coughing, snoring, moaning and sleep-talking filled the dormitory, half hell, half farmyard. There was never silence in the dormitory, not lasting more than three seconds at any rate, and by that time of night the room stank of rotten bodies and putrid breath.

Yasir, a heavy-smoking Afghani with serious bronchial problems, was lying on his side on the bunk next door, his long craggy face eighteen inches from mine, wheezing like an asthmatic donkey with a crisp packet stuck in its throat. I turned over to the other side of the bed and, two bunks away on the bottom bed, Abuzuike, a Nigerian guy, was reaching the climax of his twenty-seventh wank of the night, his hand going like a piston in overdrive under his rough blanket. Everyone wanked in Zone 22. Even the devout Christians wanked. But Abuzuike wanked for Nigeria. Barely were the lights out and he was off, hammering one out, like he was in a competition with himself to see how many he could squeeze in per night. By day, he moped around the *atrad* a picture of listlessness and misery, shoulders stooped, feet shuffling, eyes somewhere in the middle distance. In the factory he was in constant trouble for causing congestion in the manufacturing process because he was so slow and idle at his machine. Eventually, Ergin was forced to move him off the machines and give him the easier job of distributing and collecting piles of cloth around the floor. But at night he came alive. He was always the first in bed, and whenever I woke up or couldn't sleep he too always seemed to be awake, lying on his back with his blanket shaking above him. He was just about to ejaculate, judging by the acceleration of his hand, when a Vietnamese suddenly sat up at the far end of the room and jabbered something in his native tongue. The moment he fell silent, one of his compatriots down at my end started babbling a response, and for five minutes it went back and forth like a long-distance telephone conversation. The Vietnamese, for some reason, were by far the chattiest sleep-talkers.

As ever when I woke up in the night, I ended up on my back staring at the wooden ceiling and listening to the rats and mice, scurrying and gnawing, a couple of feet away on the other side of the thin boarding. There were vermin all round the Zone, but they were concentrated above and below the *atrads*, drawn by the smell of the food in the cupboards and the bags of clothes they could unravel and steal for bedding. The only people who didn't mind the rats were the Vietnamese, who liked to eat them. They could skin one faster than the rest of us could take our clothes off, and then they would bribe the boiler-room guys to let them cook it in the fires of the furnace. They ate anything, the Vietnamese: insects, weeds, birds, mice and rats. Boodoo John said they even ate dogs and cats, but I think he was joking. 'If it moves or grows, cook it' was their philosophy, and it served them well because as a rule the Vietnamese community was probably healthier than any other in the Zone.

Whenever I woke up early it was always a relief to hear the sound of the Zone buzzer, telling us we had ten minutes to get dressed and lined up outside for exercises, and that I was able to escape the fetid, germ-ridden, vermin-infested, shit-stinking wankhole that was our dormitory and get out in the fresh air, no matter how

247

cold. But that morning, my mind was heavy with dark thoughts and worries about Lucy and I was one of the last to get dressed and line up outside. I hadn't spoken to her for almost three months, since the failure of my appeal at the beginning of December, and although I had written her ten letters in just under two months I was yet to receive one from her. Boodoo John reassured me that the postal system, which came via the embassies and through the prison administration, was incredibly unreliable. The suspicion was that they used to sit on letters for weeks and months on end and then give them to prisoners in a big bundle, so that the earliest ones had become virtually meaningless by the time they were read. The fact that I'd not heard from Mum and Dad either supported his explanation, but still my mind filled with paranoid thoughts: Had she left me for someone else? Had the pressure got to her? Was she seriously ill?

I stood shivering outside the factory gates waiting for the guard to get to the card with my name on it and summon me across Sniper Alley and into the relative warmth of the factory floor. The dark novelty of arriving in a new prison had worn off after a couple of weeks in the *atrad*, and I had long since surrendered myself to the mind-numbing, soul-crushing daily routine of the Zone. Like everyone else in the factory, I'd quickly become a human automaton on the production line, mindlessly, silently chalking hundreds of faint marks on the jackets through the cut-out buttonholes of the cardboard model, throwing the jacket on to Baska's pile on my left and taking another jacket from the heap on my right. Every day was Groundhog Day: exercises in the cold, head-count, wash, porridge, factory, sun comes up, ten-minute cigarette break, factory, head-count, soup, factory, ten-minute break, sun goes down, head-count, another head-count, porridge or soup, write a letter, smoke a cigarette, bed . . . all carried out in a cold so bitter and unforgiving it was physically painful at times.

The smallest incidents, magnified by the mindless monotony, assumed a crazily disproportionate significance. When, three days earlier, the dark pinprick of a Russian military transport plane had rumbled overhead as we smoked our cigarettes during morning break, we'd stood out in the yard watching it as though we were witnessing the transit of Halley's Comet, 100 black-hatted heads slowly turning from east to west until it disappeared into the grey distance. It was the first plane I'd seen since the day of my arrest at the airport almost nine months earlier.

My head was bowed with anxiety, the images from my recurring nightmare still lodged in the forefront of my mind as I joined the file of black figures tramping across the white expanse of the yard, then through the factory door, and walked down past the rows of sewing stations to my table at the end. The machine operators blew and coughed into their cupped hands to try to warm them up before getting to work; Maximovich, puffy-faced from another night of vodka abuse, patrolled the aisles itching for an excuse to exercise his riot stick, which he wagged behind his back; three men silently, sullenly began to distribute piles of cloth from their baskets; Ergin stood at the top end of the room by the entrance, hands behind his back, overseeing the start of production as the first sewing machines spluttered into life. The piece of chalk I'd been using for over a week was now no bigger than a peanut and it was difficult for my frozen fingers to grip as I took it from my trouser pocket. My hands were numb with cold and it was as if I was trying to hold the chalk wearing gardening gloves or using someone else's hands, because there was no sensation. I placed the cardboard model over the black smock, lightly brushed the stub of chalk over the four cut-out buttonholes, then nodded towards Raza as I tossed the jacket into his pile and turned to my right to pick up another. Raza was now operating the button machines after Baska had replaced Rakim as the Zone horseman.

And so it continued for two hours, just as it had done the day before that, and the week before that ... pick, chalk, chuck ... pick, chalk, chuck ... pick, chalk, chuck ... the repetition of it slowly squeezing the life out of me so that by the time break came at ten o'clock, my brain was fully in idle mode, just a black screen, the last coherent, interesting thought having sunk to the bottom of my consciousness an hour or so earlier.

Suddenly Molloi, the young Vietnamese boy from Ergin's office, came bursting through the door on my right from the big delivery area, shouting in Russian: 'Quick! Quick!' and waving to us to follow him. Maximovich was back in his office, and was usually sleeping off his hangover by this time, so we stopped what we were doing and hurried next door. Babushka, the grey mare, had given birth and a slimy little foal was lying on a bed of straw in its makeshift stable, which had been set up inside for the greater warmth. It was desperately trying to stand up, while Baska, his arms and black shirt smeared with fluid and blood, cut away the umbilical cord and afterbirth with the confidence and expertise of a vet. We all jostled for position to get a closer look and it was difficult to say what was the more shocking, exhilarating and uplifting: the spectacle of that vulnerable, bamboo-legged grey horse emerging into the world, bursting with new life and energy – or the incredible joy and awe that lit up the faces of the prisoners as I looked along the line. It was as if we were witnessing a miracle.

The rumour had started after lunch and it took no more than two minutes to spread from the chesspiece work-shop, through the delivery area where the new foal, now a week old, was still being stabled, round the floor of the sewing factory and finally into the office where Ergin was congratulating me on my button-chalking efforts and hinting that I might be promoted to be his assistant if I kept up the hard work. Mafia, returning from a visit to the chess workshop, walked through the door with a look of excitement on his face. 'Shop open tonight! Ikram at doctor and saw truck with boxes and bags!'

Back on the factory floor, the room was abuzz with chatter among the machine operators for the rest of the afternoon, blowing away the usual atmosphere of grim boredom and weariness and only falling quiet when Maximovich or one of the other factory guards came back to patrol the floor. Normally we returned to the shelter of the *atrad* for the fifteen minutes or so between the head-count in the factory yard and the final one back in the Zone, but on this occasion most chose to remain in the three exercise yards, as close to the gate as possible, jumping up and down and jogging on the spot to keep warm. When the first blast of the alarm rent the freezing night air and the electric gate was buzzed open, 300 men stopped short of breaking into a run to take up their positions for *preverka*. The 'shop', such as it was, was situated at the far end of the office building closest to the kitchen/canteen area, opposite Atrad 3, and the general aim of the mob was to find a position as close to it as possible to be first in the queue. Everyone being present, the head-count took no longer than five minutes before the guard walked away, shouting, '*Magazin!*' – triggering a barely restrained rush towards the far end of the admin building. Within a few moments I was one of only half a dozen people left standing on the concourse; 300 others had formed into a line that was more scrum than queue. The only ones who hadn't sprinted into the mêlée were the very poor prisoners or the better-off ones, including the Dutchman Sacha Costa and Benny, who I'd learned was a Jewish guy from Latvia or Lithuania – I could never remember which one – with connections in Israel. We slowly gravitated towards each other, hands buried deep in our pockets as we walked round the corner and watched the others pushing and elbowing to try to get to the front. Two elderly women stood behind hatches handing over items as the mob of bodies pressed forward.

'So what's the big fuss?' I asked, blowing into my hands and kicking the toes of my boots into the ground behind me.

'Nothing – unless you want an onion, or some black tea, plain biscuits or boiled sweets,' said Sacha, in English.

'If they're lucky, there may be some sachets of coffee and milk powder! Fucking pitiful, isn't it?'

Sacha, who'd used to own a successful marine transport business, was four years into a twelve-year sentence for smuggling 500 kilograms of hashish into Russia. He insisted he was innocent, claiming he had been stitched up by a Russian guy who had hired a sea container from him and used it to smuggle the drugs. The guy had been convicted but, unknown to Sacha, he had won his appeal, claiming they had been Sacha's drugs. When Sacha and his young family flew into southern Russia for a holiday with his wife's parents a few months later, he was arrested at the airport. You never knew whether people were telling the truth in Zone 22 – and no doubt there were many who didn't believe my claim that the Customs officers had exaggerated the weight of my hash so they could get me for smuggling. But I believed Sacha. Benny was doing time for smuggling two kilos of hash, but I never heard him claim his innocence. (It just bothered me that his sentence was only marginally longer than mine, even though he was carrying fifty or sixty times more than me.) Like so many others, he'd made the mistake of flying back from the sub-continent on a cheap flight via Moscow.

In silence we watched 300 grown men jostle each other to get their hands on a couple of sweets and a couple of cups' worth of tea. The ones stepping away from the hatch stashed their handful of goods into their pockets, grinning as if they had just won the lottery and been given a presidential pardon all at once. It was a part pathetic, part heartening spectacle, like an aid truck in a famine zone, and I wasn't too sure whether to be happy or sad for them.

'Most of them only have a few *kapeets* – pennies – in their account, which is enough to buy maybe three or four sweets or a couple of biscuits,' explained Benny.

'Account?' I asked, surprised.

'Yeah, have you not opened yours yet? You get money paid in from home, and you can buy stuff from the shop or use it for phone calls.'

'*Phone calls!* What do you mean? Phone calls?' I asked, turning round to face him.

I had been in Zone 22 for almost two months, all the time with my ear close to the ground and my eyes wide open, trying to learn about prison life as quickly as I could, but not once had I heard anyone mention using the telephone!

'Come on, we'll show you,' said Sacha, and we walked round to the front of the building and stopped in front of a peeling light-blue noticeboard with faint Russian script in black, just about readable in the light from the distant floodlights. Icicles hung down from the gutters above, and a spray of frozen snow obscured half the wording.

'This board lists the rights to which prisoners are entitled, such as the delivery of food parcels, medical treatment and so on,' said Sasha. 'It's been there for fucking years and it doesn't mean much really. The governors and guards have created their own version of our rights over the years, but one of the original ones on here states that prisoners in *obshi* regime are allowed to make two phone calls every three months . . . and before you get too excited, this is the catch . . . *to a number in Russia*. Most people don't use the right because they've got no one in Russia to make a call to. It's one of their sick jokes. We're foreigners in here, but we can't call abroad even if we pay for it. But maybe you should do what I do, call your Embassy and see if they will patch you through to the UK to ... what's your girlfriend called again?'

'Lucy!' I blurted out with a grin, exhilarated by the prospect of being able to talk to her. The image of her smiling face flashed into my mind. 'Yeah, Lucy! She's my girlfriend!'

'Well, first you have to open a prison account and write a *zevlanya*, a formal application, to make the call, which will take a few days to clear. I'll help you write the application back in the *atrad* if you like.'

Sacha spoke Russian fluently and he translated at the rate he wrote out the *zevlanya* at the kitchen table: 'I, prisoner Tig Hague, born on December X, of Y address in the United Kingdom, charged with *statya* 228 and 118 for the possession and smuggling of illegal contraband, hereby submit a formal request to the Russian state for permission to make a phone call, lasting no longer than five minutes, to the British Embassy and that I, Tig Hague, further undertake to pay, in full, the sum of X roubles to the Zone 22 authorities ...' It probably took less time to write out the Treaty of Versailles.

The following evening Sacha and I went to see Raisa Petrovna, the almost friendly liaison officer, submitted my *zevlanya* and filled in a form to set up a Zone account.

'Ask her how long it will take to get permission to make the call to the British Embassy,' I said to Sacha.

'Two to four days. It depends.'

'On what?'

'On whether they're feeling in the mood or they can be fucking bothered to say yes. They generally like to keep you sweating for a few days.'

And so I waited, for the full four fucking days, growing ever more agitated and impatient as my application sat in a pile somewhere in the office. Once the hope of being able to talk to Lucy, or to Mum and Dad, had been dangled before me, I was able to concentrate on nothing else. At night I lay awake for hours, cursing the wankers in the office for denying me five minutes of joy. 'Man, they'll do anything in here to wipe the smile off your face,' Boodoo John said as I paced around the kitchen on the third night, rubbing my bum where I had fallen on it on the ice outside the *atrad*. 'Sad thing is, no matter how much you come to expect the shit, it never gets any easier. Wherever you got hope, they're going to replace it with frustration and misery. It's prison policy.'

I had just returned from seeing Raisa Petrovna to ask about my application, by making an imaginary phone with my thumb and little finger, lifting it to my ear. Puffing out my lips, raising my eyebrows and stooping my shoulders, I gave myself the look of a hopeless simpleton in the hope that it might excite her maternal instincts, or at least a spasm of sympathy, and encourage her to go and chase up my application with the governors. But she just shrugged and held out her hands, and I exhaled loudly and stomped from the room, trying to rein in my fury. As I marched back across the yard to the *atrad* I kicked the snow a couple of times in frustration, and was taking a third swipe when my other foot gave way on the ice below. The momentum from my swinging boot sent my body spinning up into the air and I landed on the frozen ground with a mighty thud, my bum and lower back taking most of the weight. For a couple of minutes I hopped around in agony, brushing the snow off my clothes and arching my back to relieve some of the pain, and when I turned round to motion to the observation room to let me through the gate, half a dozen guards were standing in the window, jack-knifing with laughter, their distorted shadows stretching out over the white expanse outside. The Undertaker was enjoying himself so much he was clapping at the same time.

The following night I returned, this time with Sacha in tow, to quiz Raisa about whether there was still a problem, having once again paid off the *atradnik* with two Marlboro and a teaspoon of instant coffee. She looked almost proud to be able to tell me, via Sacha, that the governors had considered my application and on this occasion they were willing to grant my request. With a half-smile she motioned me through to the guards' observation room, where an old rotary dial-up phone, the same as Regime's but black, sat on a table in the corner on the right as we walked in. There were four guards in the room, two in chairs with their backs to me watching a game show on TV, and two standing by the window, who looked at me with the customary indifference bordering on disdain. She dialled the number of the British Embassy herself and waited for an answer. I chewed my nails as I looked over the heads of the seated guards and out of the window towards the shadowy forms of the prisoners smoking in the exercise yards of the *atrads*. Raisa suddenly started talking in Russian into the receiver, then handed me the phone and walked from the room.

'Is that Tig? Hello, I'm Alla. I'm new in the Embassy. I'm working on your case. I've been speaking to Lucy and your mum and dad very much. They are very worried for you. Can you write them a letter? How are you anyway?'

'I'm all right, I'm all right. Just. It's a terrible place but right now I'm coping, and I'm learning all the time,' I said, my head crowding with things to say and panic spreading through me that they'd not received one of my letters. 'I've written about ten letters to them in total over the last couple of months! Why haven't they got them? I haven't had any from them either. What's going on?'

'I'll check for you with the state prison authorities here in Moscow. By the way, we will be visiting you soon with some food, and clothes and cigarettes, once the weather starts to improve in the next few weeks. Can you send a list of your requirements, but remember you are only allowed basic foods . . .'

'The woman down here at the Zone said I've only got five minutes on the phone, so we must be quick. I have to set up a prison money account for phone calls and I'll need Mum and Dad to put maybe 5,000 roubles [about 200 pounds] into it. Tell them I'm sorry and I know how much they've sacrificed already and that I'm going to pay them back every bloody penny when I get home . . . But I've got to speak to Lucy. Please, can you put me through right now? Try the home number first. She'll probably just be getting in from work.'

The sound of the distinctive 'trim-trim' British ringtone of the phone in Lucy's mum's house in Waltham-stow triggered a flood of adrenaline and I took three rapid, deep breaths to try to calm myself down when the phone clicked.

'Hello?' It was Lucy.

'I've got Tig on the line for you, Lucy,' said Alla.

'OH, MY GOD!' she screeched down the line, her voice bouncing off a satellite dish hundreds of miles above us in space.

I couldn't talk.

'Tig, Tig ... are you there? Can you hear me?'

'Babe, I'm here. I'm here for you. I'm always here for you,' I said finally, trying to keep my voice steady and not show her that I was crying. 'How are you? What's been going on? How is everyone? Are you coping? How's your mum?'

'They're all good, Tig. We're all doing great. It's horrible without you, but don't worry about us ...'

'What's your news? When are you coming out? How's Mum and Dad and Rob? Are you working?'

'Yeah, yeah, everyone's great, Tig. All missing you like hell ... All right, Mum, I'm just coming. It's Tig! I'll be with you in a minute ... Yeah, I'm still temping at Wiggins in the City. I'm saving up to come and see you, Babes, in the spring. Your mum and dad are coming first, once your dad's all right to travel with his new hip ... OK, Mum, just give me two minutes ...'

'You're coming out? You know you're only allowed one visit a year!'

Raisa Petrovna tapped me on the shoulder and held up her index finger.

'Luce, I've only got a minute. I can't tell you how much I miss you. I love you so much. The thought of seeing you again is the only thing that gets me through each day here. It's bollocks in here, Babe. Fucking freezing. Everyone's ill, or fucking mad. I've got about three mates. I love you, I love you, I love you ...'

'I love you and miss you too, honey. So much. I'm dying to see you. All right, Mum, I'm coming ... Tig, my love, I've got to go,' she said impatiently. 'I love you. Stay strong ...' And then the line went dead.

23

Sacha was waiting for me back in the reception area, and looking into my puffy, bloodshot eyes he patted me on the shoulder. As we approached the door the guard on duty at the desk, who was still wearing his blue fur-lined trooper hat, wagged his finger and said, 'Zanpolit,' pointing back down the corridor.

Zanpolit was leaning back in his chair, already wearing his long leather coat in preparation for leaving, and he was jangling the keys of his 1980s Ford Escort. He was very proud of that car. Most of the prison officials lived in the little wooden houses in the village around the Zone and walked to work, but Zanpolit was one of the few to live further afield. Each morning he accelerated through the main gates and parked up with a flourishing rev of the engine, like he was James Bond himself. None of the others had a car anything like as glamorous as his.

'Hague Tig, I understand that tonight you have opened your account with us. Let me congratulate you. Let's hope Alla in the Embassy is quick to send you some money,' he said, Sacha translating. The bastard had been listening in on my conversation. 'As a former banker I'm sure you understand better than most how money helps to make the world go round. I'm sure you will know how to spend your money wisely in here.'

He paused, and I filled the awkward silence by saying

clumsily, 'Thank you, Zanpolit. Those are kind words.' I stood, Oliver Twist style, looking at the floor and holding my black woolly hat out in front of me.

'It's a great coincidence that tonight we were saying how much the guards' room needed a new television and how useful it would be to have a video recorder for the Zone. And it got me thinking: I wonder if Hague Tig would like to make a contribution, now that he is soon to have a Zone 22 bank account!'

Zanpolit chuckled at his little joke and ran his hand through his heavily gelled hair, adding, 'So what do you say, Hague Tig? Do you want to be a popular man in the Zone, and make a little contribution towards the improvement of our little community?'

'Well, er ... of course ... well, yes ... how much?' I stammered.

'Well, as your friend Sacha was recently kind enough to make the full contribution to pay for some important pieces of furniture, perhaps you would like to match his generosity, and the administration can then continue to look on both your parole applications favourably when the time comes. I think 100,000 roubles should cover it.'

'And if I'm unable to raise the money back home?' I asked.

Zanpolit put on a mock-serious face and got up from his chair. 'Well, Hague Tig, some of those guards have set their hearts on this for a long time, and you wouldn't want to be the one to disappoint them, would you? You know how they are with their black marks. But perhaps you like it in here so much, you want to spend an extra six months with us?'

The freezing cold of the Mordovian winter had one very small consolation for us: the steam from our breath meant we could sometimes have a crafty cigarette without having to crowd under one of the four little pagoda-style shelters that had been designated as the smoking zones. If a guard caught us smoking outside the shelters we were automatically handed a black mark, but in the factory compound, where Maximovich and the other guards tended to stay inside during break, we could risk it in the colder months. During the ten-minute break one morning towards the end of March, I lit up a Marlboro and, cupping it in my hand and scanning the compound for an approaching guard, wandered over to the stables facing the factory to say hello to Baska and see the foal, who'd become the unofficial Zone mascot. For three weeks since her birth the little grey had been the centre of attention in the factory area. Baska had called her 'Nadezhda', which means 'hope' in Russian, and during every break almost the entire workforce filed outside to stroke and pat her and watch her prancing about the little paddock area on her tall skinny legs. There was something enchanting about Nadezhda. Perhaps it was the animal's innocence, the fact that she had no idea she was living in a shithole among miserable criminals and mean-spirited guards; or perhaps it was her youthful exuberance and the happiness she showed as she trotted around the paddock, showing off to us. Whatever it was, Nadezhda was more than just an ungainly young grey horse to us. She was a rare source of joy.

It had snowed heavily overnight and half the factory area lay under a thick blanket of white, while the other half had been shovelled into great piles around the ramshackle wooden stable block and the perimeter of the tarmac square in front of the factory. Nadezhda was roped up to a hook outside the stable door as I approached, and I stroked her nose and mane before stubbing out my cigarette with my boot and going inside. Baska was shovelling the manure and dirty straw into a wheelbarrow and struggling to manoeuvre himself between the two big horses, Babushka, Nadezhda's mother, and Molloi, a hot-blooded black colt.

'All right, Baska?' I smiled as he looked up from between the two horses and jumped towards me as Molloi twitched and fretted.

He leant his spade up against the wooden slats of the wall and handed me Babushka's rope, pointing outside with his other hand. '*Idi, anglichanin, spasiba.*' The closest I'd ever been to a fully grown horse was in the paddock at Epsom on Derby Day, and I was nervous as I led the mare out into the slippery paddock where the ice and snow lay in hazardous patches.

I stroked the animal's nose, patted her back and talked nonsense into her ear, then Baska signalled to me to bring her back inside and handed me the rope around Molloi's head. The colt was a much livelier beast altogether than his stablemate and he seemed to take an instant dislike to me, backing away as I tried to guide him out through the door. When Baska gave him a word of encouragement and a gentle slap on his haunches, the horse made a sharp bolt through the door, forcing me to jump aside and pull back on the reins as he dragged me into the snow. For a few moments the horse tugged his head from side to side and we were both growing jumpier by the second. He was so strong, and the more I pulled the rope, the more he tried to resist. The other prisoners, under the smoking shelter, had all turned round to watch as Molloi pushed me round in circles with his hindquarters, both of us slipping and sliding on the pools of ice, him whinnying and me cursing at him to stand still. It wasn't so much that he was trying to run away, he just didn't like being handled by me.

Suddenly, in one quick movement, he barged me with his flank, the rope slipped from my hand and I found myself cornered between the wall of the stable and a giant pile of fresh snow that reached up to my shoulder. Molloi's back legs were just three feet away; he flicked one of them out at me, violently, and the waft of air from his hoof told me he had missed my face by no more than an inch or two. He was a big, powerful horse, Molloi, and he was going to cause me some serious harm unless I managed to get clear. If he got me in the head, I was a goner. I was starting to panic, because I had nowhere to run and he was scraping and flicking his hind legs as he backed towards me. I withdrew into the corner between the stable and the wall of snow, and when I saw Molloi lining himself up for another kick, I immediately hurled myself out of the way, shouting, 'BASKA!' before disappearing upside down in the giant pile of fresh snow. For half a minute or so I wriggled around trying to extricate myself, and I was panicking even more now. It was a little like being turned over by a giant wave in the sea, and I couldn't work out which way up I was until, finally, I emerged into the sunlight with half a foot of snow on my hat. Baska, who was holding Molloi by the rope, and the rest of the prisoners were creasing up with laughter. Even the sniper in the watchtower was chuckling, and soon my own shoulders were bouncing up and down with amusement too. For half a minute or so, 100 prisoners rocked and fell about, holding their stomachs and pointing at me, and I could feel the tears of laughter starting to ice up as they streamed down my cheeks.

I hadn't laughed so hard since Dad and Rob had come to visit me in Moscow. I had wound myself up into a frenzy of anguish over the abrupt end to my phone call with Lucy, but all the tension flooded from me as I laughed like a madman, covered in snow from head to foot.

24

I first noticed the signs of the spring thaw when I was leaving the office building after breakfast following a visit to the doctor about my ongoing chest infection, which had flared up again and was refusing to budge even after I'd given up smoking for a couple of weeks. The fear of TB haunted me every time I coughed or felt a stabbing pain when I breathed in deeply. The glands in my throat were still up, I felt weak and tired from the moment I woke, and at night I'd been sweating like a Turk in a *hamam*. What was really freaking me out was the fact that the tetracycline antibiotics I'd bribed off the doctor with a full jar of coffee and sixty smokes had done sweet FA except make my diarrhoea even worse than normal. 'Cushion bum', as she was known to the African boys, had written me out a sick note, signing me off work for three days. I was standing outside the door of the office before heading back to bed, hacking into my sleeve while bending forward with the pain, when I felt a drip land on the back of my exposed neck. I looked up and saw that the icicles that hung along the entire length of the guttering were all dripping like leaky taps. The chest infection had left me feeling cold and shivery, but when I exhaled, for the first time since I'd arrived in the Zone, I was unable to see my breath. Spring was on its way.

They say there are two seasons in Mordovia: a long

unforgiving winter and a short unforgiving summer. Spring and autumn are no more than brief breaks between the two, little interludes of mildness and moderation between the extremity and intensity of the cold and the heat. By the time April came I'd begun to wonder whether Mordovia had a summer at all, because the snow and ice still lay thick on the ground, and the twiggy crowns of the silver birch trees beyond the barbed wire on the Zone walls were as bare as they had been when I had arrived in the dead of winter. But within a few days the icicles were gone, the snow had turned first to slush and then to mud, the trees started to bud and the birds began to sing, and by the middle of the month the only signs of winter were the piles of compacted snow in the shadows of north-facing buildings that never saw any direct daylight.

Every new sign of life was echoed in the mood of the Zone. Even Time itself seemed to have been frozen to a standstill in the depths of winter – March felt no further into the year than January – but once the ice had released its iron grip, there was a sense that life was free to start moving forward again. And the further and faster it moved, the closer I came to seeing Mum and Dad, and then Lucy, and to regaining my freedom ... Spring was the first milestone on my journey out of Zone 22. But the change in the season was also a depressing reminder that my real life effectively remained on pause as the world beyond the prison walls moved on without me.

I went to bed for three days, desperate to get myself healthy before Mum and Dad arrived the following week. I was going to look bad enough as it was. My head was shaved almost to the scalp, I was a stone and a half below my optimum weight, and although there were no mirrors in the Zone I could tell from my reflection in the windows that my face was bony and gaunt. It was going to be traumatic enough for them as it was to visit their boy in a prison camp in the middle of one of the most miserable godforsaken regions of Eastern Europe, but to find me doubled over in agony and hacking my chest to shreds every few minutes might well be too much for them to bear.

For three days and nights I did little but sleep. I drank as much water as possible and I ate my remaining four tins of fruit (three peach slices, one mandarin segments) in an effort to try to get some Vitamin C into my system. My food and cigarette supplies were almost exhausted, and for the previous three or four weeks I'd been living off nothing but three biscuits for breakfast, prison soup for lunch and a small bowl of noodles in the evening. Occasionally I made an appearance at breakfast in the canteen, but mealtimes were fraught occasions, and the guards were handing out black marks at a rate of roughly one every ten days for the most minor 'offences', like, quite literally, stepping out of line, or not greeting them with proper respect, whatever the fuck that meant. The authorities were happy for prisoners to skip meals because it meant there was more food to go round, but only a few of the better-off prisoners, like myself, could afford the luxury of staying in the *atrads*.

After four days, the day before Mum and Dad arrived, the doctor said I was well enough to return to the factory, and although the fatigue still dripped from my limbs and my chest felt like a slab of raw meat, the infection was entering its final 'clear-out' stages.

A mixture of excitement and nerves had taken hold of me from the moment I woke up and got dressed into my civilian clothes: black polo neck, blue jeans and loafers. Not since my appeal hearing back in early December had I worn the clothes of a free man, and I felt a little self-conscious as I pulled them on, before shaving as close as my old Bic razor would allow and polishing my shoes to a fine buff. When I walked out of the wash area into the corridor, the others were waiting for the buzzer to signal the start of the day's work. Boodoo John looked me up and down and gave me a builder's wolf-whistle, and Julian slapped me on the back and said; 'Hey, look at the English gentleman!' They didn't say it, but I knew they were happy for me.

It was a warm, bright morning as the guard led me out of the main gates and into the visitors' bungalow, which was situated beyond the mesh-and-barbed-wire fence to the rear of Atrads 1 and 2, but within the outer concrete wall of the Zone. Raisa Petrovna was sitting behind the desk in the small reception area at the entrance when I was led into the building. She looked up and smiled as the guard unlocked the barred gate and waved me through into the long dark corridor. Off to the left were a kitchen and two bedrooms, as functional and drab as the Zone itself: peeling, off-white walls, dark linoleum floors, plastic chairs, brown curtains in the bedrooms, prison issue sheets and blankets and small hard pillows on the beds.

I was expecting to have to wait for Mum and Dad, and

I was startled when I walked into the living room at the end of the corridor to find them standing there, smiling from ear to ear. I took a step back, almost bumping into the guard behind, and Dad said: 'Who were you expecting: Arsene Wenger and the Chancellor of the Exchequer?' I swept towards them and into their outstretched arms and for a minute or so we just clung on to each other, like rugby players in a huddle. I was determined not to cry. I wanted their visit to be a happy occasion so that they could go home with some positive images and memories to sustain them over the rest of my sentence. Mum was sniffing and dabbing her nose with a tissue, but she was holding back the tears too. Dad was giving it the comedy treatment, just as he had done when he came to visit me in Moscow.

'So how's life in the five-star hotel then? All right for some, isn't it? The rest of us have to work for a living...'

Mum interrupted him. 'They're not feeding you properly, are they?' she said, running her hand up and down my ribcage like it was a xylophone.

'No, no, they are, honestly, Mum,' I protested. 'It's much, much better than Moscow. You mustn't worry about that. It's ten times better than Moscow in here, honestly. It's clean, it's pretty safe. It's just bloody boring, Mum, and it was bloody freezing too, but it's warmer now. Anyway, you two are looking brilliant considering...'

I didn't mean to say 'considering', and I was lying, too, because I thought they looked at least two or three years older: greyer, more drawn, worry lines etched into their brows. Mum had lost at least a stone and there were dark bags under her eyes. Dad's hair was now completely grey. Look what I've bloody done to them! I thought to myself, and the shame coursed through me.

The living room was no more than the size of a small front room in a terraced house. Against one wall there was a brown sofa made from cheap fabric, covered in stains and rips accumulated over twenty or thirty years. The two armchairs were brown and mouldy too. An old black and white television, a corner table, a brown carpet, faded orange wallpaper and a picture of some dogs playing cards, hanging at an angle, completed the decor. The whole place stank of stale smoke and the sweat of a thousand convicts.

Dad winced as he eased himself slowly into one of the armchairs, his new hip clearly still giving him a bit of grief, while Mum and I sat on the settee and started firing questions at each other. The rest of the day we chatted and chirped like the sparrows bouncing around on the windowsill outside, all talking across each other to pass on news and ask after one another.

I knew that Mum and Dad were only going to put a positive shine on life back home, but their faces and voices betrayed them when they said that everything was probably going to work out fine with Garban Icap when I got out.

'So have you heard from them recently?' I probed.

Mum let out a long sigh and leant forward.

'Tig, darling, you'll get another job. Don't worry. We didn't want to tell you, but they terminated your contract back in November after you were found guilty . . .'

I had long suspected that Garban had sacked me, or were going to – relatively junior positions like mine could be filled overnight – and I'd known from the beginning that everyone was going to shield me from bad news at home as best they could, but the confirmation still came like a stab to the stomach.

'I'll make you a proper cup of English tea,' said Mum, pushing herself up off the settee. 'I brought you some PG Tips from home, and bags of goodies from the supermarket in Moscow. It's not quite like Tesco's but there should be enough to keep you going for a month or so . . .'

'And the Embassy driver who brought us down from Moscow has delivered all the little *contributions* to the Zone: the video camera, the TV and the computers . . .' interrupted Dad, giving me a wink.

'So, Dad, how have we been paying for all this, plus the lawyers, the travel to and from Moscow, my food parcels, my Zone bank account, the *contributions* and everything . . . Where's it all coming from, Dad? I hope it's not your pension or savings . . .'

'Let's not worry about that, son,' he laughed, getting up from his seat and ruffling my hair. 'Everyone's rallying around, boy. Your family and friends. We know you'd do the same, wouldn't you? We look after one another. That's what friends and family are for. That's the last thing you should be thinking about. You've got enough on your plate.'

'I want to pay everyone back when I can, Dad. Tell me, seriously, what's the total cost so far?'

'Forget it, boy. Forget it. Let's just say it's less than

273

Thierry Henry earns a week, put it that way! It's not important. Let's just get you home, boy.'

They were doing what I was doing: giving an edited, upbeat, glossy version of the truth, sparing one another too much reality.

By the afternoon of the second day, we had exhausted most of our news and we sat in silence for long periods, playing cards, smoking and reading. We didn't need to speak to enjoy the pleasure of our reunion. Dad even managed to watch some Russian TV on the ancient set in the corner, snoring from time to time in his chair while Mum and I dozed and chatted every now and then on the old brown sofa. For a few hours it felt like I was back in the front room in New Eltham again.

But as I watched their heads bouncing up and down as they nodded off, still exhausted from their three-day journey from south-east London to Mordovia via Moscow, I thought of all the picture frames on their mantelpiece and dresser at home, proudly showcasing me at various stages of childhood, from baby to toddler to goofy teenager and flanker for Kent Colts to BA (Honours) graduate from Leeds University in my mortarboard and gown; and I thought of all the hopes they must have had for me as I grew up. And what had it all come to? A prison camp in the Russian wilderness! How had I repaid their love and support over the years? By becoming a convicted drugs smuggler! I squirmed on my bum at the thought of them having to tell the neighbours what had become of me, and how the rumour mill would be doing overdrive in their circle of friends. I imagined them all down at the newsagent's and baker's in New

Eltham, shaking their heads: 'Good gracious, have you heard the news about the Hague boy? Who'd have thought he'd turn out to be a wrong 'un? Seemed like such a decent lad. Just shows you, doesn't it? You never know, you just never know ...'

In the evening, a new guard came down the corridor to check on us and I immediately stood to attention when he walked through the door. Unlike the guards before him, who had made me stand until they'd gone, he motioned to me to sit down and then nodded politely to Mum and Dad. I knew all the guards by sight, but I'd had little contact with this character, who looked a bit sinister with the dark lenses of his reactor glasses obscuring his eyes. I'd given him a few cigarettes in bribes to let me go over to the office building, but that was the extent of our contact. He was a little younger than Dad, but they shared the same stocky build.

He pointed to me on the sofa and wagged his finger, looking at Dad at the same time with a half-smile on his face.

'Correct, sir, he's a very naughty boy!' said Dad, entering into the humour, and joining him in wagging his finger at me.

The guard then bent down and made a spanking gesture on an imaginary young boy.

'You're right! I should have been a bit firmer with him when he was a lad and he would never have ended up in this mess!'

The banter continued for a minute or two, and when the guard went to leave he walked over and shook Dad and Mum by the hand, and Dad got to his feet to say goodbye. I followed the guard into the corridor and beckoned him into the kitchen, where Mum's shopping was sitting in half a dozen bags on the small formica table. I took out a bar of chocolate and a packet of Marlboro and handed them to him, but he threw up his hands in protest, exclaiming: '*Nyet! Nyet!*'

'*Spasiba, spasiba,*' I said, genuinely grateful for his show of humanity in front of my folks.

'They seem really nice, the guards here, compared to the ones in Moscow, Tig,' said Mum with a big smile as I walked back into the living room. 'It's a much better set-up. I'm glad you're in better hands now, my love.'

'Yeah, yeah, er, they're all pretty decent in here,' I replied, lying through my teeth. I thought of the nice Israeli guy, David, who had died a few weeks after my arrival during an argument with one of the guards. David, a diamond smuggler in his early sixties, had gone to the admin office to ask when he was finally going to be allowed to see his wife in the visitors' block. She'd flown all the way from Tel Aviv to see him, but on arrival at Zone 22 was told that her paperwork was incorrect and she'd have to return to Moscow to sort it out. He'd talked of little else but her visit for months on end, and when he was told that she was sitting ten yards beyond the wall but he couldn't see her, he had a heart attack and passed away on the floor of the guards' room.

'No, yeah, Mum, they're much better, the guards here. It's good. It's all right. Much better . . .'

The following morning Raisa Petrovna came down into the kitchen where we were sitting at the table having tea to tell us that the Embassy driver had returned to take Mum and Dad back to Moscow. She did that by mimicking someone turning a steering-wheel, and saying: 'Broom! Broom! Moskva!' which made Dad giggle.

We all stood up holding our chipped, stained cups, not quite knowing what to say, then all at once we burst out, 'Well, it won't be long now!' and promptly fell about laughing. Another silence followed, and eventually Mum put her arm around my waist and drew me to her, tight. Her voice was starting to break as she said: 'You carry on being strong, my boy. I love you so much.' And she buried her face in my chest to hide her tears. Dad gave me a big bear hug and we filed down the dark corridor into the reception area where, followed by two guards, we stepped straight outside into the murky morning light. Through the barbed-wire gate I saw the black Volvo of the British Embassy parked up across the road with the driver leaning against the bonnet smoking a cigarette. Behind him, a trail of smoke rose from the chimney of a small dilapidated wooden bungalow. A strange-looking brown dog, long and low like a sausage dog but with the big face of an Alsatian, stopped and cocked his leg on the wheel of the car and I heard Dad shout: 'Oi!' I didn't dare look back as the electric gate buzzed open and one of the guards led me back across Sniper Alley towards the *atrads*.

It must've been just before eight o'clock, because as I walked up the side of the *atrads* the sewing and chess workers were starting to form up in rows in front of the gates ready to be called through to the factory area. A misty haze hung over the trees beyond the Zone walls.

Without thinking, I turned round and through a gap in the walls I could see Mum and Dad approaching the car. A horrifying shriek ruptured the still morning air. All the workers spun round and as I turned the corner of the building, I saw a general commotion just outside Atrad 3's exercise yard. Guards poured out of the office building, pulling their truncheons as they ran; the sniper in the tower opposite was aiming his rifle towards Atrad 3. Two men were scuffling on the ground, rolling in the dirt and yelling, while others tried in vain to pull them apart. The guards arrived and began to thrash the prisoner on top of the other guy, who was screaming in agony. After a minute, the guards stopped beating the man and pulled him up by his collar. It was Cosmos. He was bellowing incoherently and struggling with all his strength as four guards tried to restrain him, while the other guy writhed and wailed on the ground, clutching the side of his head. As Cosmos was put in a half-nelson and led away up towards the offices, Fam, the young Vietnamese, Philip and another guy went to the aid of the man on the ground. As they sat him up against the wall, I saw that he was one of the Tajik guys called Mo, who worked in the chesspiece workshop. His hands were covered in blood and he held them to the side of his head, alternately groaning and shrieking. As the doctor emerged from the offices, escorted by a guard, slowly Mo took his hands away from his ear to show his wound to the others. All of them recoiled in horror at what they saw, and Fam put his hand up against the wall of the building and started retching. I remembered, with a jolt, that Mum and Dad were no more than 100 yards away beyond the wall, easily within earshot of the uproar, as I edged closer along the fence towards the scene. Cosmos, meanwhile, continued to shout protests and wrestle with the guards as they dragged him away towards the solitary confinement block. Philip was leaning with his back against the mesh fencing, staring dumbfounded as the doctor knelt down to treat Mo.

'What was all that about, Philip? What's going on?'

Philip could barely say it.

'Cosmos bit his ear off.'

25

After a night in solitary, Cosmos was sedated and taken away to Zone 3, a high security prison under '*ossoboni*' regime for the most dangerous criminals, while Mo, the Tajik guy, was put on the train to the hospital Zone where I'd stayed for a week of check-ups before coming to Zone 22. 'He'll come back from there with no ears at all,' was the joke doing the rounds as we lined up on the tarmac to be called through to the factory area the following morning. I winced at the memory of Mo's shrieking and Cosmos's demonic howling, and wondered what dreadful thoughts must have been going through Mum and Dad's minds as they drove away to Moscow.

'Hague Tig!' shouted the guard, putting my name card to the back of the pack as I made my way through the quickly diminishing ranks of workers and joined the flow of black uniforms through the gates. For the first time since I had arrived in the Zone, I noticed that not one of us was wearing a hat, but from a distance, and especially from behind, it was still difficult to tell people apart because our shaved heads were no less of a uniform than our hats had been. Ergin was waiting in the gloomy foyer area as I pushed open the heavy door to the factory, and I nodded to him as I immediately veered left and began to head into the long manufacturing room towards my station at the far end, just as I had done almost every day, bar Sundays, for three months.

'Tig! This way,' said Ergin, heading into his office.

Molloi was already busy on his sewing machine in the corner and he smiled as I walked in, but Mafia, the lazy bugger, was sitting on the table swinging his legs, looking sulky.

'Your button work was being excellent,' said Ergin. 'You are fastest chalker I've seen in Zone 22. One chalk with you is for two weeks. Well done. I want promoting you to working for office. You are my right arm now.'

'Brilliant, thank you, Ergin,' I said, shaking his hand, genuinely thrilled to be away from the factory floor.

To say I was proud of my button-chalking work would be an exaggeration, but I did feel a quiet sense of satisfaction at the end of the day if we'd succeeded in meeting our quota of jackets or maybe even exceeded it. I had to feel good about something. I liked hearing the sound of the Zone buzzer at the end of a shift, when I returned to the relative warmth of the *atrad* to tick off another day, having avoided a black mark or a crack across the shoulders with Maximovich's riot stick. I was one of only a handful to escape the drunken wrath of his truncheon, although once, when he was even more pissed than normal after returning from lunch outside the prison, he looked at me wildly and raised the stick across his face before staggering away up the aisle, laughing to himself like a madman with a dark secret.

In the unlikely event of my parole application running to schedule, I had worked out I had roughly 450 days to survive in Zone 22, and each one that passed felt like a small footstep closer to home and to Lucy. The passing of a day became an event. Back in London, days, even whole weeks, merged into each other as time slid by almost unnoticed; in Zone 22, I was conscious of every hour of every day. I was focusing on a small point far in the distance that moved that tiny bit closer every day. I may not have been the most skilful worker in the factory, but nobody laboured harder than me, with the possible exceptions of Molloi in the office and Baska before he took over the horses. If I'd worked any slower, my mind would have started to drift and the dreadful monotony and misery of the place would almost certainly have driven me to distraction and to despair. But it wasn't just for my sanity and for a sense of self-worth that I worked hard, I did it to win promotion to the office, where I would be less exposed to the callous whims of the guards and therefore less likely to get a black mark.

My greatest fear wasn't the hard work, or the malnutrition, or the boredom, or the illness, or getting beaten up, or thrown in solitary confinement – it was having an extra six months nailed on to the end of my sentence. If I got my head down and made a show of working hard, it was less likely that Maximovich and the other factory guards would pick on me. Some of the guys in the factory just didn't give a shit because their sentences were so long there was no point playing the parole game and trying to impress the guards. The guards didn't like the defiant 'go-fuck-yourself' attitude of the long-termers because they saw it as an affront to their authority or machismo, or even their Russian pride. ('Nigger' was a word I heard every day in Zone 22.) Every other day a guard would give a prisoner a blow across the shoulder-blades with his stick and shout at him to work faster ... or to stop smiling ... or to stand up when he walked past ... or for looking at him funny ... At first I didn't like seeing a fellow prisoner wince or yelp in pain – even if it was one of the scary or devious wankers – but after a few weeks I was secretly pleased to see them take a lashing because there was only a limited amount of thrashings that even a poorly educated, dumb-fuck, prejudiced, backwater prison guard could reasonably hand out in a week. The lazy, cocky guys were effectively drawing the fire away from the rest of us, and that was just fine by me.

If the sewing factory had been a real company, I had become a middle manager, and the perks of my promotion were a break from the maddening monotony of work on the floor and the privilege of being able to talk to someone without the fear of getting a truncheon across the back. It wasn't quite being made head of the European Derivatives desk at Garban Icap, but it had been a goal worth working towards all the same. I had learned quickly that in prison you took anything, no matter how small, that made your life that little bit more comfortable. If someone offered you a cigarette, you took it, whether you smoked or not. If you were given food you didn't want or didn't need, you kept it and traded it, or gave it to someone as a favour because you knew that person would repay you somehow, one day. I remembered Zubi screaming at Pasha in my first week in Piet Central because he rejected the small sardine-like fish the *bilander* man had handed through the hatch. It was a horrible, crappy little fish and I was looking at Zubi and thinking: What's the big fucking deal? But a few weeks later, I understood. A small fish was a rare treat, and Pasha could have given it to me or Zubi. Hang on to everything in prison because everything has a value. (Pasha, weirdly, never arrived in Zone 22. No one had heard of him, although one prisoner told me that he knew of a guy fitting his description who'd gone nuts on the train down and was taken away to Zone 19.)

Promotion from the factory floor to the office was a massive step up for me, but it came with its own demanding challenges. Our main job was to organize each project for the factory. We took charge of each delivery of cloth and worked out how to convert a pile of dyed rags into the amount of products that the authorities demanded in the time allotted. The hardest part of working in the office was dealing with Maximovich the master guard, who spent his life in one of two states, drunk or hungover, and it was difficult to say which one made him the more bad-tempered and unreasonable.

He spent most of the day in his dark little office next door smoking cigarettes and drinking vodka, coming out every hour or so to patrol the factory floor and harangue the workers. Other times he'd come into our office, pull up a chair, put his feet up on the table and regale us with what he obviously thought were hilarious tales. I didn't have a clue what he was saying most of the time, but when Ergin and the Vietnamese boys forced out a laugh, I joined in too. But his moods changed in the bat of an eyelid. On my second day in the office he came and sat down with us, drunk as a lord after a long lunch, and began to tell us about the woman he'd just fucked in the back of his van. Ergin was translating for me as Maximovich slurred and wove his way through the story, and the joke, as far as I was able to work out, was that the special 'fuck-rug' Ergin had been forced to make for him was not comfortable enough and that he was going to give it either to his mongrel dog or his 'fat, ugly, monster' of a wife, whichever one was nicer to him when he got home.

Maximovich must have been at least fifty years old, but he fancied himself as a bit of a cool dude and a ladies' man. He wore his greying brown hair swept back like an ageing rock star, and his clothes looked good on him, compared to the other guards, because Molloi had altered them so that the length and cut were just right for the contours of his plump body. He earned no more than 200 dollars a month, but that made him one of the more glamorous and eligible catches in an area where most people scratched together a subsistence living, working in the fields or doing menial part-time jobs.

Every other afternoon, he came into our office to regale us with the details of his lunchtime shag in the back of his rusty little van, leaning back in his chair, slurping on a strong cup of *cheffir* and drawing on his cigarette, like a Wild West sheriff, as we sat and chuckled nervously across the table. We all hoped that the women of the area continued to oblige Maximovich, because when he hadn't got laid he tended to return to the factory wild and foul-tempered with drink, marching up and down the aisles, shouting and smashing his truncheon on the workers and their stations.

One afternoon he threw open the door to our office,

as if he was walking into a saloon for a shoot-out, and stood there swaying and hiccoughing.

'It will be summer soon! Make 200 summer caps for the prisoners. I want them in a week.'

'No problem, *nachalnik*,' said Ergin. 'Where are the materials you want us to use?'

'Materials? I don't know, use what you can find!'

For the next few days the four of us scoured the Zone for suitable materials, even scavenging through the bins, begging fellow prisoners for old clothes and trading our cigarettes for odd pieces of cardboard and plastic bottles that we could cut up to make stiff peaks for the caps. We gathered up hundreds of pieces of cloth scraps from earlier cuttings, dyed them all black, and handed them to Molloi, who had an amazing talent for turning the most unpromising and unlikely materials into proper, functioning items of clothing, and somehow succeeded in transforming our pile of rubbish into 200 pieces of reasonably presentable headwear.

Shortly after we had finished the summer cap job, and the main factory had finished its order for padded camo trousers, Maximovich, hungover and cranky as always, announced one morning that the factory was now to produce 500 camouflage nets for the tanks of the Russian army. This time the raw material for the nets had been delivered, but they were too big to be made on the sewing machines, and Ergin asked him: 'So how are we going to make them?'

'Well, I don't know, do I?' Maximovich roared. 'You're the experts! Come up with a plan!'

Ergin, who was clever, came up with the idea of

clearing the factory floor and building some frames from pieces of old timber and metal poles, on which we could hang the tank nets. He took me with him to present the idea to Maximovich, and told him we would need about 100 nails or screws to build the frames and 100 hooks on which to hang the nets, and that we could manage the rest with what we could find.

'How the hell do I know where you're going to get 100 nails and 100 hooks from?' he bellowed, and then, pointing at me, snapped: 'You, *anglichanin*. That is your job. Go, find the nails and hooks!'

'But where? How?' I replied feebly.

'Just find them!' he shouted back, flicking his truncheon at me. 'Make them if you have to! Go on, get out! OUT!'

For the next three days, while the rest of the factory set to work on preparing the netting material, I searched the Zone from top to bottom, hunting nails and hooks and old pieces of scrap metal from which we might be able to fashion some. I got a couple of dozen from the Uzbek maintenance man in exchange for a whole packet of Marlboro, another dozen or so by persuading prisoners to remove them from their bunks, a handful by removing them from the shelves and walls of the *atrads* and the rest from the Afghan electrician who ran the workshop next to the boiler room, which I paid for with tea, cigarettes and boiled sweets. For the hooks, Boodoo John gave me some old mangled pieces of metal and, borrowing a hacksaw, a hammer and a vice from the electrician, I made the 100 hooks by bending and bashing them into shape. Maximovich had told me I had until the end of the week to produce the whole lot, and for the last two days I had to work night shifts as well as days to make sure they were ready in time.

The only benefit that came from working in the sewing factory was that from time to time there was a couple of days' break between orders and, if they could find nothing else for us to do, the guards had little option but to leave us mooching around the *atrads*. Most of the prisoners were happy doing nothing, but I didn't like the downtime because time passed so slowly and the guards, who didn't like to see us not working, were even more irritable and aggressive than normal. When we finally finished the tank nets the materials for the next assignment still hadn't arrived and we spent half a week hanging around in the *atrads* waiting for the truck to turn up. On the fourth afternoon, the inactivity was making us fractious and a restless, tense air hung over the Zone. I was out in the exercise yard, bored out of my head, leaning up against the *atrad* in the warm sunshine, smoking a cigarette and swatting away a cloud of insects. A few feet away, Chan was doing his world's strongest man impression, the blood vessels in his neck looking as though they were on the verge of rupturing as he strained to lift the largest dumb-bell over his head for the hundredth time. When he dropped it to the ground, the tyres on either end bounced violently towards Ahmed and a group of others smoking around the pagoda shelter.

'Hey!' said Ahmed, stepping out of the shadow of the shelter and walking towards Chan aggressively, gesturing at the weights. 'The weights stay by the wall. Stop throwing them around!' Chan said nothing, and the pair stared each other down until they were interrupted by the arrival of Maximovich on the other side of the mesh fence, informing Ergin and me that a big delivery had arrived and that we were to assemble a dozen prisoners to go and unload it from the truck.

As soon as we opened up the back of the truck we knew something was wrong. Everyone standing within five yards of the truck recoiled as a fine cloud of foul-smelling dust billowed out into the sunshine, all of us coughing and spluttering and muttering words to the effect of 'What the fuck?' The reek of chemicals from the bales of old boiler suits was intense, and we all looked at each other, uncertain about what to do. I went to the storeroom and fetched the packet of builders' masks that Dad had brought out for me from his work site, but after unloading a couple of the bundles our eyes were streaming and our skin became itchy and sore. We carried on for a few minutes before throwing up our hands in protest and backing away from the truck.

'No way!' said Ergin. 'I tell Maximovich, it's too danger.' He disappeared into the factory and re-emerged two minutes later, pursued by the master guard, barking a mixture of orders and insults and waving his riot stick over his head like a Cossack heading into battle.

As he staggered towards us we shrugged our shoulders and shook our heads, and a couple of guys protested to him in Russian, appealing to him to reconsider, but he was insistent and, positioning himself fifty yards away, upwind and swaying from one foot to the other, he beckoned us back towards the truck with his riot stick. The bales were heavy, and to pick them up we had to get our hands right underneath them and lean them against our chests as we heaved them into the storeroom. An hour later we tramped back to the *atrads* for *preverka* in sullen silence, wheezing, scratching and rubbing our smarting eyes. The following morning half the men woke to find their skin covered in a livid red rash and small sores, while the rest of us still had itchy skin and breathing difficulties.

There were roughly 5,000 suits in all, and Maximovich announced at morning *preverka* that our task was to cut them up and turn them into as many pairs of fingerless mitts as possible. But once we had all been called through Sniper Alley to start work, the entire sewing factory workforce assembled outside the factory, refusing to go in. Faced with the threat of solitary confinement or a black mark – with a good beating thrown in for laughs – prisoners in Zone 22 never downed tools and refused to work. This was a first for Zone 22, and there was great tension in the air as we stood around in the bright sunshine, nervously shuffling our feet in the dirt and waiting in silence to see how the authorities responded. After a while, the Zone's dozen guard dogs were brought up from their kennels at the bottom of the camp, and all but a handful of the dozen guards on duty made their way into the factory compound, encircling the prisoners, in an uneasy stand-off. The snipers, who could usually be seen leaning against the posts of their towers willing their shift to be over, were now on full alert, training their guns on the mob below.

After a quarter of an hour, Maximovich re-emerged from inside the factory after talks with some of his more senior colleagues. He ordered us all to sit down cross-legged in the dirt so that he could address us, and shouted: 'Who's refusing to work?'

There was a long silence, finally broken when one of the African boys stood up and spoke to him in Russian. Ergin translated for me: 'I'll do whatever work you want, no matter how hard, but I'm not working with this shit. It's hazardous!' Immediately, a dozen others got to their feet to show their solidarity, followed by a dozen more. After five minutes almost half the workforce was standing, but I remained rooted to the earth, paranoid about black marks and thinking: give me a rash and a cough before another six months on my sentence, any day.

Maximovich, who was sober because it was morning, called Ergin out of the crowd to offer a compromise. As it was almost summer, Ergin said, relaying the deal, we could take our benches and do the work outside. The opportunity of a break from the misery of the factory and the chance to work out in the open with the sun on their backs was a temptation the majority of prisoners couldn't resist, and Ergin accepted the offer. With a half-cheer, we got up and slowly filed towards the factory as the guards and their dogs dispersed towards the gates. I brushed the dust off the seat of my black trousers and joined the back of the queue, still coughing and scratching, and I was just passing through the door when I heard Baska let out a yell from the stables behind us. Maximovich was already inside and the rest of the guards were back in the main compound of the Zone, so I hurried over to see what was troubling Baska. As I walked through the stable door, he was leaning up against the wall with one hand, shielding his eyes with the other, shaking his head. In front of him, lying on a bed of straw between her mother and Molloi, the colt, was the dead body of Nadezhda the foal.

'Hope dead, Hope dead,' said Baska.

26

Spring meant warmth and light, but more importantly, it meant football. The melting of the snow had revealed the Zone football pitch, an uneven stretch of patchy grass and weeds next to the low wooden block that housed the eating area and the library. The whole Zone was mad about football, and when it was announced after evening *preverka* that the first game of the season would take place at the end of the week and would be contested between Nigeria and Vietnam, it triggered chaos in the *atrads* as the prisoners argued over who was going to play. Most of the matches were 'internationals', but other fixtures included Chess section versus Sewing factory, Atrad 1 versus Atrad 3, Statya versus Statya (e.g. drugs pushers against thieves), and even an inter-Zone competition, pitching the foreigners of Zone 22 against teams made up of murderers, sex offenders or fraudsters. The international teams were chosen along loosely regional lines, so Nigeria was made up largely of Africans and Vietnam of south-east Asian guys, but it was the guards who had the final say on who was going to play. Predictably, it was the prisoners prepared to cough up the most cigarettes and other treats who often got the nod, but there were exceptions to this, and some of the poorer guys who were brilliant at football tended to make the starting line-up.

In the days leading up to the game my African friends were keen to recruit my services, because, being English, it was assumed by the other prisoners that I was only a marginally less gifted footballer than David Beckham. At school, rugby had been my game and I'd been good enough to play for the Kent Colts, but my football was no more than average. I was a solid, flat-footed defender whose greatest achievement was turning out a couple of times for the school second eleven, but finally I gave in and agreed to play on the condition that I could come on as a substitute. I was extremely nervous as we ran out of the *atrads* and started warming up, because it was obvious from the first few kicks that there were some seriously talented footballers in our midst, even though only half the players were wearing training shoes on both feet. The rest wore a mixture of plimsolls, winter boots and prison issue shoes, sometimes with a different type on either foot. My Nikes may have been the flashest trainers in the Zone but I was comfortably the least talented footballer on that pitch.

Dozens of other prisoners had bribed the guards to come and watch the match, and when it got under way half the camp was strung along the touchlines cheering and screaming for their continent of origin as the tackles flew in. Some of the Africans were superb players, and Julian, from the boiler room, was an outstanding goal-keeper, throwing himself about his area with incredible bravery and athleticism. But the best player by some distance was a Vietnamese lad from Atrad 3, who, despite being the smallest player on the pitch and wearing ordinary black leather shoes, ran circles around the

Africans, and once dribbled and wove his way from one end of the pitch to the other before he was finally tackled.

The game grew increasingly frenetic and violent as the first half wore on, and I waited with increasing apprehension to be brought on. Each half was thirty minutes long, and shortly into the second I was summoned on to the pitch to try to help Nigeria overturn a 4–2 deficit. I trotted nervously over to the right of the defence. It must have been getting on for a year since the last time I'd run more than about 100 yards and by the time I'd reached the other side of the pitch I was hacking and wheezing and my lower legs felt as if they had been filled with concrete. After a short while, Julian rolled the ball to me from the area and immediately I went to get rid of it to the guy standing ten yards to my left, but I mis-hit it badly and it squirted off the outside of my trainer. The two Vietnamese guys running to tackle me were completely wrong-footed by my error, and when the ball shot past them I raced clear, to the huge cheers of the African supporters who thought I had just produced an outrageous piece of skill with my first touch of the ball. As I ran down the line looking for someone to offload the ball to as quickly as possible (before everyone realized I was shit), I could hear the chants from the other side of the pitch: 'Beckham! Beckham! Beckham!'

A couple of minutes later, my lungs still burning from my world-class run, their goalkeeper launched a huge kick downfield, curling in my direction, and as I leapt to head it clear, under the challenge of a Vietnamese, I felt something pop in my left eye and immediately put my hands to my face as I hit the ground. I left the field with my eye streaming and, after giving my trainers to one of my team-mates, returned to the *atrad*.

The following morning the eye was swollen, full of pus and red, and there was a lump on the lid the size of a golfball. Every morning after breakfast there were at least a dozen people lined up to see the doctor, half of them malingerers with minor complaints who bribed her to give them a couple of days' off work, but that day there were at least thirty people in the queue with genuine complaints, mainly breathing problems, caused by the chemical suits. I was convinced that my problem had also been caused by handling the material, or had at least weakened my eyes and made them susceptible to infection or injury. I had a legitimate complaint, but I wasn't taking any chances, and as I entered her little cupboard surgery I placed a packet of Rothmans and a KitKat that Mum had brought from England into the open drawer of her desk. All the officials and governors did the same. You never handed a bribe directly to them and they never acknowledged the gifts that were brought. It was a ritual of pretending that nothing underhand was going on, and allowed them to feel that they weren't corrupt. The doctor signed me off work indefinitely and told me to come back to see her in five days, but she didn't give me any cream or tablets, saying that with a bit of rest, it would probably heal of its own accord over time. I could tell that there was more wishful thinking than sound medical reasoning behind her claim.

For the next four days I lay in bed willing the swelling to reduce and the pus to subside, praying before I fell asleep that it would be better in the morning. But each day it grew that little bit larger, and by the time I returned to her surgery on the Monday, the eye had ballooned to the size of a tennis ball and pus was oozing out from all sides and caking around the socket. I could tell by her reaction when I walked through the door that she was genuinely disturbed by what she saw, and I braced myself for the inevitable.

'Hospital for Hague Tig,' she said, writing something into her notes.

I knew it was coming, but still my heart sank and a shiver of fear ran over me as memories of that sprawling, decrepit, lawless, forsaken hellhole flashed through my mind. The medical facilities in the Zone were extremely basic, and if a prisoner's complaint was serious he was shipped off to the hospital prison, where – as I knew from my own experience – the treatment was also almost medieval in its simplicity. Since I had arrived in Mordovia, three guys had come back from there missing a part of their body: one without an eye, one without a finger and one without a thick scoop of his calf where he'd developed a large abscess. The prison system had neither the resources nor the will to give prisoners proper treatment and the prevailing clinical approach was: if in doubt, chop it off or out. The joke in Zone 22 was that they didn't have doctors in the hospital, but butchers.

The hospital train ran on Tuesdays and Thursdays, so before going to bed I packed my suitcase for the morning, cramming it with as many cigarettes and as much coffee and chocolate as I could to use as bribes for the hospital staff. I could tell by the quiet, sympathetic way that Ahmed and the Africans spoke to me that they understood the seriousness of the situation.

'I will make sure no one touches your food and cigarettes,' said Ahmed as I headed for the door the following morning, dragging my suitcase behind me.

'Let Boodoo John have what he wants,' I replied, handing him sixty Marlboro.

Boodoo John and the other boiler-room boys were in the exercise yard to see me off and he gave me a hug and a pat on the back. The others shook my hand and wished me well. I knew they were all thinking the same thing: Tig was coming back one eye short – with a pirate's patch on his face, just like everyone else who'd been sent to the hospital prison with a serious eye infection.

Back in late December it had been with a very light spring in my step and a small sensation of optimism running through me that I had walked into that hospital reception area, looking forward to some better food and some proper rest in a proper bed. But now I pushed open the main doors with all the enthusiasm of a man heading to his execution. I had many fears about my return there. First, the hospital was a *volk*-controlled Zone and there were barely any guards around to protect people from the many deranged and dangerous prisoners wandering the campus as they wished. Secondly, serious illness was rife there, and even though the TB sufferers had a high pen running round their building to stop them getting out, there were plenty of other contagious conditions to be worried about. The hospital facilities and medications available for the patients would have shamed a Crimean field hospital, and I wasn't confident they had the knowledge or the means to help me recover. I was convinced that they were simply going to cut out my eye. But my biggest fear on arrival was that the infection was going to spread to the other eye and I was going to lose them both.

They put me in a small dormitory of ten bunks on the ground floor of the new arrivals building, with a couple of guys from Atrad 2 in Zone 22 and three from Zone 5, the camp for corrupt police, FSB and lawyers, who were kept separate from the other prisoners for their own safety. The room was as plain and depressing as a room can be: faded wooden floorboards, wooden bunks with coarse grey blankets, strip light, dirty windows. The arrangements were a big improvement on the freak-show dormitory they'd put me in six months ago, but it was slightly discomforting because everyone in the room was a recent arrival, yet to have their disease or condition diagnosed. God only knew what they were suffering from as they lay on their beds, groaning and coughing and holding their heads in their hands.

For the first three days, nobody came to give me treatment or even to inform me of my appointment time, and every time I went to reception to ask what was happening, they just shrugged their shoulders and held out their hands in ignorance. New arrivals came and went, transferred to more permanent accommodation in different buildings, and after forty-eight hours I was the only person left in the dormitory. I spent most of the day lying on my bunk and writing long letters to Lucy and Mum and Dad, because I'd been told there was no censorship of the mail in the hospital as there was back in Zone 22. I had brought with me a bundle of diaries I had written over the previous few weeks, and at the end of the second day I posted the whole lot in the mailbox outside reception.

My eye was still completely closed over, and every time I felt a throb of pain or a trickle of pus on my cheek my mind instantly filled with dreadful thoughts about what the doctors planned to do with it. I resolved that I wasn't going to agree to go under general anaesthetic and that if they were going to cut my eye out, they'd have to take me down with a tranquilizer dart.

I spent much of the day leaning on the windowsill staring out over the camp, watching the prisoners stroll at will around the massive, drearily functional Zone and praying that my eye would start to show signs of improvement. There were at least twenty large red-brick and grey stone buildings in the Zone, all in a state of advanced disrepair, and each with its own parade ground out front, suggesting that the hospital had once been an army headquarters of some kind. Between the roads and the paved squares a few scruffy shrubs filled the untended, litter-strewn flowerbeds. From time to time I nervously ventured outside to have a cigarette and to give my legs a stretch, but I didn't hang around for long because the place was crawling with all sorts of weirdos and scary-looking bastards, many of them clearly in mental distress. They walked or stood around in a state of obvious agitation, talking to themselves, shouting, pulling their hair or crouched up in a ball with their face buried in their hands. There was one guy from the building next door who used to spend much of the day leaning against the wall with his head, groaning.

But the most shocking sight was that of the men who had been sentenced to *ossoboni* regime. *Ossoboni* is the most severe regime of all, and it is reserved for the most dangerous criminals in Russia: murderers, serial rapists and the worst paedophiles. When I first saw a small group of them being walked through the Zone, I stared in horror as they drew nearer, transfixed by the grotesque posture they'd been made to assume. Crouched forward so that their back was at ninety degrees to their legs, their hands were cuffed behind them and pointing up towards the sky. It looked like a virtually impossible position to hold for more than a few seconds, but each time their arms dropped down towards their backside, one of their special guards gave them a thrash with his stick.

On the fourth day, an orderly came into the dormitory to tell me that I had an appointment with one of the doctors. (Other than when an orderly came in at meal-times with my food, it was the first time an official or a medic had come into the dormitory for two days.) My eye was just as bad as it had been a week earlier, and a shudder of dread ran over me as I began to load up with as many bribes as I could fit down my baggy trousers and under my jacket. I had an entire roll of Marlboro, a large jar of Nescafé, two bars of chocolate, a bag of mints, a lighter and a bottle of perfume, which, I figured, was probably about the going rate for an eye in there, or at the very least would buy me a few days' reprieve and a course of antibiotics. As I set off across the Zone in search of the right building, I was walking like a cowboy after three days in the saddle, trying to stop half of Tesco's from falling down my legs and praying that the chocolate bars in my pants wouldn't have melted by the time I got there.

I found the building more by luck than by design, and sat down under a bright, flickering striplight in an un-supervised corridor of plastic chairs with half a dozen other prisoners in varying degrees of pain and distress. Most of the problems presented by the patients appeared as much mental as physical, and many of them, it seemed, were recovering junkies in withdrawal who were also suffering from related illnesses such as hepatitis and lung disorders. I'd never seen such a fucked-up, grotesque, hopeless collection of human beings as were sat in that corridor, and for an hour I barely moved a muscle so as not to draw attention to myself. I was as frightened as I had been at any time since leaving Moscow, appalled by the condition of the other prisoners and terrified by the more deranged and intimidating ones. With no guards or officials to keep order, half of them walked up and down the dim corridor talking to themselves, demanding cigarettes from the other prisoners, picking arguments with each other or just stopping and staring. Others were crouching forward in their seats or rocking back and forth, moaning in pain and anguish. It was like a scene from a horror movie: a corridor full of freaks and ghouls and the living dead . . .

But I would have happily sat there for a week rather than go and see the doctor.

When finally he put his head round the door and summoned me to his room, I unloaded all my goods on to his table and then put my hands together in prayer and begged him, in English: 'Please don't cut my eye!'

'*Neeprizhivay! Neeprizhivay!*' ('Don't worry! Don't worry!') he said, patting the air over his desk and opening a set of magnifying glasses. A slight figure with grey receding hair, he came round the desk and I could smell his musty breath as he moved his face inches from mine and inspected the infection with one of the glasses. Next he made me look at an old-fashioned eye chart on the wall and, pointing at the large ones, he asked me to tell him the letters. Not knowing the proper words for them, I grunted their sound, like a caveman or an imbecile. He then handed me a card to put over my good eye and started through the chart all over again, but as my bad eye was still completely closed up – and I hoped he might have spotted that with his big magnifying glass – I couldn't see a bloody thing and so each time I heard him prompt me, I shrugged my shoulders and sighed: 'Not a fucking clue, my friend. It's dark.'

He sat back down at his desk, scrawling something into his notebook, and proceeded, at great length and great speed, to give me his diagnosis of my problem – at least that's what I thought he was doing, because he might just as well have been reading out the Russian football results as far as I was concerned. As soon as he was finished, he motioned for me to leave but I threw up my hands and cried: 'Please, please, what did you say? I don't understand.'

But he didn't understand me either, and seeing my anxiety, he sighed loudly, picked up his phone and called in a young female assistant for help. This time it took him no more than ten seconds to explain the situation and, flicking her jet black hair out of her eyes, she turned to me and said: 'Doctor saying five more days of ugly eyes and you having the operation.'

'No, no, no,' I said quietly, barely able to speak. 'Please, no! What about antibiotics, or cream, please don't cut my eye out, please don't cut my eye out . . .'

For five days I lay on my bunk frozen with worry, staring at the ceiling with my good eye, yearning for my other one to heal. On the morning of the fifth day – the deadline for my eye – the swelling was still as large, tender and infected as it had been, and the mounting panic and dread I'd felt all week started to give way to resignation. I began to feel almost indifferent about losing it. By then a greater fear had emerged, that the infection, having proved so stubborn, was inevitably going to spread to other parts of my body, or even into my blood, and I began to convince myself that, in fact, it was sensible to have the bad eye taken out after all.

For hour after hour that day I watched the door, waiting for a guard or functionary to stick his head round and beckon me with his finger, but the morning passed and still no one came, then the afternoon and still no one. The sixth day passed in the same way. On the morning of the seventh, I woke to find a pool of pus on my mattress and when I put my hand to my eye, the swelling had reduced by almost 50 per cent. By the end of the day, after washing away the gunk, I was able to see through the narrowest of slits, and by the next, the eye was half open. It had become frantically itchy, which I took as con-firmation that finally, after two weeks, I was on the mend.

In all I spent ten days in the little dormitory after my one appointment with the doctor, and throughout the entire time not one nurse or official came to visit me. No pills, no cream, no treatment, no appointments and, thank God, no operation. They just forgot about me. My eye was saved by an admin error, a clerical cock-up, a bureaucratic oversight. On the morning of the tenth day I went down to reception and, seeing the improvement in my eye, the man behind the desk, said: 'The train is today. You want go home Zone 22?'

'Yeah, why not?' I said. So I caught the train 'home'.

I could never have imagined it even a few weeks earlier, but a sensation of relief, bordering on happiness, washed over me and I exhaled loudly as I stepped out on to the platform of Zone 22 and, accompanied by one of the guards, strode across Sniper Alley and towards the office building. The sun was starting its final descent over the horizon and the football teams were filing back towards the *atrads*. The match was over now and, under the vengeful eyes of the guards, who hated the sight or sound of us having fun, everyone had gone back into prisoner mode and fallen silent. But as we passed by in opposite directions, the African boys and one or two of the others gave me a big grin or a wink, and I smiled back, pointing to both my eyes. Zone 22 was shite, but it was better than having my eye dug out in a lunatic asylum.

I still had a few provisions left, and when I lifted my bag on to the reception table to be checked, the guard helped himself to two packets of Marlboro and a bar of chocolate, not even looking at me as he slid them into his pocket. Little Alan, the office dogsbody, appeared at the open window and with a big smile and a wave said: 'Welcome again, English. Hey, you still have many eyes!'

27

'A friend of yours from Moscow arrived in the Zone while you were in hospital,' said Boodoo John as he rotated his fork in his bowl of noodles. 'Tall black guy with a big moustache. Gotta lot to say for himself . . .'

'Zubi?' I interrupted, the metal legs of the grey plastic chair scraping along the floor as I pushed away from the table. 'Where is he?'

'He's got another week in quarantine before they put him in Atrad 3. He was telling everyone before *preverka* the other night how he was going to show us a few things about how to deal with the guards. He's going to have a hard time in here if he carries on playing Mr Big, and not just from the guards either. He wants to see you, anyhow.'

After washing my bowl under the tap in the washroom I put it back in the food cupboard, took out all but two cigarettes from a packet of Marlboro and dropped in two teaspoons of coffee. I could tell the young, spotty *atradnik* didn't like my impatience as I darted into the little office that the duty guards shared with Ahmed and slid the cigarette packet under his weaponry magazine, which was sitting unopened on his desk. The cover of June's issue showed a missile streaking towards a fighter jet against a brilliant blue sky. Slowly he got to his feet and sidled to the entrance to the *atrad*, where he signalled to the observation room to let me out.

I was excited about seeing Zubi, and I'd often thought about all the kindness he'd shown me back in Moscow. Yuri, the guard who had bantered with Dad, was on duty in the guards' room and he waved me down the corridor as I walked in. Zubi was sitting on his bunk brewing up some noodles in a bowl at his feet. He was whistling to himself and his head bobbed up and down as he swayed from side to side.

'Have you not learnt to cook anything decent yet?'

Zubi spun round and leapt to his feet. 'Hey! English boy!'

We gave each other a bear hug and slapped each other on the back and made whooping noises.

'I was told you were having your little English eyes chopped out! But you look, you look, er, OK ... thin but OK, man. You look real thin. You been working out and jogging?' Zubi moved around restlessly as he spoke, as if he was nervous of me.

We both laughed. He didn't look great either. His eyes were baggier and his shoulders were stooped, and in spite of the bravura and the banter there was an air of insecurity about him now. His confidence had gone. He was just front.

It was clear from the moment we greeted each other that we were two different people from the ones that had met in Piet Central that muggy evening in July. I was the stronger, savvier one now. I was in control. I had been in Zone 22 for five months and it was my turn to offer the advice. Zubi's appeals had been drawn out over months, but at the end of it his ten-year sentence, with parole in five, remained unchanged. It was hard to see how a rebellious, cocky personality like his was going to survive in a 'black' prison like Zone 22, where you need to go equipped with discretion, hard work and humility to get by. The last time I'd seen him in Moscow he'd seemed a broken man, but now all the attitude and mouth was back, though this time it was ringing hollow. My heart sank as I listened to him telling me how he was going to show 'the pussies in Zone 22 that Zubi don't take no shit from no one'.

'Zubi, trust me, my friend. It's different in here. You're not going to get on with people if you give it the Mr Bigshot stuff. It just doesn't work. They'll slowly grind you down. They'll keep extending your sentence at the slightest excuse, they'll throw you in solitary, they'll give you the shittiest jobs, they'll turn on you at every opportunity ...'

'Yeah, yeah, yeah. Thanks for the advice, English boy, but Zubi knows how to handle himself, wouldn't you say? Zubi's smarter than these dumb hillbilly mother-fuckers. Zubi can run rings round 'em. Zubi don't take shit from no one ...'

'Well, good luck, Zubi,' I said, surprised to hear myself raising my voice. 'I'm trying to help you, like you helped me. I think you've got it wrong. That's all I'm saying. You say you're smart, but you're acting dumb if you ask me. You're heading for trouble, I'm telling you. Trust me ...'

'Fuck you!' said Zubi, pointing his finger at my face. It was hot in the room and sweat ran down from his temples and clung to his black T-shirt. 'What do you fucking know anyway, English boy? Zubi'll do it his way, and you do it yours and we'll see who gets the best results in here. If you want these fuckers to walk all over you, then that's fine, you just let them humiliate you. But Zubi's still got some fucking pride!'

I was grateful for all Zubi had done for me in Moscow, and that was never going to change, and I'd also go to his help if he was in dire trouble, but what I wasn't going to do was jeopardize my own chances of getting out of the Zone. If that meant spiking our friendship, then so be it. As I trudged back to the *atrad*, waving the fucking mosquitoes away from my face, I resolved to distance myself from him over the coming weeks. I didn't want to associate myself with a troublemaker and undermine the relationship I had been trying to build up with the administration over the previous couple of months. I'd been working hard and keeping out of trouble, I'd paid Zanpolit a visit every three weeks or so, dropping in a jar of coffee, some cigarettes and other luxuries. I'd arranged for Mum and Dad to raise the funds for the TV, video recorder, two computers ... Slowly I was prising my way, if not into his affections, then at least on to his radar, so that come the end of the year I'd be in as strong a position as possible before launching my push for freedom. I was just one of dozens, a hundred even, all trying to win Zanpolit's favour and get themselves promoted up the parole ladder. While I used gifts of cigarettes and chocolates to advance my case, others used information about other prisoners and even about other officials and guards. Whatever the currency, we were all working in the same volatile, highly competitive market.

From the moment Zubi was transferred to Atrad 3 two days later, he started standing up and challenging the regime. From a distance, I watched him ambling slowly into line at *preverka*, I heard him talking loudly in the exercise yard to show the guards he wasn't scared. He puffed his chest out and he strutted like a peacock wherever he went. He was put to work in the chesspiece section of the factory, where he immediately fell in with a group of the most intimidating, troublesome Africans in the Zone. He wasn't leading an uprising exactly, but by his disrespectful, insolent manner towards the guards and his show of contempt for the regime he was storing up trouble for himself. The guards restrained themselves at first, almost willing him on, letting him talk his way into a position where they would feel justified in making his life a living hell. Zubi was an asset in Moscow; now he was a liability and it was dangerous for me to associate with him. Slowly, without making it obvious to him, I backed out of our friendship.

Zubi's arrival made me realize that all friendships in prison were either limited, or conditional, or both. They were limited in two respects: first, because there was no more than a handful of people in Zone 22 I'd even consider as friend 'material', and second, because the regime in which we lived was so strict and tightly controlled that it was impossible for a relationship to develop naturally with the very small handful of people in the Zone who spoke passable English or French and didn't fall into the categories of scary bastard, weirdo, cultural alien, religious freak, slippery two-faced informer or crashing bore. And what relationships I did strike up were conditional in that I chose my 'friends' because they could improve my life in some way. Some befriended people for their cigarettes and food or because they came from the same country, others because they wanted protection or influence. Prisoners of the same nationality (*zemliaki*) tended to gravitate towards each other, which made them tighter, but as the only Briton in the camp that wasn't an option for me. I became something of a loner, loosely affiliated to the Africans. I liked Ergin, I liked the African boys as a group, I felt an elder brother's affection for Molloi and Mafia, I felt some kind of connection with Sacha and Benny because we were 'Westerners', but as spring quickly surrendered to the heat of the summer, it struck me that the only person in Zone 22 I would even consider calling a 'friend' was Boodoo John. But, even then ... would I ever go for a beer with him on the outside?

The truth was that I didn't want friends. There wasn't space in my little world to fit them in. All my emotions were drained by my love and thoughts for Lucy and my family, by my shame and guilt, by my fears of what was to become of me in Zone 22, by my effort not to rise to the provocation of the guards and by my anxiety about how to restart my life again on the outside when I eventually got out. There was simply nothing left in the tank to give. I just wanted my 'friends' to be people I could rub along with OK, who wouldn't grass on me or fight me, and at the back of my mind I was always aware that when I left the Zone I would never see my fellow inmates again. What was the point in making another friend, only to abandon him like I'd abandoned Zubi?

28

It was the beginning of June and I had been back in the Zone for a week, ticking off the days to my parole day, when a rumour spread around the factory like bushfire that a female visitor had arrived and that it was me she had come to see. The first I knew of it was when I walked on to the factory floor from the office, carrying a new bundle of material, and some of the African boys immediately started taking the mickey. 'Hey, English is going to get his nuts wet tonight ... English boy will be *pushin' the cushion*, eh? ...'

After years of working in the office building, Alan and the other prisoners employed there had become masters at identifying the nationality of passports from the quickest glimpse. Alan had let the word out that morning that he had spotted Raisa Petrovna processing a burgundy red passport. That meant the visitor was almost certainly from Europe – and that could only mean they were coming to visit one of two people: me or the Dutch guy, Sacha. My heart jumped at the thought that Lucy might be just a few hundred yards beyond the prison walls, and I could barely sit still when I returned to the office. We hadn't spoken since our hurried five-minute chat on the phone three months earlier. All the letters she'd written me had turned up in a bundle in April and I knew she was planning a visit some time in the summer, but

I didn't know exactly when. They didn't tell a prisoner that he had a visitor until a couple of hours before they arrived in the accommodation block. It was a way of keeping happiness to a minimum. After an hour, I could stand the tension no longer and went next door to see Maximovich, who was sitting at his messy desk with a blank expression on his face. The top two buttons of his olive shirt were undone and he was flapping the collars up and down to try to cool himself down. Two dark patches spread out from under his arms.

'*Spasiba, nachalnik*,' I said, nodding respectfully. 'Visitor for me?' He shrugged his shoulders and blew the air through his lips, as if to say, 'I don't know and I don't give a fuck,' and he waved me away as if I was a fly as he slouched back in his chair.

Around four o'clock, towards the end of the shift, I'd given up hope, convinced that the rumour of my visitor was no more than that, just a phantom hope. It was by no means the first time a rumour had come to nothing in Zone 22, where we were so desperate for excitement and novelty, anything to talk about and distract us from the monotonous grind, that we were all constantly fuelling speculation and peddling gossip. It was a way of keeping hope alive.

As we began to pack away the materials and tools and tidy up, one of the guards opened the door and flicked his head behind him, urging me to follow him. A burst of adrenaline coursed into my system and I jumped to my feet, trying not to rush or smile and betray my excitement. The guards didn't like to see us smiling because they took it to mean that the regime obviously wasn't harsh enough and that they weren't doing their jobs properly. Ergin gave me a little salute and the Vietnamese boys just grinned as I bounded from the room. Every fibre in my body was yearning to break into a sprint and cry out with joy, but I had to hold myself in check as I followed him out into the muggy June heat, out of the Zone and into the reception area of the visitors' block.

Raisa Petrovna was grinning as she handed me a form that I had to fill in before a young, pale, spotty-faced guard with spiky blond hair led me through the first of two barred gates and down a long, unlit corridor into the little visitors' apartment where I'd stayed with Mum and Dad. I knew that as Lucy and I weren't married we were only entitled to three hours in each other's company before I returned to the Zone and she was driven the twelve hours back to Moscow. The guard sat down on the chair by the door as I paced the room, looking down the corridor and listening for signs of her arrival. It was part of the same unofficial prison policy that outlawed smiling and laughter that when a prisoner was presented with a reason to be happy, like a visit from a loved one (except when it was a mother) or the arrival of a food parcel, the authorities would make a concerted effort to remove as much of the joy from the occasion as they could. So when your visitor arrived, they kept you waiting as long as possible in order to eat into the time that you were officially allowed together, and when you received a food parcel, the guards, who checked the contents for illicit possessions, helped themselves to what they wanted before they handed it over. So it was that day, as I waited for an hour while they made Lucy sit in the reception area, fifty yards down the corridor, just for the sheer spite of it. It was agonizing because I knew she was there, although out of sight and sound, and I had to suppress a rage of hatred and frustration as I fidgeted and walked up and down the room, desperate to lay eyes on her after seven long months. Every minute we waited was a minute less we'd have together. The guard must have noticed my discomfort, and I looked at him from time to time to try to stir up some sympathy, but he just leant back in his chair, a combat boot slung over a knee, yawning, drawing on his cheap Russian cigarettes and wiping the sweat from his brow.

But what an entrance when she did come! All I could see was Lucy's dark profile against the light as she stood at the end of the corridor waiting for the guard to unlock the barred gate, her mane of wavy brown hair bouncing around as she waved at me with both hands. When the guard let her through she came bursting down the tunnel, letting out an almost primeval scream, 'Aaaaaaaaaah!' as she dived into my arms and smothered my face with kisses and tears. I was crying too, but I was holding back because the guard was sitting just a few feet away and I could feel the contempt of his glare as he watched us embrace. I wanted to dance around the room with her and burst out laughing, but I knew the risks that came with overt displays of happiness and I just held her to me as tight as I could and whispered in her ear, over and over again, 'I love you so much, Lucy!'

After twenty seconds or so the guard grunted at us and motioned for us to sit down, Lucy on the old brown sofa and me on the orange armchair across the other side of the room. Physical contact with visitors was not allowed unless they were your wife or your parents. For two hours Lucy and I sat facing each other, five yards apart, tears running down our cheeks as we talked, while the guard sat halfway between us like a tennis umpire, making sure we didn't touch each other. The prison authorities said this policy was a form of discipline, a means of control, but to me it was a form of torture, for us both. The woman I loved, and who loved me, had spent three days travelling to the other side of Europe to see me; she had spent the better part of two thousand pounds in flights, hotels, petrol and provisions for me – money she could not afford, working as a temp in the City, and had had to borrow from the bank; she was only allowed to see me for two hours after their malicious delaying tactics, and then – to rub our noses a little further into the dirt – we were made to sit on opposite sides of the room to each other, like strangers on a bus. What sick, perverse Soviet bastard thought that one up?

When the guard went to the kitchen to plunder his fill from the supermarket shopping Lucy had brought for me from Moscow, I darted across the room to give her a hug. I leant down and buried my face in her neck, breathing in the familiar smell of her shampoo and perfume, but almost immediately I was swivelling round as the guard shouted '*Nyet! Nyet!*' and pulled me away from her by the arm, pushing me back across the other side of the room. I was so enraged by the little shit that I had to restrain every instinct in my body from throwing myself at him and pummelling his zitty face into the floor. I slowly sat back down, glaring at him, while he looked back at me with mocking contempt, a half-nervous smile riding up his cheek.

It must have been at least 30 degrees outside, the hottest day of the year so far, and Lucy, bless her woollen socks and jumper, was clearly in some discomfort. The last time she'd been to visit me, back in December, the temperature had been 15 degrees below; she had no idea that Russia also had blistering hot summers, so she'd packed only her warmest clothes, and arrived in the Zone wearing her fake fur coat! She couldn't take her woollen top off because she was wearing only a bra underneath, so I gestured to the guard that she was feeling the heat and pointed to the window for permission to open it, but he just shook his head. I threw him a full packet of Marlboro Reds from the roll Lucy had brought me, but still he refused, so I threw him another ... and another ... until finally, eighty Western cigarettes to the good, he got up and opened it – about six inches.

'Stupid thing is, Babes, that if we were married we'd be allowed to hold each other and this cock wouldn't be in the room,' I sighed, exasperated. 'You could even come and stay the night! A sleepover! But being in love, without a certificate to prove it, is no good. How screwed up is that?'

'Well, why don't we get married?' said Lucy, wiping her forehead with a tissue.

'You're kidding! What? In this dump? Where would we go for a honeymoon? Solitary confinement? Lucy, I'd marry you tomorrow if I could. One of the thoughts – well, more of a dream really – that has kept me going all these months, is the image in my mind of you and I walking up the aisle, arm in arm, husband and wife . . . besides, they wouldn't let anyone get married in here. They don't do happy occasions in here.'

'Well, you never know. It may be one of your official rights. If we did get married, I'd be able to see you twice more before you get out. As it is, we won't see each other till next year . . .'

We both looked down at the floor as Lucy's voice trailed away.

'Anyway,' she continued. 'I think it would be romantic to get married in a prison! How many people can say that?'

'Yeah, that'd be something NOT to tell the grandchildren.'

If the plan – and I'm absolutely convinced that it *was* a policy – was to ruin my happiest two hours since flying out of London almost a year earlier, then the authorities of Zone 22, and especially the little pizza-faced wanker of a guard, were able to reflect on a job well done. When we got up to say goodbye Lucy and I walked towards each other for a hug, but when we were about a yard apart, the guard rose from his chair and brought his arm down between us, turning to me and shaking his head.

'Please, come on . . .' I protested.

'Will you marry me?' Lucy said, tears running down her face as she turned round at the doorway.

'Yes!!'

Lucy smiled through the tears and disappeared down the corridor to make the long journey back to Moscow.

*

I tried not to show how much the little bastard Joe-90 of a guard had upset me as he escorted me back through Sniper Alley and into the Zone. Back at the *atrad*, I paced up and down the exercise pen like a wounded animal, kicking the dirt and aggressively swatting away the swarms of mosquitoes and midges that had recently arrived with the hot weather. In the smoking shelter I drew on my cigarettes with a fury, exhaling long and hard into the muggy air. Boodoo John and the African boys were talking in a huddle near the entrance but they kept their distance and said nothing. For once, no one asked me for a cigarette. Like a madman muttering to myself, I cursed the guard, I cursed Zone 22, I cursed Russia. *Fucking Russian bastards!*

Chan, as ever, was near the wall of the *atrad*, drenched in sweat as he held the two smaller weights out at his sides, slowly bending his arms to bring them up to his shoulders and then back down again, over and over. For a brief moment our eyes met and locked as I ground out my cigarette butt with the sole of my trainer and started pacing up and down the small yard, spinning on my heel each time I reached the fence. I was walking a line about two yards in front of Chan, and each time I passed him he gave me the eyeball, like it was pissing him off that I was in his personal space. I stared back at him, my anger about Lucy's visit giving me the courage not to be intimidated by him. I was enjoying pissing him off, dumping my frustration on a guy who'd spooked me from the day I'd arrived in the *atrad*. Normally he scared me shitless, but right then, seething with fury, his menacing stares went straight through me and he could see I wasn't scared ... so he gobbed on me.

I'd turned round at the fence nearest the door to the *atrad* and was striding back to the other side, head down, wiping the sweat from my brow with my sleeve, when I heard Chan clear his nose and spit noisily in my direction. As I put my right foot forward a streak of gluey, green phlegm landed with a slap at the ankle of my baggy black trousers. In one motion I swung round, bringing my left fist down towards Chan's head, but he ducked and my momentum carried me past him so that I slammed against the wooden wall of the *atrad*. I tried to turn round but Chan was on top of me, smashing his fist into my ribcage, each of the three blows sending a streak of pain up the side of my chest. I swung out with my right arm and my elbow caught him on the side of the head and he stumbled backwards. As I turned round, a hand grabbed my shirt and pulled me backwards and aside as Julian, Eke Jude, Boodoo John and Hulk steamed past and shoved Chan hard into the corner of the yard. They didn't throw a single punch between them but just put their bodies between him and me, with Julian and Eke Jude pushing right up to him and towering over his squat frame. Chan stood with his fists out in front of him, ready to take on all-comers, staring at me between the bodies as I stared back at him, trying to get my breath back.

Boodoo John peeled away from the posse, put his arm on my shoulder and said: 'You OK?'

'Yes, I am. Thank you, my friend.'

29

After making so many cock-ups and wrong decisions in the weeks following my arrest in Moscow, when I arrived in Mordovia I'd been determined to learn how the system worked as quickly as I could. My Russian began to improve: by June I knew all the important words relating to prison life and the parole procedure and I had a wider grasp of the language, albeit a fairly basic one. When I went to see Zanpolit on the pretext of asking him about an aspect of my case but really to butter him up with a few bribes, I was able to hold simple conversations with him. At the same time, I was milking Boodoo John, Ergin and Yevgeny the librarian for information about the Russian judicial system, finding out how I could work the system from the inside, and how Lucy and my family could ratchet up the pressure on the outside. The better I could communicate and the more I learned, the more confident I began to feel about getting out of the Zone on time.

Roughly once a week I bribed my way into the admin offices to see Zanpolit and shuffled across from the *atrad* with various items of Western goods stuffed down my pants and trousers. He sometimes greeted me with an easy smile, almost as if he was genuinely pleased to see me, immediately opening the deep drawer of his desk for me to unload the offerings from my underwear. You never got more than a few minutes with one of the governors, but in that time Zanpolit would reassure me that he was certain, when it finally came round, that my case would be put to the top of the pile, and that he was confident, with his influence over the local judge, that it would be looked upon favourably. The message he was sending out to me was: 'Don't worry, it's all under control.'

What's more, I'd agreed to every single one of his invitations for me to make a 'contribution' to the Zone, each time calling the Embassy and asking for the funds to be paid into my prison bank account, or arranging for the Embassy to buy the goods directly and deliver them when they sent down a driver with some more provisions, every two months or so. Since March, my family had bought 'the Zone' a new television, a video recorder, two sofas, two computers and a large quantity of expensive paints, wallpaper and brushes, not to mention an endless supply of cigarettes, coffee, chocolates and a few more expensive luxury items such as lighters, pens and watches. It was no surprise that not one of these larger items was ever seen in the camp, all of them being shifted straight out the back door and into the homes of the top officials. I didn't give a toss if they went to the moon so long as they were winning me favour with the administration and smoothing my passage out of the place.

I was in a strong position, I thought. My supplies were good, I was playing the *udo* game with increasing skill and I'd so far managed to avoid falling foul of the guards. With them, just as I did with the governors, I played the humble, grovelling prisoner, repenting the error of his ways by working hard and avoiding trouble. When a guard entered the room I always made extravagant displays of respect, whipping off my hat, standing to attention and looking straight down to the ground. With the more severe guards, like the Undertaker, I sometimes even found myself making a little bow to them, just to be on the safe side. It was just as well that the vindictive, callous bastards had no idea of the true regard in which I held them. To me, with the exception of Yuri, they were all low-life scumbags, no better than the majority of the prisoners they treated with such contempt and brutality.

So it was that slowly I grew in confidence that I was going to be one of the fortunate ones and get released at roughly the time that had been scheduled by the court in Moscow. All the fundamentals of Zone life were as severe and unforgiving as ever, and the incredible heat, bringing with it a plague of mosquitoes, made the boredom almost unbearable at times. The heat was every bit as intense as the cold had been in the winter. The other prisoners kept telling me that the summer was the harshest season of all in Mordovia, but I didn't believe them – until it arrived. When we were shivering and sneezing in the dark depths of the winter, the sunshine and the heat were an appealing prospect, but once the temperature quickly began to climb into the mid-30s, we were soon panting like dogs and willing the rapid return of winter. But as the year headed towards its longest day and the light had barely faded when we retired to the dormitory, I was keenly aware that the day when I'd be a free man again was drawing ever closer. For the first time since my arrival, I was waking up in the morning buoyed by the confidence that I finally enjoyed some control over my destiny again. I was no longer a hapless victim of fate.

We'd been ordered to spend the evenings after work repainting the inside of the *atrads* from top to bottom, using paints and brushes that Mum and Dad had been obliged to buy in Moscow and which they'd brought down during their visit. One *atrad* was to be redecorated at a time, and while the work was going on we had to sleep in the Zone dining area, between the kitchen and the library. In the mornings we stacked up the bedding against the wall, and once the final sitting of the evening meal had taken place we cleared away the tables and benches and laid our mattresses on the floor. The new sleeping arrangements created a stir of excitement in the Zone as we set up our new home, like boy scouts heading out on our first camping trip. Any change from the grinding routine generated a buzz among us, and in what, by some distance, was the greatest act of leniency I'd experienced in Zone 22, the governors agreed to a request from all three *atrads* that we should be allowed to stay up a couple of hours later in order to be able to watch the European Championship football finals, live from Portugal. With a three-hour time difference, the games didn't finish until one in the morning, but the whole prison was so crazy about football – even the Afghans were obsessed – that everyone was prepared to sacrifice some sleep to watch the games. Those of us who could afford it donated as many goodies as we could into a bribery pot in order to secure the governors' approval, and on the strict conditions that there was no noise and that production in the factory didn't suffer, the authorities consented.

Every day there was constant banter and arguments over who was going to win the match, and soon prisoners started betting against each other on the outcome. The stakes were no more than a few cigarettes and never greater than a whole packet, but soon half of Atrad 1 was involved and a syndicate developed, run by a Vietnamese guy called Dang. I wasn't that interested in getting involved, because I already had plenty of cigarettes and I didn't feel comfortable about taking more off someone else, so I kept out of it for the first couple of nights. But on the first Sunday of the competition England were scheduled to play France in the evening and a few of the guys started taking the mickey that the French were going to stuff us. In order to prove how convinced I was that England were going to win, I said: 'OK, I'll bet a whole packet of Marlboro on it!' There were seventy of us crowded around the little black and white telly with the flickering screen that we had placed on a dining table at the far end of the room, and my bet was looking good when Frank Lampard headed us in front before half-time. We looked in total control until Zinedine Zidane scored two goals in the last two minutes, and then incredibly we'd lost. I didn't care about losing the fags, but England's defeat was especially painful to take. All my wider hopes felt as if they were riding on the outcome; to have them so cruelly dashed at the death was a bitter experience, and I lay down to sleep in an almighty stinker of a mood, the laughter of my taunters ringing in my ears.

Gambling of any sort was strictly prohibited in the Zone on the grounds that it encouraged violence, so we all understood the importance of keeping our private syndicate a secret within the *atrad*. We didn't even let on to the other *atrads*, and for all we knew they might have been running their own book. Dang wrote down all the names of the gamblers and the amount that we'd bet in a small exercise book, which he kept hidden under a floorboard.

The competition was a couple of weeks old and had entered the knockout stages when at *preverka* one morning the FSB *koom*, a stocky guy in his mid-thirties with a heavily pock-marked face, emerged from the offices holding a piece of paper. The governors only ever made an appearance at *preverka* when there was trouble, and the moment he stepped through the swing door and walked round to face the columns of men from Atrad 1, we all threw each other anxious glances and started nervously shuffling our boots in the dirt.

It sounded like a roll-call of the dead and wounded in action as he solemnly and slowly read out a list of thirty names, including mine, ordering us to skip breakfast and start forming an orderly queue outside his office. When none of us moved, he screamed: '*Idi!*' There was no chance of returning to the *atrad* to grab some bribes. There were so many of us that the back of the queue started outside the building, and three guards looked over us to make sure we stayed in line and didn't speak to each other. I was roughly tenth in line and I studied every face that began to emerge from his office, every two minutes or so, for signs of what I could expect. Everyone, to a man, looked worried, and Dang, the Vietnamese bookie, was positively distraught when he came out, rubbing his face with his hands and swearing to himself under his breath. I was cursing myself for the casual stupidity with which I had drifted into the syndicate and put my parole in jeopardy, and I was fidgety as fuck when I knocked on the governor's door and walked in.

Immediately, as a matter of routine now, I took off my black baseball cap and gave him the full Oliver Twist treatment – sad, doe-like eyes, turned down mouth, rapid blinking and nervous foot-shuffling. I couldn't have looked more fucking humble if I'd worn sackcloth and rubbed manure on my face. My Russian was good enough now to understand about half of what he said, and he was speaking quickly, which didn't help, but as far as I could work out, he was saying that I was in almost as much trouble as the two 'bookie' ringleaders, because, whereas most of the others had been betting a few cigs here and there, I'd been betting whole packets.

At first I went the route of total denial, giving him the 'What me, ref?' look, total disbelief etched across my face, but that too was a mistake because from under his desk he pulled out the exercise book and, turning one page at a time, read out my name, the match and the bet placed.

'Hague Tig, England–France, England to win, one packet Marlboro ... Hague Tig, England–Croatia, England to win, one packet Marlboro ... Hague Tig, Sweden–Denmark, Sweden to win, one packet Marlboro ...'

With each match my heart sank that little bit further, and by the time he'd finished and snapped the book shut

I knew he was going to hit me with some form of punishment, perhaps a spell in solitary, or extra duties around the Zone. I'd built up a relationship with Zanpolit, and with Regime to some extent, but I'd barely come across this character. His main job in the Zone was to censor incoming and outgoing mail, and the only time we'd crossed paths was when I went to collect or deliver a letter. I had no influence over him at all, and as he rubbed his chin, mulling what to do with me, I closed my eyes and stared at the dull red linoleum floor, praying. When he spoke he did so quietly and gravely, and I could barely hear what he was saying at the beginning when he was spelling out the gravity of my error, but then he paused and I looked up.

'Hague, Tig . . . *nyet udo.*'

'What?' I blurted at him.

'Hague, Tig . . . *nyet udo.*'

It took several seconds for me to understand that he was giving me a black mark, scrubbing my parole date.

'No! No! No! Please, no!' I pleaded, rushing towards his desk. 'You can't take six months of my life away for having a bet on a fucking football match. Please . . . You can't do this! . . . Not six more months!'

The prospect of serving an additional six months in Zone 22 made me physically sick. On the way to the sewing factory from the office building I retched every few yards, my empty stomach offering nothing but yellowy bile, and when I reached the office I slumped into my chair and buried my head in my arms. The others said

329

nothing and Ergin gave me only the lightest of tasks to carry out over the days that followed, as I slouched around the Zone in a dark trance, unable to focus on anything but my own misery. I was stupefied, as if I'd been hit on the head with a mallet, and I withdrew into myself to the extent that I could barely even hold a conversation with Boodoo John. When we ate in the evenings, I pushed my noodles round my bowl in sullen silence. He let me stew, only occasionally trying to draw me out of my despair with a gentle question or a simple observation to which I replied with monosyllabic grunts.

Dang and I were the only ones to be given black marks because he was the bookmaker and I was his biggest punter in terms of the size of the bets I laid. The rest had just bet a handful of cigarettes at a time, and were either handed a warning or given extra duties to perform around the Zone. Previously, when something had gone wrong in my life, I'd been able to take some kind of action to address the problem. If, for instance, I made a mistake at work, I took the criticism from my superiors on the chin and then went away and worked harder to atone for the error. But in Zone 22, there was nothing I could do but plead for mercy and forgiveness. I went to see Zanpolit, but he just shrugged and said it wasn't his decision. I went to see Regime, but he got angry and said I'd broken prison regulations, abused the generosity of the governors and had only myself to blame. I called the British Embassy, but they said they were powerless to intervene in, let alone overrule, prison policy.

It had taken over eight months to rebuild my confidence following the shock of my conviction, and in two words — '*nyet udo*' — my fragile new-found optimism had been pulverized and scattered to the hot summer winds sweeping the plains. A few days earlier I could almost have reached out and touched my freedom, but now it had disappeared over the horizon again and I was back to where I'd started when I'd arrived in the Zone. And what was to stop them handing me another six months, and another after that? The desolation played tricks with my mind, accentuating the difficulties of life in the Zone: the heat became more intense than ever, the work more monotonous, the guards more vindictive, the food more tasteless, the dormitory smellier and stuffier and noisier ... But it was the mosquitoes that drove me to the brink of full meltdown. They'd been growing steadily worse as the summer wore on, rising up from the surrounding swamps and descending upon us in black clouds. They emerged in the late afternoon, getting more numerous and insistent as the sun began its descent, and by the time night fell, they hovered across the Zone in swarms, driving us wild with irritation as we cursed and flailed our hands around our faces and slapped our skin like lunatics. I did up the top button of my shirt and pulled the cuffs of my sleeves as far over my hands as possible, and I started smoking more heavily than ever in the belief that the fumes brought me some protection against the bastards. But there was no getting away from them, and for the entire summer my face, neck and shaven scalp, and various patches of my body, were covered in swollen, itchy red lumps. At the same time my head swarmed with dark fears of what diseases or viruses the insects were carrying, especially when I stood outside smoking furiously and looking through the mesh of the exercise yard at the sick inmates of Atrad 2.

The worst place in the entire Zone during the summer was the dormitories, where the heat, the smells, the noises and the mosquitoes joined forces with the dark, fretful fears that haunted me every night to torment me and push my powers of endurance to breaking point. Towards the end of July there was an especially hot night and I was lying under my sheet, sodden with sweat from head to foot, scratching and slapping and flailing and tossing from side to side. The mosquitoes were out in greater numbers than ever, mocking me as they buzzed in my ears and helped themselves to my blood at will. It was about three or four in the morning, but all but a handful of us were still wide awake, moaning, sobbing and cursing, and the last remnants of my resistance began to dissolve. Not since the days following my conviction had I cried as I did that night, and I didn't care who heard. I hadn't quite lost my head, but my heart was gone.

I didn't sleep for even a minute, and in the morning I tramped up to the factory with a thick head, puffy eyes and a lumpy face, scratching and wheezing and coughing. I used to find the spitting of other prisoners disgusting, but now I joined them in gobbing my phlegm into the dust as we filed through the gates and up to the main door. I didn't give a fuck any longer.

Ergin had been growing increasingly fed up with my black mood and most days were spent working in tense silence, broken only by the occasional burst of the needle from Molloi's sewing machine in the corner. At the end of the day, Ergin held me back and said: 'Stop the sadness. You must being positive. Do something. Call Lucy or your mother. Remind why you fight to get out, why you must keep hope.'

Like the robot I'd become, I followed Ergin's instruction and after *preverka* I went to see Raisa Petrovna in the office and wrote out a *zevlanya*, written request, to make a phone call to the Embassy. I dropped a bar of Lindt into her drawer and said: 'Tomorrow.' The next night, as the rest of the Zone headed for the football pitch, Petrovna led me through to the phone and dialled the number herself. Yuri, the guard who was nice to me, was the only other person in the room – the rest had either gone home or were patrolling around the football match – and he gave me a nod as I waited for her to hand me the receiver.

'Hello Tig, how's it going?' said Alla, as sunny and upbeat as ever. For once the sound of her cheerful voice failed to lift my spirits.

'Sorry, Alla, but I need to talk to Mum and Dad or Lucy,' I said, rubbing my face with my other hand. 'Going crazy in here. Put me through to someone, can you? Don't care who it is. Just need to talk to someone before doing something stupid. You've got to help get me the hell out of here. Can't do another six months, Alla, can't do it, can't do it ...'

'I'm doing that for you now, Tig,' she said. 'Try not to worry, we'll do everything we can from here. Try to be strong.'

I could hear the phone ringing in London and it was Mum who picked up.

'Mrs Hague, I've got Tig for you!' said Alla. 'I'll put

the receiver down my end. Go ahead and talk, you two.'

'Oh, Tig my love. Wonderful, I've been dying for you to call. You'll never guess what?'

'What?'

'You're getting married, my love!'

'Am I?' I replied, eventually.

30

I should have been used to the wild yo-yoing of my emotions by then, but this swing from utter misery to crazy happiness was almost violent in its change of direction and it took several days for me to calm down, clear my head and enjoy the wonder of the news. No date had been fixed, Mum said, because Lucy, with Alla's help from the Embassy, was still battling with the bureaucracy of the Russian prison and legal system to arrange one. But the fact that it was going to take place at all, and that Lucy was going to be able to visit me at least another three times before I was released, expelled the most furious demons from my mind once again, and lifted me out of my gloom with a sharp yank. I'd thought Lucy was joking, or just trying to keep my spirits up, when she'd talked of getting married in the Zone, and I didn't believe the system or the governors would permit it anyhow. But she'd meant it, and now it was going to become a reality. Almost as quickly as it had deserted me, my strength and optimism returned. 'Good to have you back with us,' smiled Boodoo John one evening over our noodles. 'You been away so long, I was wondering if you were ever coming back.'

I was given further cause to celebrate when the news filtered out from the office building at the end of that week that following a shake-up of the Russian criminal code, all current cases were eligible for review under the new sentencing guidelines. Rumours about the new code, known as *pepravka*, had been circulating for weeks, fuelled by prisoners coming back from the hospital Zone with stories of Russians leaving other Zones in their droves after their sentences had been slashed, but no official pronouncement to that effect had ever been made in Zone 22 and most of us dismissed them as the wild fantasies of desperate men. It was only when Ahmed and Sacha went to see Regime after *preverka* one evening that the truth of the speculation was confirmed, sparking a mood of excitement across the camp. It was as if a dormant forest fire that had been smouldering beneath the surface had suddenly erupted into flame again. Out in the exercise yard, there was a buzz of chatter that I'd never previously heard in the Zone. It was the unmistakable sound of hope.

Only those for whom life was worse on the outside – or whose sentences were so long they had no reason to rush – opted not to join in the mad scramble at the end of the summer to have our cases re-considered over the days and weeks that followed. The rest of us started filling in forms, making phone calls and writing letters to lawyers, embassies and our families, to push our cases forward for re-evaluation. Yevgeny, the librarian, suddenly became the most popular paedophile on the planet, as we all flocked to him for legal advice and help with writing our applications in Russian. Yevgeny was an elderly American of Russian origin who had once enjoyed a highly successful career as a translator, and could even boast the Vatican among his impressive list of former employers before he'd been sentenced to twenty years for a catalogue of disgusting crimes. The guards called him the 'monster', but it was difficult to imagine this tall, greying, heavy-set man in glasses committing hideous acts of child abuse because he was always gentle, courteous and extremely generous in helping other prisoners with their legal papers or teaching them Russian. Besides, he was the only man with the knowledge, the ability and the will to help us, and we were more than happy to set aside our feelings of revulsion if the old pervert was able to advance our attempts to secure a reduced sentence.

Zanpolit, meanwhile, cleaned up on bribes night after night, with queues of twenty or more lining up outside his door to make inquiries about the new regulations and to try to push their cases up the list of his priorities. My hope was to have my sentence reduced by about three to six months, meaning my parole date would be brought forward by six to twelve weeks. It wasn't much, but even getting a single day shaved off my time spent in Zone 22 was worth the effort.

I could live with the mice but it took a while to get used to the rats. There was no getting away from either of them. They were everywhere: under the floorboards, in the roof, behind the walls, in the food cupboards and in our luggage. We saw the mice every day, scurrying along the skirting boards of the *atrads* and darting between cracks and holes in the floorboards. A whole community of them chewed their way into my black Samsonite suitcase and set up home there for the winter. When I opened the case in spring to take out my warm weather clothing, half of it had been chewed to shreds and turned into a series of nests. As I lifted the lid about a dozen little brown creatures swarmed out and disappeared across the dormitory floor. But I didn't mind the mice. I even felt a strange affection for them, just as we all had done for Nadezhda the foal, and the other two horses. They never caused us any real bother. But the rats were something else altogether, and no matter how many times I saw one I never felt comfortable about sharing a building with God only knows how many of them.

The rats tended to come out only once the sun had gone down, and they made a lot more noise than the mice as they scampered along their runs throughout the night. Every now and then, maybe once a week if they were desperate for food, we saw one during the day, racing across the floor of the *atrad* to safety under a shower of flying boots and shoes. Boodoo John was the best shot, and by the end of the summer he had the most 'kills' in the *atrad*, stretching his tally to six for the year with a superb shot by the food cupboards as we came in from *preverka* one evening. I was standing in the corridor when a bloody great big brown rat, the size of a small cat, burst out of the food locker area and made a run towards the toilets, where they came up through the holes in the floor. In one fluent motion, Boodoo John hurled his boot at the fleeing creature and knocked it dead from ten yards.

As always, Boodoo John picked up the rat by the tail and immediately sought out the nearest Vietnamese to sell him his catch for a handful of boiled sweets or a few cigarettes. On this occasion he sold it to Nguen, who promptly bribed the guard to leave the *atrad* and then hurried down to the boiler room, where he skinned and gutted the rat in the shower area and roasted it in the giant furnaces. The resourcefulness of the Vietnamese was truly astonishing, and the reason why they were the least malnourished group in the Zone was because they supplemented their diet with every non-poisonous living entity they managed to get their hands on. Many of them had been brought up in poor villages in the jungle and were experts at living off the land. There was no creature that they were squeamish about eating. Once, Dang and Mafia caught a long snake during morning break-time up in the factory yard and within minutes they had stripped and gutted it with a knife they used for carving chess-pieces. That evening the entire Vietnamese community sat down to eat roast snake steaks for their dinner. On another occasion some of us were having a cigarette under the smoking shelter outside the factory when Fam appeared with a giant caterpillar. He let it crawl through his fingers a few times before throwing it up in the air, catching it on his tongue and swallowing it. Their knowledge of wildlife was incredible, and they often brewed up herbal concoctions for their ailments from plants they found growing around the Zone. For weeks I watched at break-time as Mafia and Molloi went over to the stable block, poured a jug of water over a tree stump and then covered it back up with straw. One day I went over and asked Molloi what they were doing and he pulled back the straw to reveal dozens of mushrooms they were cultivating.

I rarely heard the Vietnamese complain about their fate or their treatment in prison. Their philosophy in a nutshell seemed to be 'Life is shit, whichever side of the barbed wire you're on, so you might as well just get on with it.' Most of them had virtually nothing they could call their own: no bank accounts, no private food supply, no cigarettes. What they did manage to acquire through some form of *divzhenya*, such as doing a favour for another prisoner, they put into a kitty from which they shared everything out among themselves. The Vietnamese lived very much as a community and kept their distance from the others.

The Afghans were the same, although they did mix with the Turks and the other Muslims for their daily prayers. One evening I ended up watching a documentary about the Taleban – or rather I ended up watching the Afghans watching the documentary. All of them in Atrad 1, about a dozen in total, crowded round the little old black and white telly, gleefully pointing out places and Mujahideen fighters that they recognized. The programme highlighted the extreme poverty and violence in their homeland, and it was easy to understand how the Afghans in Zone 22 had left home and turned to crime in order to cobble together some kind of a livelihood. Whatever life they'd led in Moscow, or even in Zone 22, it can't have been any worse than their existence back home.

So too with the Vietnamese in the Zone, and there was one incredible episode in particular that highlighted their resourcefulness as well as their community spirit. It was in the evening, late in the summer, and I could feel the first chill of approaching autumn as we headed out to the *atrads* to watch the football match between Vietnam and Nigeria – a fixture that had been played about a dozen times over the summer. The game was in full flow when the Vietnamese goalkeeper let out a cry of excitement, pointing up towards the main gates, and we all turned round to see a guard striding towards the admin building, carrying a writhing hessian sack under his arm. The Vietnamese let out a great cheer, while a few of the others started booing and grumbling.

'What's going on?' I asked Boodoo John.

'There's a stray dog in that sack and the Vietnamese are going to eat every last part of it. They'll even make a stock from the bones,' he said, with obvious disgust in his voice. 'They've been saving up cigarettes for months. The going rate's about 400 cigarettes, I think. A dog is a feast to them. They eat cats too, but there's not much meat on them. It makes me feel sick . . .'

An elderly Vietnamese called Baw, a former butcher who worked in the shower area, hurried over to the offices and came out a couple of minutes later holding a very strange-looking beast: a kind of sausage dog, with a disproportionately big head and ears, as if it had been put together by a committee of idiots. I realized after a few moments that it was the dog I'd seen cocking its leg on the Embassy car that had come to drive Mum and Dad home in the spring. And it certainly wasn't looking too comfortable with its new owner as it wriggled crazily in his arms.

'How's he going to kill it?' I asked Boodoo John.

'He'll take it down to the shower room, slit its throat, skin it, gut it, carve it up into different cuts and wash the blood down the drain. Then after the match, they'll cook it up in the boiler room fires: meat, eyeballs, tongue, penis, tail . . . nothing is wasted.'

As Baw headed down towards the boiler room, skirting the side of the football pitch, the ball was kicked in his direction and an Afghan spectator swung round and bumped straight into him. Baw was startled, and as he rocked back on his heels the dog leapt from his arms and, almost as if it knew its number was up otherwise, made a frantic dash for freedom. Immediately the match erupted in uproar as all the Vietnamese players and spectators threw up their hands in horror and started running after the dog as it bolted back towards the admin offices. They were virtually hysterical, all of them yelping and screaming as they ran this way and that, all over the compound, to try to corner the animal.

Meanwhile, every other prisoner in the Zone was roaring with laughter and cheering his lungs out for the dog. It was like a Benny Hill scene – even the guards were laughing – and it went on for about ten minutes before the dog dashed through the front door of the admin office just as Zanpolit was walking out. That, we all thought, was curtains for the dog, but one of the African guys working in the office let it out of the back door and within a minute the chasing and the cheering had started all over again. We screamed ourselves hoarse as the Vietnamese threw themselves on the ground trying to scoop up the weird-looking creature, but it was too quick and agile for them and after a while it escaped into the guard dogs' kennel area in the bottom corner of the camp, next to the solitary confinement block. As soon as it was inside, the dog dug a hole under the fence and within a minute it was on the other side, bounding away to freedom. As the Vietnamese wailed in despair, the rest of us let out a giant roar, clapping and punching the air in delight. The match was cancelled because the Vietnamese were too upset to carry on, and as they bickered among themselves, and harangued the butcher for dropping it, we all wandered back to the *atrads*, grinning and chuckling, somehow all deeply touched and inspired by the dog's bold escape. So it was possible to get out of there after all! was the vibe we were all feeling. That bizarre-looking dog lifted all our spirits, and for the following few days the mood in the *atrads* was noticeably upbeat.

Until, that is, the guard brought the dog back in.

This time there was no drama, nor canine heroics, and a gloom fell over the *atrads* as we stood in the exercise yards and watched the dog being carried down to the boiler room, squirming desperately under the Vietnamese's arm. As the door shut behind them, it was as if a small part of us died, just as it had when Nadezhda the foal had been found dead.

Later in the evening, Molloi came back to the *atrad* kitchen where a small group of us were sitting around in silence eating noodles and drinking tea. He was carrying a little metal pot which he placed on the table in the middle of us; taking off the lid, he lifted a rack of ribs from the steam and asked us, '*Sabaka?*' ('Dog?') Molloi burst out laughing as the rest of us leapt up in disgust or pushed back our chairs, watching him run the dog bones along his lips. The Africans found the eating of dog more offensive than anyone else, and Boodoo John and Julian stomped out of the room in protest. In the night Molloi and Hung, another Vietnamese guy, howled and whimpered in their sleep, just like dogs, spooking the Africans, who moaned and covered their heads with their blankets until Boodoo John got out of bed and shook them awake.

31

As the heat of summer began to fade, the days grew shorter and the chill winds of returning winter sent brief warnings of the great freeze to come, the majority of us in Atrad 1 spent our evenings writing out our applications, in Russian, to have our cases reviewed under the new *pepravka* ruling. Like most of the others, my Russian was not good enough to write it myself, and so for a few evenings over a fortnight I bribed the *atradnik* with a couple of cigarettes, and made my way to the library to ask Yevgeny, the paedophile, for some help in composing our formal applications and covering letters to the Russian justice department. Each night there were at least a dozen of us crammed along the benches of the wooden table in the middle of the small, book-lined room and, like a schoolmaster, he came to us one by one to help. All our cases were different and needed to be fashioned individually.

Yevgeny was generous with his time and advice, and he always greeted me with a smile and an enthusiastic welcome. 'Hey, Tig! Great to see ya! Sit yourself down and I'll be right with you,' he drawled in his American accent.

He couldn't have been more friendly, or more professional in his execution of the formal documents; and neither, even if he had been a leading Moscow lawyer, could he have been more knowledgeable about the Russian legal and judicial system. But never for a minute did I feel comfortable in his presence. Every time I looked at his kindly face, the words 'monster' or 'kiddy-fiddler' jumped into my mind and I had to shake my head to rid it of images of vile abuse. Sometimes he stood over me at the bench, breathing down the side of my neck and leaning against my back, and if there was space on the bench he liked to sit down next to us and press his leg up against ours. He was especially fond of the young Vietnamese prisoners, and it made me feel queasy when I watched him stroking their backs or hair by way of supposed encouragement or congratulation when they completed a sentence correctly.

Yevgeny never asked for payment, but the prison code, the principles of *divzhenya*, demanded that we all brought him something in return for his time and expertise. I always used to bring him a couple of teaspoons of coffee, a piece of chocolate or a few boiled sweets. What he really wanted was a blowjob or a fumble under the desk, and there was gossip that a handful of other desperate prisoners, with nothing else to offer him, were prepared to indulge him in that respect to get their applications completed. My application and letters were almost done when I made a fourth visit to the library – and vowed never to return after witnessing an incident that will take years to eradicate from my mind. It was getting on for ten o'clock, time to hurry back for bed, and there was only Yevgeny, myself and a Vietnamese boy called Lanh left in the room. I was sitting at one end of the table and Yevgeny was at the other, squeezed up against Lanh as they crouched forward over a mess of papers and files. Yevgeny was sitting side on to me, half-turned to face Lanh, with his right elbow on the table and his fingers pressed into his face, making the knuckles turn white. The room had fallen silent for a couple of minutes when I began packing up my own documents. I was getting to my feet when I dropped my biro and quickly bent down to pick it up from under the table. As I stretched out my arm to reach it, I saw Lanh's hand slowly pulling up and down on Yevgeny's erect penis. The shock of the spectacle made me recoil and I cracked my head on the underside of the table, letting out a yelp of pain as I emerged and stood up rubbing my scalp. They were both looking at me, Lanh in terror and Yevgeny with a weirdly serene smile. I stared back, unsure what to say.

'You won't tell anyone about this, will you, Tig?' said Yevgeny in his strong American accent. 'You'll only get Lanh into serious trouble.'

I don't know why we didn't guess straight away that *pepravka*, the reconsideration of our sentences, was going to be one more triumph of grim, attritional disappointment over wild hope, just like everything else in Zone 22. We knew from repeated experience that there was no such thing as a free lunch in there, but we never stopped believing otherwise. The system stamped on our hopes and ground them into the dirt at every possible turn, but a few weeks later those hopes would spring back with as much vigour as ever. It was physically impossible to stop hoping, almost as if it was a survival mechanism passed on in our genes.

When one or two of the prisoners found that their sentences were actually increased on review, the stampede of applicants quickly turned into an orderly, slightly anxious queue which, after weeks of bureaucratic delays ran into months, became a mere trickle. A handful of the long-term prisoners in Atrad 3 saw their sentences slashed in half under the new rules, but for the rest of us, all *pepravka* did was clog up an already congested parole system still further while creating tension, rivalry and chaos among the prisoners scrambling and elbowing to get to the top of the *udo* list. It was not a single, sudden dashing of hope, but a drawn-out disappointment, a creeping realization that nothing was going to come of reviews except a long wait and, eventually, a negative reply. By the time the cool northerly winds began to sprinkle the Zone with the yellowing leaves of the surrounding birch trees, the subject of *pepravka*, such a hot topic of conversation just a month or so earlier, was no longer even mentioned. Such was the speed with which hope was born and died in Zone 22.

I leant my head and shoulder against the wall in the corridor as I waited my turn in the queue to use one of the two basins in the wash area, depressed at the thought of another day's mindless toil, chalking out the outlines of jacket designs until my body ached with the repetition of it. There was about ten minutes to go before we had to be lined up outside the factory gates, and I was starting to grow impatient, when Alan rushed through the door from the exercise yard, a toothy grin wreathed across his face. The weather had turned dramatically in the previous few days as the winds blew in from the Arctic north, bringing occasional flurries of snow, and Alan brushed off the flakes from his woolly hat as he strode towards me.

Alan was always rushing into the *atrad* bursting with rumours and gossip he'd picked up in the office building, about the delivery of a food parcel, or news that the shop was going to open that night. He liked the thrill of conveying good news to others, but more often than not the rumour proved to be exactly that – a rumour – and the excitement he generated faded away and left a sense of anti-climax hanging in the air. The week before he had sparked a bushfire of feverish anticipation when he had come flying into the *atrad* to say he was convinced that a parole hearing in the local court was going to be held the following day and that there were twenty names on Zanpolit's list. We believed him every time because we enjoyed the revival of hope that his conjecture stirred up in us.

'I think she's here, English!' he said, his eyes wide open. 'Your girlfriend!'

'What makes you think that then, Alan?' I said, standing upright and looking through the window of Ahmed's office towards the offices, half-expecting, stupidly, to see Lucy standing outside waiting for me under the gently falling snow.

'I saw Raisa Petrovna with a pink passport, and heard her talking about a girl who stayed in the village last night! I think it's your Lucy.'

I enjoyed the sensation of optimism spreading through me like a charge of electricity, but at the same time I tried to play down the possibility that she was truly there, just a few hundred yards away beyond the barbed wire fence. There was no crueller feeling in Zone 22 than that of high hopes being dashed. I'd tried only to believe good news when it happened, and until then I nailed my bursting hope down as best I could. Within minutes of Alan's arrival the entire *atrad* was alive with chatter that I had a visitor and it was difficult not to feel buoyed up by the rising tide of expectation. When I had a visitor or a food parcel, everyone knew that there was going to be a lot more goodies in circulation, boosting the *divzhenya* economy, and that was a cause for celebration; but a visitor was also an event in its own right because it somehow acted as a link between the Zone and the free world beyond, reconnecting us to the lives we had once had and to which we would one day return.

The rumour mill was in full swing by the time we filed through Sniper Alley into the factory, and a lot of the guys were winking and smiling at me. Molloi was behind me, whispering excitedly: 'Mrs Tig's here! Mrs Tig's here!' I knew the bastards were going to make me stew in uncertainty for as long as possible, but when nine o'clock passed, then ten, then eleven, the doubts started to swarm in my head. It was just another fucking pathetic rumour. I was standing in the office with Ergin, sifting through the latest delivery of old cloth, but my mind was elsewhere and I wasn't working well. Ergin could see how restless I was, and said: 'Go ask Maximovich if she's here.' I found him in his office, feet up on the desk, smoking and staring vacantly out of the frosted window. I nodded respectfully and slipped three Marlboro on to his desk. 'Visit for me today?' I asked, but the hungover fat bastard just shrugged and exhaled loudly as he slid the cigarettes into his breast pocket. Back in the office next door, I was slouched in my chair ignoring the pile of cloth heaped up on the table in front of me and drumming my fingers in time to the rat-a-tat-tat of Molloi's sewing machine when a guard entered the office and pointed at me. He was one of the older ones, with a bit of a paunch and a hang-dog expression frozen on to his face, and I managed to suppress my smile as I sprang to my feet and followed him out of the building, being perfectly programmed not to behave in any way that would give the sour old bastard the slightest cause to penalize me.

I had to stop myself running all the way back to the *atrads* to collect my wash gear and civvy clothes before hurrying down through the lightly falling snow to the boiler room to get cleaned up. Julian and Boodoo John had their shirts off, their upper bodies covered in sweat as they shovelled coal into the furnace, as I burst into the room. 'Lucy's here!' I shouted above the roar of the boilers, and they both broke out in smiles and high-fived me as I swept past them and started quickly peeling off my clothes. As I pulled my T-shirt, the final layer, over my head, I became conscious of how badly I reeked. The accumulated grime, particularly in the sweaty months of summer, made us smell like stray dogs, or old-style tramps. The water from the single shower – where I'd been taken on my first night in the Zone – was boiling hot, and for a few minutes I savoured the rare moment to myself. Even when I crouched over the toilet there were people watching, but there, behind the shower curtain, I was alone. No matter how hard I scrubbed, the musty, acrid stench ingrained in my skin remained, and I towelled myself furiously, then smothered my body in some old Gillette body cream that had been sitting in my locker since I arrived.

The only civilian clothes I had were a pair of black jeans and a blue roll-neck jersey which my parents had brought over to Moscow, and the loafers I was wearing when I got arrested, but I felt like James Bond himself when I slipped them on and smoothed down my wet hair. I may have smelt like a bar of British Rail soap and my clothes may have been hanging off my skeletal frame like washing on a clothes-horse, but Christ, I felt cool. I'd been slowly losing weight ever since my arrest fifteen months earlier and by now my body weight was down about 15 to 20 per cent, leaving me with little more than my skin, my bones and my vital organs. My black jeans kept sliding off my hips and I had to use some old yarn I found on a shelf as a makeshift belt.

I returned to the *atrad* and waited, my heart thumping. Hour after hour went by and still nobody came to summon me. I went out into the cold to pace up and down in full view of the observation window, hoping they'd put me out of my misery, but the two guards on duty just stood there, staring blankly. They were just playing with my head again. I smoked one cigarette after another until my mouth felt like a cat litter tray.

It had gone three o'clock, and I was almost insane with impatience and frustration when a guard finally motioned me towards the gate and buzzed me out of the exercise yard, where two others were waiting to escort me out of the Zone. As I started to make the long walk down towards Sniper Alley, at the Zone's perimeter, a handful of guys heading up to the factory began to cheer and shout crude jokes through the mesh. One of them went into a kind of skiing motion with arms and bended knee, jeering: 'English boy, go get willy wet!'

My heart was racing by the time the guard unlocked the big metal gate to the visitors' apartment and walked me down the dark corridor to the dim light of the small living room at the end, where the ceremony was to take place. I was so nervous and excited I couldn't stand still, and I wasn't allowed to sit, so I rocked back and forth on my feet while the young guard on the door – the evil little git who hadn't let us touch each other the last time – stared at me with his dead eyes, chewing his gum. I heard the gate being unlocked and down the corridor I saw Lucy's silhouette rushing through the gloom. Tears were running down her cheeks and she brushed past the guard and into my outstretched arms. She was smiling. Really smiling. 'We're getting married!' she kept saying over and over, squeezing me so tight I felt my pathetic frame was going to snap.

She was looking beautiful in her tight jeans, pointy boots and a beige top. Alexi had warned her on her first visit not to go looking too sexy or wear anything too revealing because that would only draw unwanted attention and envy from the guards and the locals. She may have dressed down, but to me she looked better than a Bond girl.

I wanted to say something perfect to acknowledge my

happiness, but the words 'Do I smell?' came out of my mouth instead.

'You smell beautiful, you smell great,' she said, which I knew was a lie because I honked of cheap soap and kennels and tramps.

I was crying hard now, but trying to control my happiness. I held her tight but I said nothing, trying to let my body do all the talking. The fuckers would punish me later if I made my happiness too obvious.

I heard the sound of footsteps heading down the corridor. Alla, the girl from the Embassy, was the first to enter. She was much younger and better-looking than I had imagined from our conversations on the phone, but I was surprised, for some reason, that she had black hair, not mousy blonde as I had pictured her in my mind. She gave me a hug and a shy smile, as if she was ashamed or embarrassed that we were to be getting married in such a horrible little room. There was a grey woman there too. You should lose that hairstyle, love, I thought as she strode in. Her hair was pulled back so tightly it looked as if it was going to wrench her hard-set little face off. She must be the registrar, I figured.

There was also one of the junior prison officials, the seventeenth in command or something. I didn't know his name, only that I hated him. The last to enter the room was Regime, the prison number two and world-class wanker to boot. 'What the fuck's he doing here?' I whispered to Lucy.

'Prince Charmless is going to be the witness to our wedding, my love,' she replied, with a plastic grin stuck on her face.

There was an awkward silence as everyone shuffled around the room to find some space. The seventeenth in command turned to me and motioned me into the kitchen. Lucy and Alla had brought down several bags of shopping, and the official couldn't even wait until the ceremony was over before snatching his share of the spoils. I looked on with contempt as he rifled through the bags, taking out cold meats, cheese and chocolate and putting them into another plastic bag. When he'd finished, he looked at me with his mouth open as if to say, 'Yeah? And what the fuck are you going to do about it, English boy?' Then he walked out of the kitchen, down the corridor and out of the building.

The living room was still awkwardly silent when I went back in. I took Lucy's hand and noticed that she was wearing her mum's wedding ring. I smiled at the gesture. Sandra had already given us thousands of pounds towards the bribes and legal fees, and now she'd given Lucy her ring.

'Wow, what an amazing gesture from your mum,' I said quietly, but Lucy didn't return my smile. Instead she looked at her feet, struggling for words.

'Mum's died,' she whispered. 'I wasn't going to tell you. Cancer. Six weeks ago. Spread from her ovaries into her bladder. She fell ill not long after you were arrested.' My face melted as if it was made of wax. I sat down on the sofa with my head in my hands. I'd only written to her a few months earlier to ask for Lucy's hand in marriage. 'I'm going to look after your girl when all this is over,' I'd written. 'I'll look after her for the rest of my days. I promise. I know the wedding isn't perfect and not what you would have wanted, but trust me when I tell you I'll make sure your little girl will always be safe and happy with me.' She'd never got the letter. It struck me like a blow to the stomach to know that Lucy had been dealing with her mother's illness and death as well as all the crap and stress I'd dumped on her. With a shudder I remembered my first call to her from the Zone, when I'd got upset that Lucy cut me off to go and see to her mum.

As I rose to my feet, wiping my eyes, the registrar clicked open her briefcase and took out a pile of documents. Lucy and I stood, hand-in-hand, facing the others. Regime was standing to the registrar's left, next to the tatty brown sofa, with his peaked cap pulled down to his eyes. Alla, who was to translate, was to the right of them while the armed guard stood at the door, clutching his sub-machine gun aggressively, like I was going to choose now as the moment to jump through the fucking window. The registrar gave us a weak smile as the ceremony began. Regime just stared into the middle distance, as if on military parade, his mouth turned down and his jaw set solid.

Lucy didn't stop squeezing my bony hand as Alla stumbled awkwardly through the translation. I could tell that she was making up half the words as she went along, trying to make them sweeter and more romantic than they really were. When she said, 'Your love will see you through these hard times,' she started crying and she didn't stop for the rest of the ceremony, choking back her tears through every broken sentence. Lucy was crying too but I was desperately trying to rein myself in.

I managed to hold back the tears but my body shook uncontrollably, almost noisily, like a bag of bones.

I was getting married to the girl I loved, but I couldn't wait for the ceremony to end. It was relief as much as joy that I felt when the formalities were over and we signed the Russian document confirming us as husband and wife. The registrar invited us to kiss each other and the other three applauded as our lips touched. Alla was clapping away madly, her face wet with tears, but Regime was giving it the slow-hand treatment, as if Lucy and I were some kind of terrible comedy act he was trying to shoo off stage in a provincial music hall.

We stood around in silence while the registrar packed away her documents and books and then, one by one, we shuffled towards the corridor as Regime led the way to the kitchen for the 'reception'. The kitchen was even smaller than the living room, and even bleaker. There was no 'decor' to speak of, just a two-plate stove, a small fridge, a wooden bench, a table and two chairs, and it was incredibly claustrophobic as all six of us, including the armed guard, tried to find some space in which to stand without having to touch each other. Alla reached into her bag and pulled out a bottle of Russian sparkling wine that she'd smuggled in to prevent the guards or governors taking it. She went to the one cupboard in the room and took out an assortment of plastic beakers and chipped, stained coffee mugs.

No one was saying a word, and I felt nervous because Alla was taking liberties by not getting permission from Regime as she popped open the cork and started pouring the wine into the cups and mugs. Without having to move from where she was standing, she passed around the mugs, handing me mine last of all. Before Regime had a chance to butt in, she raised her beaker and said: 'Cheers! Here's to the happy couple!' But as we all went to take a sip, Regime jumped towards me like a redneck's dog let off his leash, shouting in Russian: '*Nyet! Nyet! Nyet! Nyet anglichanin!*' He snatched the mug from my hand and put it down on the table, then bent down to the shopping bag at his feet, took out a can of Diet 7 Up and thrust it towards me.

'Well, sod this!' snapped Lucy. 'If Tig's not having any, nor am I!' And she reached into the bag, took out a can of her own and scowled back at him. Her boldness gave me a thrill.

A terrible tension charged the room for a couple of minutes as we sipped our drinks and looked at the floor. Alla tried to say something to Lucy and me, but we weren't really listening. I was too busy dreaming about kicking the shit out of Regime.

Revelling in the awkwardness, Regime downed his mug of sparkling wine and immediately threw back what should have been mine. He picked up the half-empty bottle from the table and said in English: 'Cheers!' Then he turned on his heel and walked out of the room. The wedding reception was at an end.

Alla, bless her, didn't need telling that Lucy and I wanted to spend as much time together as possible, and after quickly updating me on the progress of my case, she disappeared down the long, dark corridor. When we heard the heavy metal gate at the entrance being locked and bolted, Lucy and I returned to the living room and gazed out through the bars at the grey sky and the snow-covered compound.

'So, my darling wife, where would you like to go for our honeymoon?' I asked, putting on a posh voice.

'Well, my love, I've always fancied the Seychelles myself.'

'I was thinking more along the lines of Barbados or Mustique. I have heard the weather is perfect at this time of year.'

'I'm not sure we could afford that, what with saving up for the house and everything.'

'Well, what about this for a plan? I know this charming little place, just along the corridor from where we're standing. It's got two lovely squeaky metal beds, and a little wooden table to die for.' I held out my hand before leading my wife down the corridor.

We took out the table separating the two single beds and pushed them together. Lucy's girlfriends back home had given her a pair of pyjamas as a wedding present, and they'd sewn 'Mrs Hague' in sequins on to the bottom. We tore off our clothes and jumped quickly under the old sheets to escape the cold. Like everything else in the apartment, the beds stank, even though Lucy had brought clean sheets with her. I didn't want to guess how many murderers and rapists had sweated into the mattresses over the years. We lay facing each other and chatted about our weird little wedding for a while, then drifted off to sleep.

I have no idea what the time was when I begin to stir and found Lucy's warm body wrapped around mine. Lucy was still more asleep than awake, but she was clearly feeling as amorous as I was. For the first time in God only knows how many months I was feeling all dreamy and happy, when suddenly there was an almighty crash as the door was thrown open, smashing against the wall. An armed guard, wearing mirrored sunglasses, strode in and stood at the foot of the bed, glaring down at Lucy. He'd barely taken one step into the room before I'd sprung out of bed like a jack-in-the-box, stark-bollock naked, and was standing to attention in every sense. '*Anglichanin, kitchen for shopping!*' he barked, and walked out through the door, expecting me to follow. Lucy pulled the sheets over her head as, trying to catch my breath, I danced around on one leg attempting to pull my trousers on.

I spent forty-eight glorious hours with my beautiful wife, lying in bed or sitting wrapped in each other's arms on the sofa, trying to milk every last minute of the experience and commit it to the memory bank for the harsh winter months ahead. Not until the snow outside the window had started to thaw in five or six months' time was she going to be able to come back and visit. I barely let go of her for two full days. When our time was up and the Embassy car arrived to collect her, we hugged for five minutes without saying anything, and our silence was far more eloquent and emotional than any words of consolation and encouragement we might have offered one another at that moment.

'Farewell for now, Mrs Hague!'

'Farewell, Mr Hague!'

She disappeared down the dark, windowless corridor

and the heavy metal gate clattered behind her, leaving me alone in the living room, where the smell of her perfume lingered in the air and on my clothes. I lifted my shirt to my nose and breathed in deeply. The young guard who had ruined Lucy's first visit to the Zone came and led me out of the building. As we turned towards the Zone gates I saw the black Embassy car pulling away slowly across the road, the exhaust pipe billowing a cloud of fumes and steam into the cold afternoon air. Lucy caught sight of me out of the corner of her eye and started blowing me kisses. I waved back and blew her one big kiss, but as I did so the guard shoved me in the small of the back, making me stumble forward. Instinctively I spun round and snapped in English: 'Go screw yourself! I'm saying goodbye to my wife, you little prick!' I was as shocked as he was, and for a few seconds we stared at each other, unsure what to do next. I'd never spoken to a guard like that before, and for a moment I feared he was going to explode and march me in to see one of the governors, but his reaction was quite different. He looked embarrassed, almost cowed, by my outburst and simply motioned to me to continue walking.

As we crossed Sniper Alley and began to head up the side of the *atrads* to the main concourse, I became aware of a change in my manner. I held my head high and swung my arms with all the confidence of a guardsman on parade – not, it struck me, because I had told the spotty young guard where to get off, but because I was now married to the woman I loved and no fucking guard could ever take that away from me. Nor, when I lay awake at night at my wits' end, could the guards come and take away the thoughts of her that I conjured in order to comfort myself, and the dreams of our future life together. That was beyond the reach of even the most vindictive bastards. That's why I'd told the guard to go fuck himself!

The most difficult part about being in prison had been living without the woman I loved, and my greatest fear always was that she was going to leave me. Only now that she had gone did I truly understand what Lucy had done for me: she hadn't gone to such lengths to arrange for us to become man and wife because it was a sensible, obvious thing to do. What she had done was create a lifeline for me, a means of survival, a source of strength to help carry me through the last difficult period of my sentence. She could have waited until I was released to get married, in a church, in a flowing white dress, with all our family and friends present. But by spending four months battling the bureaucrats to organize the ceremony, and by travelling 2,500 miles across the world to get hitched in a smelly little prison visiting block – the most unromantic setting imaginable – she was making a massive statement of her commitment to me. My eyes welled up, but a smile spread across my face as I realized what that beautiful little angel had done for me and I strode into the exercise yard a different man from the one who had left two days earlier. I can handle anything now, I thought.

32

Udo was an obsession in Zone 22. Parole meant just one thing – freedom! *Udo* ate up our thoughts and our conversations like an insatiable animal. Except for those who were in for the long term, say anything longer than five years, everyone else in the Zone was scheming their escape, using every means at their disposal to bring pressure to bear on their claim. Bribes in the form of goods and information were handed over to the governors, legal loopholes and technicalities were researched in the library, and those with influential embassies pressurized them into action as best they and their families could.

At the other Zones, the Russian ones, parole hearings took place twice a month in the nearest High Court. At Zone 22 they happened every six to eight weeks, which meant there was a massive backlog of cases. At any one time there were between fifty and seventy-five prisoners, roughly a quarter to a third of the entire prison, waiting for parole. Part of this congestion was caused by the confusion in legal circles caused by the new Russian code of criminal law, which had come into force only a couple of years earlier. But it was mainly that there was no urgency in the system to see us released, and no pressure from the outside to motivate the Zone officials and local judges who held our destinies in their hands.

It was rare for more than a dozen prisoners to be released at one hearing, so there were always a few dozen inmates who were left crushed by the news that the judge hadn't got round to considering their cases. It was easy to understand why Zone 22 had come to be known as the 'Forgotten Zone'. We were the system's lowest priority. No good reasons, only vague excuses, were ever given for the failure of the system. The standard line the governors peddled to desperate prisoners was: 'You've been in for however many years, what's another few months?' In a handful of cases, those months had become years.

Udo was spoken of as a race, a competition, in which timing the burst for the line was the key to winning. Following Papi's advice, my plan had been to launch my push for parole in the middle of autumn: that gave me roughly the four or five months I needed to move up from the back of the grid, through the congested pack of applicants ahead of me, so that come the final laps in February I was in with a realistic chance of a podium finish. Like any race, there were going to be dangerous manoeuvres, bumps, collisions and acts of chicanery along the way, and some of us were going to see our hopes crash and burn. We all played by the same ruthless set of rules. It was every man for himself, and at the end of it there was going to be a handful of winners cracking open the champagne and a whole lot of losers left to start the race all over again.

My chances looked to have gone up in smoke before the starting flag had even been raised when I'd been given a black mark in the summer. But the night after Lucy had left, I had a plan to get me back on track, a plan so bloody simple it made me chuckle out loud when it came to me as I lay on my bunk scheming my escape.

Without looking up, Zanpolit pulled open the deep drawer on the right hand side of his desk as I slid my boots through the melted snow on the linoleum floor left by the procession of inmates before me.

'*Nachalnik*,' I said, nodding my head and standing two yards closer to his desk than I'd done in the past so that I could look straight down at him. He looked up at me and glanced over at his drawer, which had been emptied of earlier bribes. I looked at the drawer and stared back at him as he furrowed his brow, bemused that for the first time in a dozen visits I hadn't walked straight round and unloaded some goods for him and his wife. He put his right arm out over the drawer to indicate that he was ready to receive my offerings.

'No,' I said quietly, continuing to stare at him impassively.

There was a pause.

'No?' he replied, leaning back in his chair and linking his hands over his groin. 'No?'

'No.'

'Hague Tig has no more Nescafé, or Marlboro?'

'I have Nescafé and Marlboro, thank you.'

'He forgets today?'

'No, I don't want to give you any.'

Silence.

I continued to stand with my legs apart, holding my woolly black hat with both hands in front of me. Zanpolit got to his feet and walked towards the first of the three windows on the wall to his right. Outside, the light snow-fall was brilliantly lit up by the camp lights. A guard ambled past the window, his fur trooper hat turned down over his ears, his Alsatian at his side.

'Hague Tig is angry with Zanpolit?' he said, with his back to me.

'No, the British Embassy is angry with Zanpolit.'

Zanpolit turned round sharply, quickly trying to wipe the look of alarm from his face.

'The British Embassy?'

'Yes, my wife told me they are disappointed with you. My family gives you many gifts, and you give me nothing. No support, nothing. You only take. They are angry about my black mark, Zanpolit, and they are surprised that you have made no effort to change the decision.'

'Is Hague Tig threatening me?'

'No, Zanpolit, I'm just telling you that the British Embassy is preparing a letter for your superiors in Moscow. They like to see fair play.'

'A letter? So what do they want?'

'They want the black mark overturned, and they want my name on the parole list when my time comes in February.'

'And what if that is not possible?'

'I don't know, Zanpolit. It's not my decision.' I paused for a few seconds before continuing. 'But I do know my family will always be very generous to you. They have many gifts for you . . .'

Zanpolit ran his hand through his gelled hair a few times while he thought, before swivelling round and saying, 'Come back and see me at the end of the week.'

My mouth was dry and sticky, as it always was when I'd been lying through my teeth, and I gulped back two mugs of freezing cold tap water as soon as I returned to the *atrad*.

'Did he go for it?' asked Boodoo John, sticking his head through the doorway of the washroom.

'Hook, line and sinker.'

Two nights later I slipped the *atradnik* two Marlboro and made my way across to the office building.

Zanpolit was leaning against the front of his desk, his legs stretched out in front of him, one foot over the other, and his arms crossed tightly against his chest.

'*Nachalnik!*' I said, nodding respectfully.

'You tell the Embassy all is good with Zanpolit, all is good with Zone 22 and I will help Hague Tig.' He walked round to the other side of his desk, picked up a document, tore it in half and then into quarters and eighths and sprinkled the shreds into the wastepaper basket below.

'Your parole is February again,' he smiled, as he leant over and pulled open his drawer.

'Thank you, Zanpolit, thank you,' I beamed, suppressing a powerful urge to shout with joy as I approached his desk. He turned away and examined the snowy landscape print on his wall as I reached into my pants, pulled out a sweaty jar of Nescafé Gold Blend and placed it into his drawer. From my jacket pockets I took out sixty Rothmans, a bar of Lindt, a metal lighter and a Parker fountain pen and laid them alongside the coffee before sliding the drawer shut.

'Thank you again, Zanpolit,' I said, as he looked inside

the drawer and I walked backwards towards the door.

'Don't expect more favours from me. I will do my best to make sure your name is on the February list for parole, but the rest is up to the judge.'

'I understand, thank you.' The race for parole was back on.

33

I was as confident and optimistic as I ever had been as I joined my competitors in preparing to start making the first moves. Lucy had brought down 1,000 dollars' worth of goods – mainly cigarettes and coffee – and together with a large parcel delivery, sent by Mum and Dad via the Embassy, my bribery stocks were full. Even after the guards had helped themselves to the bags in the accommodation block when Lucy came, I still had twelve medium-sized jars of Nescafé Gold and twelve small (the large size was too big for my locker and my trousers), twenty-four bars of Lindt chocolate, a dozen salamis, a few pens and lighters and 5,000 Western cigarettes. Anything with English writing on it was considered a luxury, but in a nation of heavy smokers Marlboro Man was king and Mr Rothman the next in line to the throne. In order to avoid drawing attention to the amount of food I had after a delivery, I started paying 'rent' in cigarettes to some of the African boys in return for the use of their lockers.

I faced stiff competition from my main rivals who were also up for parole at the end of February. In addition to the scores of prisoners whose parole date had already passed and who would be pressing their cases harder than ever, there were a handful of characters with whom I was in direct competition: Benny Baskin, Ergin and Boodoo

John in particular. All three of them were big hitters with strong cases for prompt release, and it was highly unlikely we'd all go at once. Those who didn't would have to wait a couple of months, at least, for another shot, and the realization of this was going to put a strain on our relationships as we all set about trying to win Zanpolit's favour.

Benny's case looked the strongest of all. He could speak Russian like a native, he was on first-name terms with Zanpolit and he had bribes to burn. Boodoo John had no money and only basic Russian, but he was a model prisoner who had earned widespread respect for his quiet, unassuming manner and five years of hard work in the toil of the boiler room. By coincidence, we were both due for release on 15 February, and though we joked over our noodles about walking out of the Zone arm-in-arm, we both understood the uncomfortable fact that we were rivals for freedom.

Ergin's Russian was also very good; he too was in Zanpolit's good books and he had recently been appointed as the head prisoner in Atrad 1. He also had one very influential contact in Moscow, who moved in high judicial and political circles and who had written a letter in his support. Ergin thought he was in pole position. In the sewing factory we talked of little else but *udo* and he kept saying to me, 'Tig, watch what I do and learn from it and maybe you'll be out a couple of months after me.' He meant it kindly, but it really fucked me off.

My store of bribes and my good relations with Zanpolit, Raisa Petrovna and to a lesser extent Regime were good assets. Papi had advised me to concentrate all my efforts on one 'cop', but I realized after a few months that if I had bribes to spare, there was no harm in sharing them around with the others, especially since the other governors all had a say in who got parole. So every third or fourth visit to the office building, I went to Regime or Raisa instead of Zanpolit and gave them the chocolate, the cigs and the coffee. (Raisa had become noticeably friendlier since Lucy had bought her off with a new double bed to make sure our wedding took place.) It became increasingly important that I kept her on side, because I needed to start using the phone as much as possible. In the first twelve months inside Zone 22 I'd made no more than five or six calls – and that was stretching my luck – but from early December I started phoning the Embassy every fortnight to put pressure on them to begin exerting some influence over Zanpolit. The Embassy was my only trump card.

The networking began every evening after the final head-count of the day. We returned to the *atrads* and milled around anxiously, waiting for signs that Zanpolit had returned to the Zone after his evening meal, trying not to let on to each other that that was what we were doing. It was one of the unspoken rules of the race that we didn't acknowledge that we were networking. Sometimes Zanpolit decided to park his Ford Escort inside the Zone and we watched him twirl his keys around his finger and whistle his way towards the admin office before making our move. Every night it was like a dramatic performance being staged right in front of us: when the lights went on in Zanpolit's office, the curtain was effectively up, and Benny Baskin, for instance, would steal through the dark, hunched against the cold, and disappear into the low wooden block opposite. Moments later, I'd see him standing in Zanpolit's office, smiling from ear to ear as he tried to work his charm on the young governor. Ten minutes later, Ergin or Boodoo John or any of the other dozens who had pinned their hopes for freedom on the man, made the walk across the tarmac to have their go. And so the evening continued, until Zanpolit decided he'd had enough, turned off his light and went home with his briefcase full of goodies, leaving those left in the queue and shivering in the exercise yard to melt away and try again the following day.

On the surface, the monotonous grind of daily life was no different from the way it had always been. The routine never changed. Head-counts, meals, factory work, bed ... head-counts, meals, factory work, bed ... head-counts, meals, factory work, bed ... the cycle was as endless as it was soul-crushingly predictable. But below the surface, tensions were constantly simmering, hopes were burgeoning and nerves were fraying. The spectre of parole haunted the Zone. There was no greater, more dramatic event than a parole hearing if a prisoner was in the frame for release. But there were no set dates for the hearings and we were constantly guessing, speculating and yearning for news of the next one. Parole hearings took place when the judges at the local High Court of Zubova Paliansky decided to have one, and since my arrival in the Zone they'd been taking place roughly every six weeks. In order to try and keep a lid on the tensions that news of a hearing stirred up throughout the Zone, they never gave us any advance warning of when one was to take place. Instead, we watched Zanpolit's every move, waiting for him to walk out of the office building carrying a bundle of our blue files in his arms. That was the sign.

While myself, Ergin, Boodoo John and the dozens of other hopefuls began jockeying for position for the February parole race, dozens of others were bracing themselves for the hearing that was due to take place at some point in mid-December. Julian was the only prisoner among them that I knew even reasonably well, and I watched him become increasingly distracted and nervous as the days went by. His booming laugh was one of the few sounds of joy I'd heard in the Zone, and it often got him into trouble with the guards because it was so loud and far too happy for their liking. But by the beginning of December the foghorn boom had become a nervous chuckle as he waited for Zanpolit to make his move. It was Julian's third parole application, and after the pain of two setbacks his desperation this time round was plainly visible. The suspicion was that they were stalling his release because he'd worked in the boiler room longer than anyone and they didn't want to lose his expertise at maintaining the ancient machinery. A cool character normally, he became fretful and withdrawn, biting his nails and pacing up and down the exercise yard, along with the other hopefuls, hoping to see Zanpolit emerge from the offices.

We were all at work when the news raced round the factory that Zanpolit had finally gone to court with his blue bundle, and that evening all the parole candidates to a man donned extra layers of clothing to stand out in the freezing cold and await the governor's return. The names of the successful applicants were never released until after *preverka* the following morning, but still they waited for his return, pressed up against the mesh fencing, stomping their feet and blowing furiously into their hands. And when his brown Ford Escort finally sped through the gates, the headlights sweeping two shafts of bright light across their expectant faces, every-one started shouting at him for information as he stepped from the car. 'How many names on the list? . . . Please tell us tonight . . . Zanpolit, when will we know? . . . Was the judge in a happy mood?'

The following morning we took up positions for *preverka* after we'd got up from the ice after our squat thrusts. There was a hum of nervous chatter, followed by absolute silence as one of the junior officials began to read out a list of those who were to go and see Zanpolit. Julian was standing two prisoners away from me, one row in front to my left, and he was peeling his thumbnail and tapping his foot rapidly as the official worked his way through the list. All around me I could hear stifled yelps of joy and congratulation and sighs of relief, like the gentle popping of champagne corks, but then the list ended and the official walked away. Julian was left rooted to the spot, his hands covering his face, shaking his head slowly from side to side.

I hated seeing a prisoner's desolation over the days that followed a failed parole application, even when I didn't know him, or even like him. With Julian, it was painful to witness. Physically, he was a big, powerful man and there was something particularly pathetic and upsetting in

374

seeing him reduced to a sobbing, hunch-shouldered wreck. It was made all the worse because, although confident of my own release, I knew there was still a chance that I was going to suffer exactly the same misery as him. For years a prisoner had one date fixed in his mind – his parole date – and he looked forward to it with growing anticipation, so that by the final months, weeks, then days, he was virtually high with excitement. When the sun set and that day passed just like any other, and the prison authorities collectively shrugged their shoulders and waved him away, ready to punish him with another six months if he complained, that prisoner's fragile hope, what little faith he had left, was shattered and it took weeks to pick up the pieces. Julian's slump in mood was dramatic and visible, and he became restless, fidgety, gloomy and inconsolable where once he had been upbeat, optimistic and bursting with good humour. There was little his Nigerian brothers or I could do to help him, other than pat him on the back and offer him hollow words of reassurance and encouragement.

'I'm sure it'll happen next time, Julian. It's got to!' I said after breakfast, as he sat in the kitchen slumped over the table, with Boodoo John and Eke Jude on either side.

'That's what I thought this time, and the time before that! The fuckers are never going to let me out of here.' He was trying not to cry, and I grimaced at the sound of his voice cracking up.

In 2004 the pressure on the parole system inside Zone 22, and therefore on the competition to get out of there, had become even more intense than normal, for two reasons. First, there had been a sharp fall in the number of new arrivals to the Zone and the guards and governors needed no telling what that meant for them: the fewer prisoners, the fewer the bribes. It also meant a decrease in the funds they received from the government. They didn't give a shit whether we were released or not at the best of times, but as the prison population dwindled, it became in their own interests to try to stall the release of the prisoners for as long as possible, especially the better-off ones like me. Without us, there would be no more Marlboro, Lindt chocolate bars and Nescafé, no more expensive lighters, pens and watches, and no more televisions, video cameras, double beds, wallpaper and sofas.

When Julian went to see Regime to find out why he was still being held in prison five months after his parole date, he was told that his application – and that of dozens of others – had failed because they didn't have the original documents from their trials. Most prisoners only had photocopies, and their originals were lodged in the vaults of court archives in Moscow and other major cities across Russia. The prospect of trying to unearth them from deep within the country's notoriously impenetrable bureaucracy triggered panic throughout the Zone. What made this explanation especially infuriating and depressing was that it was the Zone authorities, not the Russian criminal justice system, that had introduced the new stipulation. It was nothing less than a shameless attempt to slow down the release of prisoners and hang on to the source of their contraband and inside information. Groceries were being put before the freedom of men. And it was sod's law for those of us aiming for parole in February that we found ourselves also competing with dozens of inmates who should have gone in December and January, and some from even earlier hearings.

I thought I had my original documents, but after the December parole hearing I checked them to be absolutely sure and was immediately thrown into a paddy of anxiety when I discovered half of them were copies. It had been announced at *preverka* that if parole applicants weren't in possession of the proper papers by mid-January, to register them with the local court, they'd be ineligible for the next parole hearing and would have to wait until the end of March or early April for their next chance. I knew from the Zone grapevine that it could take up to three months for the bureaucracy to produce the documents they needed, and I went straight to Raisa Petrovna after *preverka* and unloaded a medium-sized jar of Nescafé Gold and two bars of Lindt before begging her, with my hands held together in prayer, to let me call the Embassy that very evening.

'Alla, you've got to do me a big favour and you've got to move fast.' I was virtually hyperventilating with anxiety as I explained to Alla about the new stipulation, and she listened patiently as I babbled incoherently down the line.

'Tig, I'll get your documents for you. I give you my word. Please don't worry yourself sick about it. Put it from your mind . . .'

'But how the hell are the Embassy going to deliver them when they won't risk driving down in the dead of winter? You can't put them in the internal post, because the bastards here will just sit on them till it's too late, and you can't risk putting them in the normal post either . . .'

377

'Tig, relax. We will find a way . . .'

'Relax! How the hell can I relax in Zone 22? How can I relax about spending one more day in this godforsaken misery pit? You've got to sort it, Alla, 'cos I'm in danger of losing my head in here, and then I'll never get out . . .'

34

Boodoo John walked round the kitchen pouring the strong black tea into metal cups as I emptied a packet of oatmeal biscuits into my eating bowl and handed them out. 'Happy New Year,' I said to each person as I made my way round the room, and they replied, 'Let's hope,' or words to that effect – all except Julian, that is. Still gutted by his parole failure, he replied, 'Well, it can't be any fucking worse than the last five.' There were six of us in all – Boodoo John, Julian, Eke Jude, Hulk, Alan and myself – and we stood in silence for a few moments facing each other over the wooden table, all still wearing our hats and outdoor coats to keep out the blood-stopping cold. The boiler had broken down for the third time in four weeks, and Julian and the other boys had only just managed to get it running again after hours of toiling down in the sheds.

'Well, here's to 2005!' said the ever-cheerful Alan, his breath clearly visible as he rolled out a toothy grin and raised his cup of tea in front of him. The rest of us wearily lifted our own cups and muttered, '2005!' and then the silence returned and we stood awkwardly, shuffling our feet, cradling our tea and looking at the splintered wooden floor. I tried to think of something upbeat to say in order to break the silence, but nothing came to me, just as it had failed to do on Christmas Day a week earlier.

The passing of another year of our lives was a cause for sad reflection, not celebration; a bitter reminder that while the world beyond danced and set off fireworks, we stood shivering and coughing in a wooden shack in one of the most desolate corners of the globe, thousands of miles from our loved ones, months and years away from the day when we would be allowed to be reunited with them.

The buoyant mood that had followed the wedding and the reinstatement of my parole date sustained me throughout November, but that surge of joy and confidence had quickly given way, first to a gnawing anxiety and then to a growing despair, with occasional bursts of outright alarm as the days passed and still there was no word from Moscow or Zanpolit about whether my original trial documents had been found and sent down to the Zone. Typically, Zanpolit and the other governors refused to tell us when the cut-off date for parole applications had been set, preferring to let us stew in sleep-thieving anxiety for as long as possible. The arrival of the New Year served only to heighten the passing of time and highlight the deadline for our parole applications. As I raised my glass and added my gloomy voice to the toast, the knot in my stomach squeezed a little tighter.

My physical condition wasn't great either. The viruses ebbed and flowed up and down the camp throughout the winter months, and there hadn't been a day since the first snows had arrived when I hadn't been either hacking my chest to mincemeat and/or running for the hole in the floor to squirt out some more diarrhoea. A couple of days into the New Year I was lining up for the first *preverka* of the day, feeling no rougher than normal as I jumped from foot to foot to keep warm, when without warning my stomach was seized by cramps and I projected an arc of vomit through the frozen night air. Luckily I was in the front row and my spew landed in the pile of cleared snow about two yards in front of me. The guard doing the head-count was three columns away to my right and he stopped and scowled as I continued to unleash streams of watery yellow puke that burnt through the snow like acid and sent steam rising up into the darkness. My head was swooning and it was a struggle to stay on my feet for the few minutes it took the guard to finish his counting. I was first in line to see the doctor after breakfast and I probably didn't need to give her the giant bar of Lindt Swiss Premium milk chocolate with raisins and hazelnuts, but I wasn't taking any chances. She wrote me out a sick note, granting me three days off work, and I immediately took to my bunk, alternately sweating and shuddering with cold and almost delirious with fever.

It was difficult to keep track of time over the hours and days that followed as I lay under my blanket, curled up on my side with my arms wrapped around my cramping stomach, drifting in and out of consciousness. Fuelled by fever, the recurring nightmare about Lucy became even more grotesque and vivid and I hurled myself from one side of the bunk to the other, over and over, trying to dislodge the stream of horrific images from my mind … Lucy, heavily pregnant, writhing on the ground, crying out for me to come to her aid. Me trying to board some form of transport but it's too crowded to get on, or the ticket collector or cabbie won't let me in; me waiting for a ride that never comes or finally getting on the train or bus or into the car but it never arrives at its destination or the plane that never lands, and all the time Lucy is screaming and wailing . . .

Almost thirty-six hours had passed before I managed to haul myself off the mattress and fetch myself a drink of water. My mouth was so dry I could barely swallow, but when I swilled back a cup of water from the washroom tap I immediately projectile-vomited into the basin, narrowly missing Ahmed, who was washing his face in the neighbouring sink. It wasn't until the following morning that I was able to hold down any water, but I was still so weak that Boodoo John had to help me across the concourse to see the doctor again. The worst had passed, but she signed me off for two more days and I returned to bed once again. At any given time of the winter there were at least a dozen of us in bed suffering from some form of ailment in Atrad 1, but this bug was proving especially virulent: there were roughly twenty of us laid up, and the room hummed to the hellish sound of groaning and whimpering. For the first three days I felt so rough that I stopped thinking and fretting about the fast-approaching deadline for parole applications, but as I began to recover, the fears slowly returned to torment me. And as always, they were especially powerful and unsettling at night.

By the fifth day, I was well enough for those fears to have transformed themselves into full-blown alarm, and I woke up with a fury of demons screeching around my head. It had been over ninety-six hours since anything solid had passed my lips, and the delirium caused by the fever had been replaced by a wild confusion made up of hunger, weakness and panic. But through the fog, I could clearly see the importance of finding out whether the documents had arrived and I knew that, come what may, I had to get across to the office building at the end of the day.

After missing the shower session that week it was almost eleven days since I had washed properly, and the smell of my own stale body odour was overpowering that evening as I took off the filthy blue fleece and T-shirt in which I'd been sleeping and sweating all week. I covered every inch of skin in soap lather, but no sooner had I rubbed it on than I washed it off with three handfuls of freezing cold water and wrapped myself in my towel, shuddering in the icy air. I could tell by the sight of my breath and the cold of the water that the temperature inside couldn't be much above freezing, meaning that outside it must have been between 20 and 30 degrees below.

Back in the dormitory I stood transfixed at the sight of my naked torso, reflected in the window darkened by the night that had fallen six hours earlier. Where once, eighteen months earlier, I had had a well-defined, healthy physique – broad shoulders and upper chest, narrowing to a small waist – my sides were now straight lines that ran from my armpits down to my hips. My ribs were starting to protrude and the skin was pulled taut over my cheekbones, making my eyes look way too big for my dark, unshaven face and sheared head of hair. The hazy red glow of the dormitory night-light accentuated the rash of raised, painless lumps that had been slowly spreading out from my chest and sides and across my back over the previous few weeks. I could barely recognize myself as I stood there, so engrossed by the ghoulish vision before me that it was a full ten seconds until the cold persuaded me to put on the first of four layers before I headed across to the admin building to see Zanpolit.

The quiet rage that had festered inside me from the time of my detention in Moscow, arising out of an inability to accept that my punishment was in any way proportionate to the misdemeanour I had committed, had been growing steadily in intensity. Now it was threatening to boil over, and that was not something I could afford to let happen when – in theory at least – I was so close to regaining my freedom. The last thing I needed at this stage was to let an outburst of temper land me in trouble. Still smarting from the humiliation of having to rescind my black mark, Zanpolit would jump at the slightest opportunity of slapping another six months on my sentence, pre-empting any intervention by the British Embassy by bulwarking his case against me with phony testimony by the guards about my general behaviour and attitude. I clenched my fists in my pockets as the dark thoughts ran through my mind, and made my way across the concourse to see the man himself, head down and huddled against the driving blizzard that swept through the barbed wire to the north of the Zone. As I walked up the three wooden steps to the office door, I was talking myself into a conciliatory, patient frame of mind. 'Just keep your cool, Tig . . . keep your head . . . be polite . . . it will all be over soon . . .'

Zanpolit grunted in answer to my gentle rap on his door, but he didn't look up as my rubber-soled boots squeaked across his floor and I dropped three packets of Marlboro and a jar of Nescafé into the open drawer of his desk. As I pulled the coffee out of my pants I saw that the notepad on which he was scribbling was littered with doodles, including dozens of mini-Swastika shapes, a large love heart which he had filled in with blue biro, and a sports car, complete with exhaust fumes coming out of the back and a few streaks behind the vehicle to indicate the great speed at which it was travelling.

I stood facing his desk, biting my fingers, waiting for him to talk. He said nothing for over a minute, until finally he looked up and raised his eyebrows as if to say, 'I can't be arsed to open my mouth to talk to scum like you. What the hell do you want anyway?'

'Have my trial papers come from Moscow?' I asked in Russian.

'Do I look like a postman?' he replied, looking down at his pad.

The anger rose up in me like bile, sudden and uncontrollable, and I had to swallow hard to stop myself snapping at him.

'Well, how can I find out?' I said, holding my arms out at my sides and shrugging my shoulders.

'I don't know. Why don't you call your friends at the British Embassy?'

'OK, I will, but when is the final date for parole applications? It must be close now.'

'Soon.'

'How soon?'

Zanpolit jumped to his feet, sending his chair crashing against the wall behind him. His face was screwed up in purple rage as he pointed at the door and screamed, 'Out! Out! Out!'

Whether it was because I was too weak and dazed or because I was no longer frightened of him, it was difficult to say, but I didn't flinch as he bellowed at me. Instead, I held his gaze and then turned and slowly walked from the room, not letting him see any of the anger and contempt that seethed within me. But as soon as I was out in the open I kicked the air wildly, spinning around in the snow that was now blowing almost horizontally through the camp. Inside the *atrad*, I leant my arms and head against the food lockers in the little room to the right of the entrance and looked down at my boots, muttering 'Bastards! Bastards! Fucking bastards!' It was generally the only space in the building where we could escape contact with other people, but looking back under my right arm I could see two pairs of feet standing behind me. Immediately, I spun round and turned on the two young Chinese guys who had arrived in the *atrad* two weeks earlier.

'Go on, fuck off, will you! Get your own fucking cigarettes and food ... Leave me alone, you scrounging wankers ... Piss off back to Peking! ...' I shouted, waving them away as I advanced towards them. I stomped across the corridor into the kitchen area, where Ahmed was sitting at the table with two of his North African friends drinking tea, and I could tell he had clocked my rage as soon as I walked into the room and turned to see Chan to the left of the door using my tea towel to dry his bowl and mug. Ahmed's eyes darted between the two of us and he put down his tea. Instinctively, I snatched the towel from Chan's hand, making his bowl fall to the floor with a metallic clang. 'Who the fuck said you could use that, Chan?' I snapped.

The table fell quiet as I turned on my heel to leave, but almost instantly I felt Chan's fist connect with the back of my neck. The next thing I knew I was bent over in the corner by the door, shielding my head as he came at me with flying feet and fists. Each withering blow into my right side sent pain shooting up my body, and I knew I had to move fast and start fighting back before he inflicted some serious damage. The last thing I needed at this stage of my sentence was a return to the hell of the hospital Zone, because that meant an almost certain end to my chances of getting parole at the next hearing. My fear of that was even greater than my fear of Chan's powerful fists and wild rage, and in one massive effort of will I sprang out of the crouching position and hurled myself at him, screaming like a banshee. The shock, more than the physical force, made him recoil and crash against the far wall. I pulled back my right arm, ready to drive a fist into his face, but as I swung my body round to deliver the blow, Ahmed waded into Chan from the right, knocking him sideways with a bone-shuddering blow to the jaw. It was a massive punch, and it stunned Chan for long enough to allow Ahmed to follow up with two further punches to the head and a violent karate-style kick to his ribcage.

Chan, though, wasn't down and out yet, and he slowly got to his feet, pushing his back up the wall as Ahmed rained blows down on him. Chan had his fists over his face and his arms covering his chest, like a boxer on the ropes, absorbing the hits, when in a sudden explosion of movement he made his move. Dropping his arms, he pushed off the wall with his right foot and propelled himself at Ahmed, landing on him with such force that the two of them crashed over the table, sending metal mugs flying in all directions. Ahmed bounced off the bench on the other side of the table and landed awkwardly on his back with Chan on top of him. The Chinaman rose above him on his knees, lifting his fist high above his shoulder, but Ahmed quickly twisted to the left and hurled him against the wall.

Like the other two observers, I was paralysed with fear, and we pressed ourselves up against the walls while a crowd formed at the doorway and people started pushing to get a view of the action. The two scrappers scrambled to their feet, gasping for breath, and immediately began to exchange a flurry of punches, forcing each other up and down the room with the savagery of their blows. The sound of fist on face was nauseating, and both were now smeared with blood as they lunged and ducked and looked for the killer opening in each other's defence. For a few seconds the frenzy abated and the two stood facing each other, swaying from one side to the other, before Ahmed feinted a punch with his left hand, forcing Chan to stick out his right to block it. Ahmed seized his chance, throwing a massive right that crashed into Chan's jaw and sent him reeling backwards against the far wall. As Chan staggered forward, he could only lift his arms halfway up to his face as Ahmed leapt towards him, jack-knifing his body in mid-air for extra power, and landed a huge head butt on the bridge of the Chinaman's nose. I heard the bone crack and watched the blood shoot in all directions as Chan crashed back into the wall and lay slumped and stunned on the floor. Ahmed, bloody and wild-eyed, stood over him panting for breath, with a hint of a smile at the corner of his mouth.

He spun round and looked me in the eyes, but said nothing. I'd rejected him in favour of Boodoo John, but he'd never stopped looking out for me. He'd told me that he was a better man than he looked. Now he'd shown me. As Chan lay slumped in the corner, groaning, Ahmed strode from the room.

It was a stroke of great good fortune that the *atradnik* was not in the building when the fight took place, because all three of us would almost certainly have ended up either in solitary confinement or with another six months slapped on to our sentence. At the very least, I would have had to kiss goodbye to any chance of getting my parole at the first time of asking. Ahmed, though, was quick to try to prevent news of the incident reaching the admin building. Within minutes of washing the blood from his face and changing into a clean black T-shirt, he was marching round the *atrad*, issuing warnings to anyone thinking about grassing us up to the guards or governors. And Ahmed, with his deep diagonal scar and intense glare, had a way of issuing warnings that made even the most devious and hardened inmate think long and hard before ignoring him. No one fucked with Ahmed. The beating he had administered to Chan, one of the meanest, toughest bastards in a Zone full of mean, tough bastards, was clearer and more eloquent than any words he might have used.

'Do you think Chan might squeal?' I whispered to Ahmed, as the *atrad* began to close down for the night and we filed into the dormitories.

'No chance,' he replied. 'He's too fucking proud. He knows there's only one way to get even with me – and that's a rematch.'

35

I stared at the cheap white clock on the wall in Ergin's office, watching the red second hand jerk its way clumsily around the dial. I was passing the time by seeing how long I could hold my breath. Ergin sat leaning forward, one leg crossed over the other, with his elbow on his knee and his fist on his chin. He was gazing vacantly out of the window, even though there was nothing to see but the grey breeze-block wall dividing the factory from the Zone. The wall was so close that he couldn't even see the grey sky above it. Mafia practised throwing a cigarette into the air and catching it in his mouth, while Molloi's head bounced up and down as he dozed in his chair. The only noise in the room was the loud ticking of the plastic clock.

It had been a similar scene in the office for several weeks by then, and the boredom of doing nothing was proving far more crushing than the boredom of doing the same thing over and over again, all day, every day. At least time didn't appear to stand still when we were working. The boys on the factory floor were busy at their machines, making blue boiler suits for another Zone, but until the next consignment and job order arrived there was nothing for the four of us in the office to do except watch the clock and wait for something to happen. Doing nothing creates a peculiar tension among people, especially in a small room, inside a prison, in the middle of nowhere, in a foreign land. For a few days, following the Chan–Ahmed fight, I sat in dread, waiting for a guard to summon me to the governors' office to be punished for my role in the fracas.

The atmosphere in the room was not improved by the unspoken but intense rivalry that existed between Ergin and me, which gave an electric charge to our friendship that was difficult to conceal. We both understood that we were adversaries in direct competition for the handful of parole places up for grabs in February, and we avoided the subject as best we could – which was hard, considering that was all either of us had been thinking about for weeks: freedom!

From time to time Ergin politely asked how my application was proceeding, and I asked about his, but our mutual displays of curiosity were no more than a sham of manners. We both knew that if it came to it, each of us would happily trample on the other's head to be the first through those giant mesh gates and away to our loved ones. Secretly, I hoped his application was quietly going down in flames, and I'd be very surprised if he didn't feel the same about my own.

Suddenly, Maximovich pushed open the door to Ergin's office and all four of us automatically stood up and took off our woollen hats. As one, we nodded our heads in respect and said, 'Good afternoon, *nachalnik*!' The master guard had clearly enjoyed his lunch break. His eyes were half-closed, one half of his shirt was hanging out and he had to prop himself up against the door-frame before he was able to speak. I imagined him half an hour earlier, parked up in a remote clearing in the pines, riding up and down on top of some poor woman in the back of his van, trousers round his ankles, his pot belly bouncing in rhythm with the rocking of the vehicle.

'You ... English boy – visitor is here. Go to your clothes,' he slurred, pointing at Mafia with his riot stick. No one moved. We looked at each other, not knowing whether he meant me or Mafia, or whether he was talking drunken rubbish and there was no visitor.

'Er, who has a visitor, master guard?' said Ergin, gently.

Maximovich's eyelids drooped lower and lower, his chin sunk into his chest and he began to sway back and forth in the door-frame. Then, with one mighty effort, he jerked his head upwards and boomed: '*Hague Tig! Visitor!*' As he finished, the master guard, all sixteen stone of him, lurched forward and did a kind of pirouette to try and right himself before landing on his back with a thump in the middle of the room. Mafia and Molloi started giggling, but Ergin waved me away. 'Go on, you go. I'll look after this fat drunk bastard.'

I strode back through the Zone towards the *atrad* as fast as I could without running, and without risking a fall on the patches of black ice that were forming on the cleared tarmac. The rich orange sun was beginning its final descent over the tips of the pine trees beyond the barbed-wire wall to the west as I racked my brains as to who might have come to visit me. Lucy, Mum, Dad and Rob had all said that the next time they saw me would be on English soil. Maybe it was Alla or someone else from the Embassy, or dear old Alexi with another food parcel, or a lawyer from Moscow … I changed into my civvy clothes in under a minute and, escorted by the duty *atradnik*, made my way down the side of the *atrads*, across Sniper Alley and into the reception area of the accommodation block. Raisa Petrovna was on duty at the desk and she waved me down the long dark corridor without a word. As soon as I walked into the living room I did a double-take. Standing by the window was a man with a shaved head, a big nose and one arm in plaster, sticking out at an awkward angle from his body.

'Jesus, what the hell are you doing here?' I blurted, my mind quickly trying to work out what the hell one of my former colleagues at Garban Icap was doing paying me a visit in Mordovia.

'Hello, Tig. Long time no see,' he said, with a strong Essex twang and a broad smile. 'Did no one tell you I was coming?'

'Er, no, Steve, they didn't. No one tells you anything in here if it's helpful or positive.'

'I brought you a present. Here, have your original trial documents. The girl in the Embassy asked me to bring them down to you,' he said, handing me a brown A4 envelope. 'See, we're not all wankers! I was just …'

'Hey, hang on a moment,' I interrupted, as the alarm bells started to ring. 'You've been sent here by Garban, haven't you? They're getting jittery because I'm going to be back in London soon. They're trying to sweeten me up, aren't they? In case I badmouth them around the City? That's why you're here, isn't it?'

'Woah! Tig, Tig, slow down!' he said, holding up his good arm. 'It's nothing like that, mate. Honestly.

Relax, I left Garban months ago. I'm on gardening leave. I came of my own accord. No one except your mum and dad and the Embassy knows I'm here . . .'

'Then what the hell are you doing here? In Mordovia! When you could be sunning yourself in the Caribbean? I just don't get it, Steve. I know we got on well enough at Garban, but we weren't exactly bosom buddies. It's all so bloody weird.'

Steve paused and stared down at the floor for a few moments before looking up. He looked sad and sympathetic all at once, his face imploring me to trust him.

'Tig, I can see why you're suspicious, but the plain truth is that, like lots of other people who worked with you, I've been feeling absolutely gutted about what's happened to you, mate. I haven't stopped thinking about it since the day you were arrested – what was it, almost two years ago now? I know it must be weird for you, finding me standing in here, but I had to come. We knew you weren't a druggie, let alone an international smuggler! Tig "The Jackal" Hague, international drugs baron! I don't think so somehow. I had to let you know that I, and plenty of others, have been really upset about what's happened. If I called and said that when you eventually got home, you wouldn't believe me, would you?'

'I don't know what to say, Steve. I'm sorry if I sound paranoid. I'm going slightly nuts in here. I don't trust anyone any more. This place is a viper's nest. It plays with your head . . . I'm really touched that you've come all the way out here to see me – and bring the documents.'

I walked across the room and we gave each other a hug and a slap on the back. 'Thanks, Steve, I appreciate you coming – *and* bringing these,' I said, waving the envelope above my head. 'You have no idea how much this little bundle means to me. These little babies are my passport out of here!'

We both went to sit down, him in the armchair in the corner, me on the smelly old brown sofa. 'So, no one twisted your arm to come out here, then?' I said, pointing to his plastered arm.

'No, this is an heroic football injury, sustained on the battlefield of Spitalfields 5-a-aside astroturf pitch . . .'

We talked for two hours before it was time for him to leave, cracking jokes and bantering just like we used to do in the pubs of the City after work at Garban. Steve had been driven down by a Russian he had hired, and it had taken them two days to get there in the treacherous, wintry conditions. They wanted to get on their way because the weather was forecast to get even worse.

'Steve, I owe you one,' I said, getting to my feet. 'The pints are on me when – *if!* – I ever get out of this hellhole!'

As he made to head down the corridor, he turned and said: 'If ever you feel you're starting to lose heart or go completely crazy, try to remember that there's loads of people back home, thinking of you and praying for your release. Stay strong, my friend. It won't be long now . . .'

'So everyone's been telling me for the past couple of years.'

Steve's flying visit to the Zone was almost shockingly strange. He hadn't been one of my greatest buddies at Garban, let alone in London, but once he'd gone and the surprise of it had begun to fade away, I felt my mood start to lift. The fact that a former work colleague, who I knew only reasonably well, had gone to such great lengths – and with a broken arm – to travel out to see me in the middle of nowhere and in the depths of winter restored some of the faith in humanity that had been slowly draining out of me over the months like water out of a leaking bucket.

In buoyant mood, a few nights after Steve had left, I decided to make my big move on Zanpolit. Nearly everything was in place: my original trial documents were all in good order and, with the help of Yevgeny the paedophile librarian, I had completed my official application forms and written the covering letters in Russian. The next stage of the plan was to make sure that I was on the list of applicants that Zanpolit would submit to court for the judge to review at the hearing on an as yet unspecified date in February. Zanpolit put the dozens of applicants in some kind of rough order, to make it easier for the judge to rule who was to walk free. To make sure I was high up on that list, I planned to hit Zanpolit with my most generous bribe since I'd arrived in the Zone. He might have shouted at me during our last meeting, but 200 cigarettes and sufficient coffee and chocolate to last his wife until the spring was likely to be enough to put the greasy smile back on his face. Messieurs Nescafé, Marlboro and Lindt open a lot of doors in Mordovia.

I was at the front of the queue in the exercise yard that evening, jumping from foot to foot to keep out the perishing cold and hugging myself to stop the flurries of snow from disappearing down my neck. The guards enjoyed looking out from the warmth of the observation room and seeing us dancing around in discomfort, and often they waited ten or more minutes before buzzing the first of us through. There was only so long you could stand the freezing cold, and often people gave up and retreated to the warmth of the *atrad*. But Yuri, the old guard who'd hit it off with Dad, was on duty that night, and when he saw it was me with my face pressed up against the mesh gate he immediately buzzed me through. I shuffled awkwardly towards the offices with two rolls of Marlboro, a jar of Gold Blend and three bars of Swiss chocolate stuffed into my baggy trousers and jacket pockets. The one advantage of growing so thin was the greater space it freed up in my clothes for smuggling bribes.

As ever, Zanpolit pretended not to notice as I unloaded the Western luxuries, but to emphasize the scale of my generosity I took out each item very slowly and placed it very deliberately and neatly into his deep drawer. I watched his eyes widen as he stole a glance at my offerings and closed the drawer.

'So you want to be my friend again, Mr Hague?'

'I just want you to get me out of here, Zanpolit. I have served my sentence. It is time for me to go.'

After the last hearing in early December a handful of applicants had been refused bail on the very dodgy grounds that the paperwork they'd put together had contained some errors. It was just an excuse to stall their departure by another couple of months, but to make absolutely sure I didn't fall victim to the same callous ploy I asked Zanpolit to inspect all my documents.

'Is everything correct?' I asked in Russian, as clearly as I could without sounding like I was talking to a five-year-old.

Zanpolit ran his bony index finger down each page of my bundle before he looked up and said: 'They are good. You need just one more: a character reference from the guard in Atrad 1, confirming your good behaviour. I will ask him for it, and next week, on 9 February, I will pass your application on to the judge at the Zubova Paliansky court.'

'And that's it?'

'That's it.'

'I will be free?'

'You will be a free man again, Mr Hague.'

'Is that a promise?'

'You have my word.'

'Thank you, Zanpolit, I am grateful to you,' I smiled back at him, clenching my fist in celebration inside the hat I was holding in front of me.

As I walked out of his office, Boodoo John was waiting outside and we gave each other a semi-hug and a wink as he headed inside. Back in the *atrad* I waited for him in the kitchen, pacing up and down with a cup of tea, almost bursting with joy. I wanted to celebrate somehow, or call Lucy and tell her the great news. 'Yes! Yes! Yes!' I muttered to myself, walking round the table, nodding my head and punching the air. 'Thank God for that! Finally! Goodbye to Zone 22! Hello, England! Yes! Yes! Yes!'

A couple of minutes later I turned round as the rickety old entrance door to the *atrad* opened and Boodoo John swept in, quickly closing the door behind him to keep out the freezing wind. I was smiling from ear to ear, but as soon as Boodoo John turned round and I saw his furrowed brow and pursed lips, I wiped the smile from my face. He walked into the kitchen, head down, brushing the snow off his black jacket.

'How did it go?' I asked him. 'What did he say?'

'Er ... it was OK. He said I had as good a chance as anyone, but ... that means nothing, does it? I got a bad vibe off him. I don't think I'm in the running this time ...' He sat down, exhaling loudly, running both hands over his cropped head as he looked down at the table. 'What about you? Did he drop any hints?' he added, trying his best to sound positive.

'Yeah, it was OK, I think,' I replied, eager not to sound too triumphant. 'It was pretty positive, if I'm honest. He said my papers are in good order and my name will be on the list.' I let out a nervous laugh before putting my arm round his shoulder and adding: 'You're going to be just fine. You're the only prisoner they like because you work hard and you don't cause trouble. You've got the respect; I've got the cigs and the chocolate. We're both going to be OK. I can feel it. We'll both be walking through those goddam gates together.'

36

It was the evening of 9 February, the day Zanpolit was
to lodge my parole application at the local court, and I
decided to celebrate by cooking Boodoo John and myself
a bowl of noodles using the last few slices of *kolbasa*.
For pudding we were going to have the last of the six tins
of sliced peaches in syrup. After that, only noodles and
oatmeal biscuits remained from the provisions that
Lucy had brought down from Moscow in November,
and from around Christmas time I'd been eating smaller
portions to spin them out. If the worst came to the worst
and my release was delayed by a few days, or even a
couple of weeks, I could always start eating the disgusting
prison meals again. The end of my ordeal was in sight,
and I wasn't bothered about going hungry for a few
weeks, knowing that soon I'd be tucking into some
proper food back in England.

Boodoo John said little as he ate, and it was obvious
that he was worried sick about getting his parole, though
he was too polite to say as much. He made the odd grunt
of appreciation as he wolfed down his noodles, exclaiming, 'You're some chef, English boy!' and slapped me on
the back as he took our bowls to wash them under the
tap in the wash area next door. But like so many others
whose fates were to be decided in the coming weeks,
he was restless and distracted. I'd been trying to make a

concerted effort to conceal my glee at the prospect of my impending release, following the tip-off from Zanpolit, but sometimes my optimism and excitement just burst out, like a nervous laugh, for all to witness. My body language, for a start, was more confident, and there was almost a swagger in my stride as I went about the Zone with my head and shoulders no longer slumped downwards and my boots no longer shuffling miserably through the snow. And for the first time in over a year, all the pop tunes that had once filled my head from dawn to dusk started to return, like signs of spring, the first shoots of new life starting to emerge from the earth. After our noodles I shuffled down the corridor in my slippers towards the TV room, whistling the Oasis track 'Don't Look Back in Anger'.

As I walked past the small office, the sullen young guard obsessed by military hardware was leaning back in his chair with his combat boots up on the table, staring through the door. Behind him, the surging wind drove the recently fallen snow up against the *atrad*, making the window rattle and whine like a kettle. I carried on walking and whistling and was halfway down the corridor when he shouted my name and beckoned me back to see him. I moon-walked backwards until I reached the door and craned my neck so that he could see only my head.

'Yes, *nachalnik*?'

'Hague Tig,' he said, sneering down his long, pointy nose. 'Your parole application – where is it? Maybe you want to stay here? Maybe Mordovia is better than England?'

'What?' I blurted out, as alarm ran through me like a

wave of electricity and I spun round in one motion, my momentum carrying me to within a yard of the table. 'But Zanpolit said ... he said ... he was going to give it to you to sign ... where is it? It should be in court ...'

'Don't ask me,' he shrugged, and picked up the magazine on his lap, lifting it up so that I could no longer see his face.

I grabbed my coat and hat, pulled on my boots and rushed outside to join the end of the queue to be buzzed over to the offices. Half an hour later I was standing in Zanpolit's office pleading with him for an explanation. Not looking up from his desk, he said slowly and coldly, as if he was trying to control his temper: 'I gave him your papers as I said, Hague Tig. Be very careful how you speak to me. Now just go away ...'

'But, my parole ... what about the judge? ... will I still make the list ... will you take my papers ...?'

Zanpolit sat back in his chair and gave me the eyeball as he ran his bony fingers through his swept-back gelled hair. After a pause, he pointed at me, narrowed his eyes, and pointed at the door.

I didn't know which of the two spiteful bastards to believe, but it made no difference anyhow because I wasn't in a position to call either of them a liar or an incompetent. Either one of them could torpedo my parole application. Humility and diplomacy and a bagload of Marlboro offered the only route forward, and the following evening, after a fretful day watching the clock and pacing around Ergin's office, I went back to the *atradnik* and presented him with eighty cigs, a small pot of Gold Blend and a KitKat. For a guard, this was a massive bribe, the equivalent of two weeks' wages, and when I dumped the goods on the table, a look of astonishment spread over his face before he quickly stuffed them into the little camouflage fabric rucksack at his feet. He nodded up at me and I left the room.

Zanpolit hadn't yet taken the bundle of parole applications to court, but time was fast running out. The Zone was on full alert, and when Zanpolit did finally emerge from the office building, weighed down with bundles of our applications, the news would spread to every corner of the camp within minutes. I wanted my file of papers to be sitting on Zanpolit's desk ready to leave, but the *atradnik* twat wanted to play mind games with me, so he held on to them and then, quite literally, leant back in his chair for a few days and watched me grow ever more frantic. Every evening, with increasing desperation, I asked him if he had got round to writing my character reference and each time, never looking up from his Guns 'n' Ammo mag, he gave me the same infuriating answer: 'When I have time, Hague Tig. When I have time.' He only needed to write one simple line saying I had kept out of trouble, but for four days he did nothing but sit in his little office reading his weapons porn, occasionally getting up to make an inspection of the *atrad* or go outside for a stretch and a smoke. Every stage of the parole process was designed to be as awkward and frustrating as possible for the prisoners, and this nasty little game, leaving it right to the final possible moment, was one more 'fuck you' from this guard. The sad wanker was trying to push my patience to the limit, hoping I'd snap at him so that he'd be able to hit me with a black mark. I wasn't being singled out and picked on. It was just an unwritten rule in the guards' contract to seize every opportunity to make life as stressful as possible for the inmates.

The anxiety made sleep difficult, and after a fourth night of fretting and cursing I could stand it no longer. I went to see the *atradnik* and begged him to sign me off. It was a demeaning experience, but I had run out of options and I was prepared to do virtually anything to make sure my application reached the court, where no bastard in the Zone could stall or tamper with it – and if that meant humiliating myself before a moronic, malicious redneck ten years my junior, then so be it. 'Please, please, *nachalnik*,' I said, my face screwed up in desperation, my hands cupped together and pressed against my heart, like a kid pleading for sweets. 'Please, help me. You are a good man ...' This was exactly what the evil little shit wanted – a display of grovelling servitude from the 'rich' Englishman. In a way, I had humiliated *him* by giving him a pile of bribes he could never afford on his wages, drawing attention to the fact that even though I was a prisoner and he my gaoler, I was still financially better off than him. Now he had had his revenge. He went to the locked cupboard on the wall by the window, took out my bundle of papers from the upper shelf and sat back down at the table. Pulling a biro out of the inner pocket of his combat jacket, he scrawled a single line on to a blank piece of paper and signed his name below. He handed me the bundle and immediately waved me out of the room with a dramatic flourish, like I was a massive fucking mosquito.

Walking backwards out of the room, and bowing as

I went, I smiled and said: '*Spasiba, spasiba, nachalnik*, you pathetic little worm, *spasiba, spasiba* . . .'

I delivered the completed application to Zanpolit that evening and sought final reassurance from him that I was still on the list of prisoners he was recommending for release. 'Hague Tig will be a free man very soon,' he smiled. The following morning, shortly before we assembled by the factory gates, I was out in the exercise yard smoking a cigarette when Zanpolit emerged from the offices in his long Gestapo-style leather coat, carrying a fat briefcase in each hand. Immediately a cheer went up along all three of the yards, and some prisoners threw themselves against the mesh fencing, shouting questions at him as he walked towards his ancient brown Ford Escort and loaded the hopes of fifty men into the boot. Zanpolit didn't even look up as he climbed into the car and sped out of the gates with a few flashy revs of the engine and a squeal of wheels that sent muddy slush and exhaust fumes flying into the air behind him.

That evening, I, Boodoo John, Julian and Ergin, together with every other parole applicant, were summoned to the offices after the final *preverka* to be handed a receipt, proving that our papers had been lodged at court. Back in the *atrad*, all four of us hugged and slapped each other's backs. The rivalry was over. We had all made the list of hopefuls, and now it was down to the judge. It was out of our hands. It was, thank God, out of the Zone's hands.

When the judge would sit to consider our cases was anyone's guess. Even if they knew, Zanpolit and the other governors were never going to let on. And so we waited and fretted and paced up and down and chewed our nails and smoked a thousand cigarettes, day after day, waiting for the news to roll through the Zone that Zanpolit was going to the court in Penza to collect the list of names of successful applicants. Concentrating on work was virtually impossible, and even Ergin, so conscientious and responsible in running the factory and so confident about being released, was clearly affected by nerves too. He fidgeted and paced the room as anxiously as the next man. Even though Zanpolit had given me his word, I grew increasingly anxious as well. Not until I heard my name being read out in morning *preverka* would I be able to relax fully. Mingled with the mounting anxiety was an almost uncontrollable excitement about regaining my freedom, a constant stream of dreams and plans about what I would do once I was released. Day and night, happy images filled my head: me running through the sliding doors at Heathrow and scooping up Lucy – my wife! – in my arms; a big family party round at Mum's; heading up to the West End with my old mates for a night of drinking and dancing. Even the simple prospect of lying in on a Sunday morning, then shuffling down the road to the grumpy newsagent in my tracksuit bottoms and furry slippers to get the papers, filled me with an almost child-like thrill. Not since the days and weeks leading up to my trial had I felt such an extraordinary surge of positive feelings.

Finally I could endure the uncertainty no longer, and I gave Raisa Petrovna my last luxury gift – a Zippo lighter – so that I could make a call to the Embassy there and then that evening rather than wait for a day or two until she or one of the other officials could be bothered to sign it off. Alla's assistant at the Embassy said she had no idea when the hearing was to take place, and put me through to Mum.

'Now, Tig, Alla at the Embassy swore me to secrecy when I called her yesterday, but she's been told the hearing is to go ahead next week some time and – let's just say it's looking very positive for you, my darling. But don't tell a soul, whatever you do. They warned me that it might jeopardize your release. As soon as I get the word from the Embassy I'm getting the first flight out to Moscow and I'm not leaving the bloody place without you! I can't wait to have you back home, safe and sound!'

I walked back to the *atrads* clenching my fists like a footballer who'd just scored a screamer, whistling into the cold wind.

Molloi came flying through the office door, yelping breathlessly, 'He's gone! Zanpolit's gone to court!' It was four o'clock in the afternoon and for the final hour of the day Ergin and I made no attempt to disguise our nerves. Neither of us was able to sit down for more than a few seconds before jumping to our feet and going to the toilet, or finding another excuse to walk to the other end of the factory. In the evening, around fifty of us paced up and down and chain-smoked in the yards of the three *atrads*, waiting for Zanpolit to return. When he finally appeared through the main gate and we saw his dark silhouette against the floodlights tramping towards the offices, we began shouting and pressing ourselves up against the fence. One of the prisoners yelled: 'How many names are on the list?'

'That's for me to know,' he replied and disappeared inside. It was the confirmation we needed that there had been a parole hearing. I was standing next to Boodoo John and the two of us embraced excitedly, slapping each other on the back. The list was always read out in the morning, and for the rest of the evening I didn't want to eat or sit down. I couldn't sleep that night, and as soon as the wake-up siren sounded I flew out of bed, threw on my clothes and ran outside for morning exercises. I was buzzing so much that I jumped and squatted like Jane Fonda herself.

We lined up for *preverka* and waited. It was still pitch black and the glare of the floodlights was reflected in the shiny, mirror-like surface of the compacted ice. Our backs, as ever, were to the office, and after five minutes I heard the door open behind me and the crunch of boots in the snow. A guard started reading out a list of names. One of the first was 'Ebubadike' which was Boodoo John's real name, and from the corner of my eye, as I carried on looking down at the ground, I saw a giant grin burst across his face. Julian's was called out soon after, and I turned to see him looking to the heavens in thanks. I didn't recognize most of the people being called out because we all knew each other by nicknames. One after another, names floated across the frozen air, and each time he drew breath before reading out the next one, I closed my eyes and waited for mine ...

But then the talking stopped. The list had ended. There was silence, briefly, followed by the sound of boots heading away into the distance. Then the slam of the swing-back door. Black figures around me began to melt away. I couldn't move. The snow was starting to settle on my hat and shoulders. I looked up to see that I was the only prisoner left on the concourse. I felt a hand on my shoulder. It was the guard Yuri, Dad's mate, wearing his trademark mirror glasses. He pushed me gently in the direction of the *atrad*. I floated back into the yard, unable to form a coherent thought or emotion. Boodoo John was waiting for me. He gave me a tight hug. The gate closed behind me with a clang. A gust of wind picked up a heap of the powdery snow that had settled against the *atrad* wall overnight and sent it swirling around the yard like a miniature tornado.

'Celebrate, my friend, celebrate. Don't commiserate. You're free. Be happy,' I said, dazed.

'I'm sorry, English boy. I really am. I don't know what to say. But you'll be next, English boy. You're next … Hang in there …'

'Well done, well done, mate! I'm really happy for you,' I said, warm tears running down my frozen cheeks as I held on to him.

37

The following morning, after breakfast, there was a small farewell party for Boodoo John and Julian in the kitchen. There was a pan of strong *cheffir* and a plate of biscuits on the table, and a dozen Africans and a couple of others took it in turns to give the pair of them a hug and have a quiet word in their ear. Boodoo John and Julian were quiet, embarrassed almost and sheepish, trying not to let their joy get the better of them in front of us. They had the rest of their lives to dance a jig and punch the air in delight. I tried to avoid these parties as a rule because there was always an undercurrent of bitterness and envy behind the superficial jollity, but this was different. These were the boys who'd watched out for me since I'd arrived. Genuine good guys. (The long-termers never even bothered coming because it was too painful for them.) As a going-away present, I gave Boodoo John my favourite fleece top, a new pair of jeans Mum had bought and my fancy Nikes. One of the other boys gave him a blazer with shiny gold buttons. None of my clothes would have fitted Julian's massive frame, so I gave him a full bottle of shampoo and 100 Marlboro. He didn't smoke, but Western fags could be used as currency on the outside too.

'You look like a pimp in retirement,' I said, giving Boodoo John a slap on the back and forcing out a plastic smile for the occasion. All prisoners wanted to look good on the day they finally walked out of Zone 22, and a few of the inmates had even started a little mini-business by getting their families to send decent clothes down so that they could sell them for cigarettes and food.

When the guard came to escort them to the prison minibus around twenty of us filed into the little exercise yard and formed a makeshift human tunnel, like rugby players at the end of a match. Boodoo John and Julian were the last through the *atrad* door and, leaving their bags by the gate, they came back and walked down the lines, shaking hands, embracing and slapping backs, all to the accompaniment of an incoherent din of cheers, banter and expressions of goodwill. Both of them were crying and, for a few moments, I forgot all about my own plight as a rush of almost overwhelming emotion washed over me. Before I knew what I was doing, I too was welling up and clapping wildly as the electric gate closed behind them. The other successful applicants were waiting for them on the concourse, an assortment of Afghans, Vietnamese and Middle Easterners – about fifteen of them in total – and immediately they started to walk up towards the factory gates before turning right down the side of the *atrads* towards the free world beyond. Boodoo John was the last man in the group and he stopped before turning the corner, put down his *sumka* and gave us a little salute before disappearing from view.

Slowly we turned to go, but within moments the sound of the siren shattered the silence that hung over the Zone, and we began to scramble on to the concourse to assemble for another day in the factory.

'You have no right to keep me here. You are stealing my freedom, my life. Why am I still here, Zanpolit?'

Now that my papers were on the outside I was less bothered about upsetting him, and I spoke to him as I would to a junior colleague at work who'd screwed up, not rude but blunt. And the plain fact that my parole date had now passed fuelled my indignation and gave me the confidence to talk to him in a way that I wouldn't have dared just a few weeks back.

Zanpolit wasn't upset for me, he was just embarrassed that his limited influence over the judge had been exposed. His pathetic charade of power had been blown wide open, revealing him as the backwater, pen-sucking, paper-shuffling, Escort-driving, sadistic, good-for-fuck-all, greasy-haired, shit-fucking little weasel that he was.

'You are not the only one, Hague Tig. Ergin and Benny Baskin are still here as well, you know . . .'

I cut him off, in English, snapping: 'Oh, come off it!' And I turned on my heel and headed to the door.

'Hague, Tig. Stop . . . *Hague* . . .' But I carried on walking and angrily pulled the door shut behind me. In the corridor outside, the queue of prisoners stared at me, wide-eyed.

Before leaving the office I filled in a request form to call the Embassy the next day. It was too late to call there and then, but the following evening I was put through to Alla's junior colleague Irina.

'Hello, Tig, nice to hear you, how's your parole application going?' she said in a friendly, sing-song voice.

'How's it going?' I seethed down the receiver. 'How's it going? I'll tell you how it's going: it's *not* going! That's what. People are walking out of here, but I'm still here and I'm going to be here for at least another two months, unless some people start pulling their fingers out and put some pressure on these bastards to get me the hell out . . . Put me through to Lucy, will you?'

Without replying, she put me on hold and the classical muzak came on. Prisoners were only allowed five minutes on the phone, and as I waited and waited I grew ever more agitated, knowing that my time was rapidly disappearing. I started abusing the muzak: 'What kind of shit, fucking violin bollocks is that? Call that fucking music? La di da di da di fucking da di da, fucking bollocks, fuck off violinist wanker, get yourself a proper fucking instrument . . .' And when Lucy finally picked up I was insane with rage and I let fly at her.

'It's me . . . Your husband . . . From prison . . . In Russia . . . Still! I'm still here! I'm thinking of retiring here I love it so much! . . . What the hell are you and everyone else doing back in England? . . . I'm rotting to fucking death in here. I need some bloody support, Lucy . . . I'm going to end up dying in this dump unless people on the outside start pulling fingers out of arses and get bloody motivated . . . I've got no bribes left, no food, there's not going to be another fucking parole hearing for two fucking months . . . What the hell is going on?'

'Slow down, Babe . . . listen to me . . .'

'Slow down? How can my life slow down any more?

414

It's at a goddam standstill. I've had enough. I'm losing it in here. I've hung on for nearly two years now, and I can't take it any more ...'

I was ranting so fast and loud that Lucy couldn't get a word in before our time was up and the phone went dead. I slammed the receiver down and slid down the wall, digging my fingernails into my face. Another prisoner waiting to use the phone touched me on the shoulder and as I stood up to leave I kicked the wall and punched a fist into my left palm. The Undertaker and another guard stood by the window, laughing.

To the anger, despair and helplessness, I could now add deep shame, which was made all the more painful by my inability to contact Lucy and tell her how sorry I was. I hated myself for the way I'd spoken to her, and as soon as I got back to the *atrad* I immediately started writing her a letter, page after page of it, pouring out my apologies and my love and my gratitude. She wouldn't receive it for months, but my urgency to communicate with her was unbearable. I was so upset and paranoid that I convinced myself she was going to leave me, once she'd done the honourable thing and seen me released. She'd stuck by me for two years, and for half of that she'd also been nursing her mum as she slid towards death; she'd given up her job to help me, she'd borrowed thousands of pounds to come and visit me, she'd had to give up her dream of buying our house together ... And how did I repay her love and loyalty? By screaming blue murder down the phone at her!

My parole date was almost a month in the past and

I resented every additional day of my freedom, of life – MY LIFE! – that was taken away from me. For days I barely spoke, not even to Ergin, who was submerged in his own world of dark thoughts. If I was asked a question, I just grunted and shrugged or replied with a 'yes' or a 'no'. At night I lay awake for hours on end, my head numb with fatigue and self-pity, my body numb with cold, listening to the Arctic winds whistling and screeching round the rickety wooden hut, and the rats and mice scuttling over the ceiling two feet from where I lay. The days passed in a dull, grey haze.

A week after Boodoo John and the others had gone, there was a strange episode when I was called out of the factory and summoned to Regime's office. I walked in to find two youngish guys, about my age, dressed in short leather jackets and designer casual clothes. One of them had a round, pleasant face and wore a baseball cap. He had his feet up on Regime's desk, which shocked me. The other guy was rummaging through the drawers of the desk, more out of curiosity, it seemed, than in a deliberate search for anything.

'Take a seat, Tig,' smiled the guy in the cap, in English, chucking me a block of Marlboro Reds. 'You must be getting pretty low on cigarettes by now.'

'I am, as it happens. Thanks,' I replied, sitting down a little nervously. He had an air about him that invited me to trust him, and when he asked me how I was bearing up, I let rip about the parole system, the governors, the guards, the mind games, my health ... I had trusted the two young plain-clothes cops in Moscow too, and they had stitched me up – but I didn't give a shit any more. I'd played the system and it had got me nowhere. So what the fuck if I spoke my mind?

'... I can't take much more of this. What kind of justice is it to hold a man for almost two years ...'

He cut me off in mid-sentence, holding his hand up above his head, and said: 'We know, we know ... If I promised you you'd be out of here by the end of March, would you believe me?'

'No, I wouldn't! I don't believe anything anyone says in here any longer. The wankers in charge are more deceitful and bent than the fucking criminals. Besides, the next parole hearing's not till end of April or May ...'

He let out a half laugh as he got to his feet and walked round to the front of the desk, reaching into his wallet and handing me a piece of paper with a telephone number but no name. 'Here's my number. Call me when you're out. We may be able to work together if you ever come back to Russia. I'll show you the good side of Russia. You'll be back in England by the end of March.'

'Yeah, right, and I've got a twelve-inch cock.'

I returned to the factory, shaking my head and trying to make sense of our five-minute exchange. I guessed they must have been FSB operatives, because no one else would have the authority to boot Regime out of his office like that. But why would they come and see me? What possible interest could they have in my case? An absent-minded English banker caught with a fleck of hashish in his jeans on a business trip. It just didn't add up, and I dismissed it as another round of mind games. The pair, I concluded, must have been in the Zone on other business and decided to kill some time by taking the piss out of the stupid English guy just for laughs. Maybe they were friends of Zanpolit's, just another pair of bastards playing tricks with our heads and our hopes, just like the rest of them. But I couldn't dismiss the meeting from my mind. If it was just a practical joke, it was an elaborate and especially cruel one, even by the high standards of Zone 22 guards. However much I tried to put it from my mind, it had sparked a small glimmer of hope that refused to be put out.

'Someone is here for you,' said Ergin, walking back into the office, avoiding eye contact with me. It wasn't my fault he had failed to get parole, nor his that I had failed too, but a feeling of mutual resentment had developed over the two weeks that had followed.

'It's probably the Embassy driver with the food parcel I requested,' I said almost apologetically as I made my way to the door. 'About bloody time too.' Back in the *atrad* I washed and got dressed into my civvies, but I took my time and ambled slowly over to the accommodation block, figuring that if I dawdled long enough I might avoid having to go back to the factory – the day shift was over in just under an hour.

I strode down the corridor, hands in my pockets, and my face immediately lit up as I saw Alla sitting on the sofa and said: 'Hey, it's you!' I walked into the room and stopped dead in my tracks, speechless with shock.

'Lucy! What? Oh my God!' We hadn't spoken since my tirade at her two weeks earlier, and I hugged her so tight I almost broke her in half as I lifted her off her feet and spun her around.

'What the hell are you doing here?' I said after a minute.

'We've been to court in Zubova Paliansky to see the judge, Tig,' said Lucy, her face dropping a little. 'We waited all day but he never came, and then the clerk came to tell us that he'd had to travel to another town to deal with an urgent case there. The plan was to flutter our eyelids and put a bit of Embassy pressure on him to make sure you were definitely on the list for his next hearing but . . . Babes, I'm sorry. It's been a horrible waste of time and money . . .'

I tried to hide my frustration, but couldn't stop myself sighing deeply and shaking my head in utter disbelief that yet another twist of fate had worked against me.

'When the hell is my luck going to turn?' I said, rubbing my hands up and down my face. 'It's like there's a bloody curse on me!'

'Tig, don't worry,' interrupted Alla. 'I'm going to keep telephoning from Moscow and I'll come back down and see him in person if I have to. I promise.'

'At least I've got to see you for a few minutes!' said Lucy, putting her arms round my neck and covering my face in kisses.

Because they'd wasted so much time waiting for the judge, we only had fifteen minutes together before the Embassy driver put his head round the door and told Alla it was time to go back to Moscow. Alla left us for a few moments to ourselves, and there was no guard this time because the Embassy were in town and they wanted to spin as favourable an impression as possible.

'I'm so sorry about the way I spoke to you, Babe,' I

said, squeezing her tight. 'I don't know what came over me. I just lost it . . .'

Lucy leant back, flicking her wavy brown hair over her shoulders, and put her finger to my mouth.

'You don't have to apologize for a thing,' she smiled. 'To be honest, I was amazed you didn't go off the handle any earlier. You've been as strong as an ox. But it won't be long now . . . Trust me.' And she gave me a little wink as she leant towards me and pressed her lips against mine. We'd learned that a short farewell was the least painful way to part, and after a final hug, she swept down the corridor, leaving me standing in the middle of the room with four bags of shopping at my feet.

After two months of living off virtually nothing but plain noodles, my body had started to crave nutritious food, especially fruit and vegetables, and as soon as Lucy had gone I reached down, pulled out an apple and devoured it in three huge bites, core and all. Then I took out another, and that too disappeared in a matter of seconds, but almost immediately I felt sick and I put a third one back in the bag. My stomach was obviously not expecting anything as nutritious as a piece of fruit. My provisions, including cigarettes, had been virtually exhausted, and a few days earlier I'd called Alla to request a food parcel. I was grateful for the shopping the girls had brought, but it was strange that Alla hadn't thought to add all the requests I'd put in over the phone.

In fact, it was a very weird little episode altogether, and I tried to make sense of it all as the guard escorted me back across Sniper Alley and round the corner to the entrance of the *atrad* to unload my bags in the communal

420

food lockers. Weird was fast becoming the new 'normal' in my life. Nothing made sense any longer. So my wife pops over to Mordovia from London to see me for a quarter of an hour. And?

Is that any weirder than going to a stag party in England and ending up in prison in Russia as a result of it a few days later? So they bang me up for almost two years for carrying a fleck of a substance with the same powers of intoxication as half a bottle of wine or three cappuccinos? So an old work colleague, with a plastered arm out at right angles, pops by in Mordovia to say hello? So my parole date passes and still I rot in prison? So a man eats a dog and then howls in his sleep? I don't know what weird means any more.

We were lining up outside Atrad 1 for the evening head-count, coughing and snivelling as usual, stamping our feet and blowing into our hands as the thick snow swirled out of the darkness and into the blinding glare of the camp lights. It was a particularly cold night and I was desperate to get back to the warmth of the *atrad*.

The day before, Raisa Petrovna had given me a fresh parole application form and, after all the delaying tactics the last time round, I wanted to make sure my papers were in order long before Zanpolit added it to the existing bundle and resubmitted them to the court. Then the guard quickly read out the names of prisoners wanted by Zanpolit: 'Baskin, Benjamin ... Ergin, Eritoglu ... Hague, Tig ...'

My heart sank. What the fuck had we done wrong now? The others melted away towards the *atrads*, and the three of us gravitated to each other and headed towards the office door, our necks and hands buried deep inside our jackets to keep out the cold. 'Don't worry, he only wants to give us the official court explanation as to why we failed to get parole,' said Benny. 'That way, he can feel better about himself and pretend he did everything he could for us.'

The three of us stood in silence outside Zanpolit's door, trying to avoid eye contact with the two guards in the corridor. Benny went in first, and when he came out a minute later he gave me a wink as he brushed past, as if to say, 'What did I tell you?' I was in next, and when I took off my hat and looked up to greet Zanpolit, he looked at me sternly.

'*Siol! Ti da moi,*' he said.

I stared at him in astonishment, unable to talk for a few moments. Eventually I said: 'Me? . . . Why? . . . What? . . . But . . .' Then in English: 'You're fucking kidding! Why?'

'*Vseo! Ti da moi,*' he said.

'I can go?'

'The British Embassy will be here in the morning.'

'That's it?'

'That's it.'

'It's over?'

'It's over.'

38

It was an unofficial rule of the Zone that prisoners who'd
won parole didn't vaunt their good fortune in case they
stirred up or provoked those left behind who had old
scores to settle, or whose own applications had ended in
failure and who were consumed with envy and bitterness.
But the reality was that it was physically impossible
for a man to contain the glee he felt on being told he
had regained his freedom. When I walked back into the
reception area, the Undertaker was on duty behind the
desk. I tossed him a virtually full packet of Marlboro Red
and stopped to give him an extravagant bow, sweeping
my black woolly hat under my body as I leant forward.
With a broad smile, I said in English: 'You will die in
this shithole, you fat, evil bastard. Goodbye.' He stared at
me, not knowing how to react. I walked out of the office
building and, as the door swung shut behind me, I
jumped off the top step and swallow-dived to my left,
into a giant heap of freshly cleared snow.

A small crowd of wellwishers and beggars gathered
around me as Ahmed opened up the food locker, and I
started spraying noodles, coffee and cigarettes around the
entrance area like confetti. Dozens of black-clad arms
reached forward to try to grab the flying produce until
everything had gone except for one roll of cigarettes.

Next, I opened my suitcase and started throwing out all my clothes, causing another unseemly scramble as I sang in a mock-operatic voice: 'And you can have my shirt … who wants some pants? … everything must go … who'll take these fine socks off me? …' All I kept was my loafers, jeans, black roll-neck, fresh underwear and a packet of letters I'd received from home. At the first buzzer to assemble for work, the group quickly dispersed and people began frantically pulling on their boots, coats and hats and streaming out through the door. Eke Jude and Hulk, who could barely speak English, high-fived me as they filed outside. Ergin and Benny, who had to wait until Monday for the prison minibus to take them to Moscow because their embassies wouldn't come to collect them, stopped and we gave each other a quick back-slapping bear-hug.

'Go on, hurry up!' I said. 'You don't want to get a black mark now!'

'Just one more day at the office,' said Ergin, looking pleased with his little joke.

Within two minutes of the buzzer sounding, the stampede had passed and the *atrad* fell silent. I went to the office Ahmed shared with the *atradnik* and looked out of the window at the three blocks of prisoners falling into line outside their respective *atrads*, the black of the uniforms forming a striking contrast with the snow that carpeted the Zone. The first shafts of morning sun found a gap in the gathering clouds and suddenly streamed through the distant tree-tops and the barbed wire on top of the far wall as the Undertaker stepped out of the office, holding the prisoner name cards, with his grey-blue trooper hat perched at an awkward angle on his fat head. Ahmed was cradling a metal mug of tea, and he stood up from his desk to join me at the window, where the sun made his deep scar look all the more gruesome.

'Ahmed, I'm sorry I didn't trust you.'

'Don't worry, I wouldn't trust a man with this.' And he reached up to touch the scar.

'And thanks for watching my back and saving me from Chan. You'd make a hell of a bodyguard . . .'

'I'd been waiting for that moment for years,' he smiled, softening his harsh appearance. 'The thanks is mine.'

'I hope it all works out for you when you finally get out of here. If, God forbid, I end up here again in the meantime, you'll be top of my shortlist for *smelniks*!'

We patted each other on the back and he disappeared from the room without a word. After changing into my civilian clothes, I made my bed in perfect prison fashion, folded up my prison uniform and left it in a neat pile at the foot of my bed. Abuzuike, the king masturbator, was off sick, lying in the neighbouring bunk, with his round black face poking out over his rough blanket. He was, no doubt, desperate for me to get a move on so he could knock out his first of the day.

'I won't shake your hand if you don't mind, mate,' I said, picking up my bag. 'Keep plugging away, though, that world record can't be far off now.'

I went outside and sparked up a cigarette under the shelter as a light flurry of snow began to fall. I'd only taken a few drags when Yuri emerged from the office building to escort me to the reception area at the entrance to the Zone. The yard gate buzzed open for a final time and together we walked in silence through the falling snow to the main gate. As we reached Sniper Alley, I stopped and turned round for one last look at the place that had been my home for so long. At the far end of the compound, I could see the Africans shovelling coal for the boilers from the vast heap, their bodies no more than hazy, dark outlines through the flurries of snow. Baska was unloading a milk churn for the kitchen from the back of his horse cart. I waved to him, and he raised a hand back and then carried on his work, as if I'd see him later.

When I turned back and began my walk down Sniper Alley, I stopped almost immediately. To my left, his face pressed against the mesh of the factory fence, was Molloi, the teenage Vietnamese boy from the office. He wore a grin as if it was him walking to freedom. 'Go! English boy, go!' he shouted. I smiled back at him and started walking, my chin high and my chest puffed out.

At the gate, Yuri put out his hand for me to shake. 'Say hello to your father from me,' he said, taking off his mirrored shades and giving me a wink as he turned to leave.

Zanpolit was waiting for me in the reception office, the gateway to the world beyond. A woman behind the glass counter gave two heavy stamps to my release documents, tore off one half and handed it to me without expression. Zanpolit opened the door on the other side of the room. '*Davai adachi!*' he said ('Off you go, good luck!'), and he gave me a gentle push in the back. The door clicked shut behind me. I took small steps through the fresh snow, breathing the air deep into my lungs. I felt light-headed, almost faint. I stopped, realizing I didn't know where I was meant to be going, but I felt perfectly calm. All I could see was pine trees, a couple of wooden cabins and snow. I lit a cigarette, turned my head towards the sky and let the snowflakes fall upon my smiling face.

Afterword

Tig's mother met him in Moscow and they flew back to London together in the spring of 2005. He is back working in the City as a broker, after his friend Steve, who visited him in Zone 22, helped find him an opening at a major firm. He and Lucy bought a house in London, which they share with their one-year-old daughter. Tig has remained in close contact with his many friends in Moscow.

Acknowledgements

I would like to thank Niall Edworthy for helping me to tell my story. My gratitude also goes to Joel Beckett, for his friendship and invaluable advice and for helping to get the whole project together; to Jonathan Harris and Justin Paige for their in-depth knowledge and support; and to Rowland White, Natalie, Sarah and the whole team at Penguin, who have made us feel so at home and helped us every step of the way towards presenting the book in its best possible form.

I would like to express a massive thank you to our dear Alexei; a life-saver. You've shown a kindness and self-lessness that makes me wonder how I can ever repay you; the way you put your life on hold to help me and my family is amazing and I am forever in your debt. Similarly to Alla, without whom we would have been lost in this nightmare, with no one to help us understand what was happening. I will never forget how you got us through the whole terrible experience with such bravery, yet always with a calm reassuring smile and a soft shoulder to cry on. Also to Pavel, Alex, Andrei, Dima and all of my other clients and friends in Russia, who tried many ways to help us, not least collecting money towards our costs.

Closer to home, Sheila, Doug, Michael and Nick deserve a particular mention for pulling strings and trying to organize a way out for me. You are true friends to me and my family. I owe a big part of my survival to the letters sent by all my friends, Lucy's friends and our families. I received 50 per cent of them at best, and can only hope that some of my replies got through. Those letters and cards kept me focused on what was waiting for me at home; they provided some shafts of light on dark, lonely days and nights and helped me to keep strong. Thank you. And not forgetting those who helped and supported Lucy and Mum while I was away, enduring untold grief and heartache with them. I know that my girls wouldn't have made it through without the support of a strong network of friends, true friends, who sprang to their help, or lent a listening ear, or gave a loving, supportive hug whenever it was needed. To John, for helping Lucy through harder times than I could even imagine; thanks for putting a smile on my face every day, bro. And to everybody else who has helped me get my life back on track since I came home and has helped replace some nasty memories with some real good ones. Thanks to Steve for keeping your promise and to Steph and Chris for giving me a chance.

I would be nothing without Lucy, my soulmate and my rock, who stuck with me through the thickest of thicks and the thinnest of thins; my heart is forever yours. To Rob, for never taking no for an answer and for always being there for me. To Mum and Dad, who must have thought they were in for an easy life once their last chick was about to fly the nest. I apologize again for the sleepless nights of worry and fear and I thank you for never giving up. And thank you to Isabella, my sunshine.